A SCHNITTKE READER

RUSSIAN MUSIC STUDIES

Malcolm Hamrick Brown, Founding Editor

Photograph of Alfred Schnittke in the 1980s
by Victor Brel.

A
SCHNITTKE
READER

Alfred Schnittke

EDITED BY ALEXANDER IVASHKIN
TRANSLATED BY JOHN GOODLIFFE
WITH A FOREWORD BY
MSTISLAV ROSTROPOVICH

INDIANA
University Press
Bloomington & Indianapolis

Published with the generous support of the Estate of Allen W. Clowes
through the Indiana University Press Music Fund.

This book is a publication of

Indiana University Press
601 North Morton Street
Bloomington, IN 47404-3797 USA

http://iupress.indiana.edu

Telephone orders 800-842-6796
Fax orders 812-855-7931
Orders by e-mail iuporder@indiana.edu

The paper used in this publication meets the minimum
requirements of American National Standard for Information Sciences—Permanence of Paper for Printed Library
Materials, ANSI Z39.48-1984.

Manufactured in the United States of America

Library of Congress Cataloging-in-Publication Data

Schnittke, Alfred, date
A Schnittke reader / Alfred Schnittke ; edited by Alexander Ivashkin ;
translated by John Goodliffe ; with a foreword by Mstislav Rostropovich.
    p. cm. — (Russian music studies)
Includes bibliographical references and index.
    ISBN 0-253-33818-2 (cloth : alk. paper)
1. Music—20th century—History and criticism. 2. Schnittke, Alfred,
    date—Criticism and interpretation. 3. Musicians—Russia
(Federation)—Interviews. I. Ivashkin, A. (Aleksandr) II. Goodliffe, J.
D. (John Derek) III. Title. IV. Russian music studies (Bloomington, Ind.)
ML197 .S2627 2002
780'.92—dc21
                                                              2001005133

1 2 3 4 5   07 06 05 04 03 02

CONTENTS

Contents

FOREWORD

I believe I have earned the right to provide this introduction, principally because I knew personally many of the composers of whom Alfred Schnittke writes, and have played their music many times.

I have read all of Alfred's essays with enormous interest and enjoyment. To tell the truth, even though I was his friend, I did not know that he was capable of such careful and interesting analysis, that he had such a profound insight into the music of other composers, and that he found in it so many regular features that were hidden from others.

It is splendid that Schnittke's essays and ideas on music are finally being published.

I was particularly interested in the essay on Stravinsky, whose music I worship. I remember that Shostakovich was once forced to put his signature to a critical article on Stravinsky published in *Pravda*, the central Soviet newspaper. At that time I was already well acquainted with Stravinsky. In the article it was asserted that Stravinsky, who was so successful in his Russian period, later suffered a marked decline. . . . When I was studying with Shostakovich at the Conservatory, I played *The Symphony of Psalms*, arranged for four hands by Shostakovich himself, who loved the work. For many years Stravinsky's music had been banned in the Soviet Union, but at that period there was already a certain "thawing out."

Then I arrived in London, where Stravinsky also was at the time. I met him at a rehearsal. He was rather like Baba Yaga[1] and looked at me with a kind of "nasty" grin. "I've read Shostakovich's article about me," he said. Then, in a tone of bitterness, he added: "Tell your friend that, whether or not he likes what I am doing, each of us has the right to experiment." I passed on the message to Shostakovich. When he heard it, he twitched nervously. By what he composed Stravinsky had indeed demonstrated his right to experiment—by his paradoxicality, in which Schnittke detects a special kind of logic. When the aging Picasso was asked, "Are you still searching for something in your work?" he replied, "No, I have already found something." Stravinsky, too, had found something in his music.

I like to recall how Schnittke wrote his *Concerto for Three*. It was his sixtieth birthday, and I asked him to compose something to celebrate it. "Perhaps I should write something for those who play my music most," he said, "and in that case it will be something 'for three'[2] —for you, [Gidon] Kremer, and [Yuri] Bashmet." As a subtitle for the concerto he wrote "Rostropovich will provide,"[3] because I commissioned it. When he had finished it, he said, "The three of you will be wildly successful," and he wrote the minuet that we were to play as an encore. That minuet is an example of the "polystylistics" of which he speaks in his essay. The music may remind you of Lully, but it has to be put in one key. Each instrumentalist plays a beautiful melody. But the chords that form the harmonies always sound inappropriate. The three players, with the exception of the one playing the melody, seem to

---

1. Baba Yaga: The witch from Russian folktales. —ed.

2. *Na troikh:* a common colloquial expression in the Soviet Union, referring to the sharing of a bottle of vodka by three people. —ed.

3. Meaning that Rostropovich should buy the bottle of vodka. —ed.

have gone wrong and lost each other. This is precisely where beauty lies. . . . When Schnittke analyzed polystylistics, he was doing so for his own work.

In his essay on timbres Schnittke refers to the music of Prokofiev and Shosta-kovich. This reminds me of my student days, when I tried to introduce one of my close friends, who later became a well-known singer, a mezzo-soprano, to Proko-fiev's music. This was for a concert at the Hall of Columns at the House of Unions [Dom Soiuzov] in Moscow. I had confessed to Prokofiev that I had a "star turn" and asked him to listen to the radio broadcast of the concert. He was pleased to do as I asked. The next morning I hurried round to see him. "I heard your 'star turn'," he said. "It was remarkable, amazing. . . . I was particularly taken by what she sang as an encore, [Grieg's] 'Solveig's Song'—her voice sounded just like a clarinet!" This anecdote is connected with the idea of timbre and the remarkable timbral instru-mental thinking of Prokofiev. One of his favorite instruments was the tuba. "How wonderful it is," he used to say, "when the tuba softly plays a low note! I have the impression that there is a beetle sitting on the note, and I listen to the note, then pick up the beetle, and move it onto another note."

In Prokofiev's music one finds more timbral effects connected with nature than in any other composer. In *Peter and the Wolf*, for example, the clarinet is the cat-instrument. And its rapid passages are like the cat climbing a tree. In the sound of the clarinet there is cat fur and fluff. Or—I do not want to offend bassoon-players—but when I hear a bassoon it always reminds me of the old grandfather [in Prokofiev's *Peter and the Wolf*]. And if the grandfather is cunning, then it has to be the bassoon! Timbral colors evoke various associations. What can be more birdlike than a flute? And the wolf is depicted with the *tripled* timbre of the French horn!

Schnittke writes, "[A]n infinitely differentiated scale of interpolating sonorities that move one to the next and that include every imaginable richness from the world of sound can be conceived only in theory. . . . [O]nly a more or less precisely graduated illusory scale is possible . . . [dependant on] the individuality of the composer, the individuality of the instrumental ensemble selected, and the indi-vidual relationship of the performer and his instrument."[4]

This is perfectly true. All my life I have tried to achieve a variety of timbres. Of course, I have studied composition and conducting, and this has helped me consid-erably. But in practice the three factors listed by Schnittke are always embodied in the actual and potential performances of music. We performers are remembered only thanks to the music we play and how far we understand that music. Naturally what perhaps matters most to us is intuition, but we nevertheless also have to try to penetrate the depths of the music with the help of analysis. One must admit that in his analytical essays, Schnittke has clearly penetrated to depths inaccessible to the vast majority of musicians. It seems as if for his analysis he used a laser and an electron microscope, but in fact it was simply his genius!

Mstislav Rostropovich
May 1999

---

4. From Schnittke's essay "Timbral Relationships and Their Functional Use: The Timbral Scale" (Chapter 22 in this volume). —ed.

Note about the Music Examples

When Indiana University Press received the typescript of Schnittke's unpublished essays on music from Alexander Ivashkin, many of the music examples accompanying the essays had been hand copied by Schnittke himself. Jeffrey Ankrom, former Indiana University Press music editor, decided that readers might not only appreciate seeing the examples exactly as Schnittke had notated them, but would perhaps also learn something from the choices he made when reducing examples from full score. Unfortunately, the paper Schnittke used had degraded from age and usage, precluding the possibility of photographing his manuscript "as is" to make plates for printing. But Mr. Ankrom was committed to his decision to share Schnittke's holograph scores with readers of this book, and after his departure from the Press, he volunteered to take upon himself the exacting task of cleaning up the examples while painstakingly preserving all the essential features of Schnittke's original notation. The consequence of Mr. Ankrom's generous expenditure of time can be appreciated in the manuscript music examples scattered throughout the present volume, which, with the exception of Examples 27.3 and 32.5–32.10, are authentic facsimiles of Schnittke's holograph scores. My sincere thanks to Mr. Ankrom for his extraordinary contribution to this volume.

Some of Schnittke's manuscript examples could not be salvaged to make facsimiles. These were expertly recopied by Justin Merritt, a composer and Associate Instructor affiliated with the School of Music, Indiana University, Bloomington.

Malcolm Hamrick Brown
Founding Editor
Russian Music Studies

TRANSLATOR'S NOTE

In *The Bible as Literature* (Oxford University Press, 1990), John B. Gabel and Charles B. Wheeler refer to the "two ends of a spectrum of possibilities in translation" designated by the terms, coined by translation theorists, "formal correspondence" and "dynamic equivalence" (p. 243). In the former the emphasis is on "the form of the original," in the latter on "the reader's ability to understand readily." They add that those involved in beginning any translation project "must decide for themselves whether to favor the demands of the form or the needs of the reader."

In attempting to put Alfred Schnittke's words into English I tried as far as possible to position myself at about the mid-point of this translation spectrum, conscious, on the one hand, of the need to let him speak or write for himself in his own somewhat idiosyncratic and often highly technical way and, on the other, of the impossibility of allowing him to do this when he was not talking or writing in English and was not therefore readily accessible to the potential reader of this book. Schnittke's Russian was, perhaps like his music, something of a law unto itself. In trying to express ideas that were often profoundly original, he used a language in which any considerations for smooth stylistic elegance were secondary to his anxiety to achieve maximum precision and subtlety of analysis. I have therefore largely resisted any temptation to oversimplify his often complex ideas in the interests of a reader who might find them too difficult to digest. Schnittke made few concessions to the vast majority of human beings, whose minds tend to move much more slowly and less penetratingly than his did.

I am fully conscious of the fact that my efforts to do justice to both writer and reader were doomed not to succeed and that there are places where I was led into compromises that may well not satisfy either. But putting Schnittke into English has inevitably and rewardingly taken me closer to him, and I am profoundly grateful to have had the opportunity to gain deeper knowledge of one of the most remarkable human beings of the twentieth century. To Alfred Schnittke and to his readers in English I acknowledge and apologize for the shortcomings of my work, but, even secondhand and in inadequate translation, the composer's stimulating ideas and his stature as a world figure are too important not to be made accessible to those who know no Russian.

John Goodliffe

INTRODUCTION

A Man in Between

Alfred Schnittke died in Hamburg on 3 August 1998 following a fifth stroke; he had been fighting this fatal illness since 1985. His funeral in Moscow on 10 August 1998, attended by thousands of people, was a tribute of honor and admiration to the greatest Russian composer since Shostakovich. "The last genius of the twentieth century," according to the Russian newspapers and, belatedly, Russian officialdom.

With Schnittke's music we are possibly standing at the end of the great route from Mahler to Shostakovich. Schnittke intensifies all their contrasts and articulates the strong ambivalence of their music. He drives this powerful post-Romantic tradition toward the very extremes of the late twentieth century, our *fin de siècle*. Shostakovich gave unique expression to the thoughts and feelings of those generations of Russians whose fate it was to live under the yoke of totalitarian power. Schnittke is often called the "man in between." A strong pulse of latent energy is undoubtedly inherent in both their musics, and extreme pessimism is common to both: many works by Shostakovich and especially Schnittke are "dying," dissolving in the world, fading into the distance of time. Indisputably, all of this has to do with time. Those wishing to listen to Schnittke's music in the future are by no means bound to feel all these concrete, time-connected features. But they will undoubtedly absorb the intense energy of the flow of the music, making it part of their being, part of their thinking, and part of their language.

Schnittke is a "man in between" different traditions. "Although I don't have any Russian blood," said Schnittke, "I am tied to Russia, having spent all my life here. On the other hand, much of what I've written is somehow related to German music and to the logic that comes out of being German, although I did not particularly want this. . . . Like my German forebears, I live in Russia, I can speak and write Russian far better than German. But I am not Russian. . . . My Jewish half gives me no peace: I know none of the Jewish languages, but I look like a typical Jew."

Schnittke was one of the most prolific composers of the twentieth century. His works are an established part of the standard repertoire for orchestras, chamber groups, and soloists. In the 1970s and 1980s he enjoyed extraordinary popularity in Russia. "His music used to be our language, more perfect than the verbal one," wrote one Russian critic. When Schnittke's music was to be performed in Moscow, Leningrad, or Novosibirsk, concert promoters used to warn the police in order to prevent overcrowding and chaos. All performances of his music were important events for Soviet listeners, for in it they found spiritual values that were absent from everyday life during the endless years of "terror," "thaw," "cold war," and "stagnation." In the West, especially during the 1980s and 1990s, his music was widely performed, from Germany to the United States, from South America to New Zealand. His works have also been recorded on more than one hundred CDs from many different companies.

During the so-called "Khrushchev Thaw" in the USSR of the early 1960s, Schnittke became interested in absorbing new compositional techniques and in finding new sound perspectives. By contrast, the 1970s was a time for retrospective analysis of stylistically different idioms (exemplified in Schnittke's well-known polystylistic Symphony No. 1) and for trying to find new meanings for the old roots (in, for example, the musical hermeneutics of the Concerto Grosso No. 1 or the Violin Concerto No. 3). Finally, from the late 1970s, Schnittke began to expand the space of his music. He wrote symphonies, concertos, and the so-called "Faust Cantata, seid nuchtern und wachet. . . ." Later, between 1986 and 1994, he completed his major works for stage: the ballet *Peer Gynt* (1986) and the operas *Life with an Idiot* (1991), *Gesualdo* (1994), and *Historia von D. Johann Fausten* (1983–1994).

Schnittke's nine symphonies reflect the various aspects of human history. The first, third, fifth, and seventh are concerned with historical and cultural entities. The second, fourth, sixth, and eighth symbolize religious or spiritual experience. Schnittke tries to find a new shape, a new angle, but remains within the true symphonic tradition. With him the tradition of the great European dramatic symphony comes to some kind of conclusion, yet in many respects he still keeps the tradition alive, for one may certainly detect the influence of German culture, German forms, and German logic. But, at the same time, he virtually destroys the symphonic tradition by revealing its erosion. In this respect, he is more the irrational Russian "destroyer" than the precise German craftsman.

Many of his ideas came from his work as a film composer. (He composed soundtracks for sixty-six films.) For Schnittke, "incidental" and "serious" music coexisted and interpenetrated each other. Inside the "neoclassical" frame of the Concerto Grosso No. 1 (1977), one finds the transformation of a cheerful song-chorale of Soviet schoolchildren, a nostalgic atonal serenade, quasi-Corellian allusions, and, finally, "my grandmother's favorite tango which her great-grandmother used to play on a harpsichord" (Schnittke's own words). In the Concerto Grosso, as in many of his other compositions, Schnittke uses fragments from his film scores. Speaking about this work, Schnittke said, "One of my life's goals is to overcome the gap between 'E' (*Ernstmusik,* serious music) and 'U' (*Unterhaltung,* music for entertainment), even if I break my neck in doing so!"

Schnittke's late compositions are enigmatic. Their textures become very ascetic, and the number of notes is reduced. However, the latent tension increases, and the meaning of his last few compositions is to be found between the notes rather than in the musical text itself. The actual musical language becomes "tough," dissonant, discordant. It is definitely not easy-listening music. At the first performance of the Symphony No. 6 at Carnegie Hall, almost half the audience left before the end. However, those who remained were enthusiastic.

In considering Schnittke's output, one might recall Charles Ives's saying: "Nature creates valleys and hills, and people build fences and attach labels." No one knows how long it may take before Schnittke's compositions are seen properly as an integral part of musical history. However, it is clear that he did express the very essence of the hectic and dramatic twentieth century, and that he pushed music out of its "local" isolation by bravely demolishing all artificial fences.

Schnittke—The Writer

It is hard to believe that Schnittke was writing articles on music all his life! His first publication appeared in the main Russian musicological journal, *Sovetskaia Muzyka*, in the late 1960s. He was continually analyzing the music of his fellow composers. It is truly amazing that, although he was so busy with his own music, he always found time to listen to the music of his contemporaries, to speak at conferences and seminars, and to publish analytical articles. The very last speech he made was the keynote address at the Prokofiev festival in Duisburg in 1990.

He had a tremendous number of social contacts and loved polemical arguments. For instance he was always ready to get seriously involved in discussions on how to teach harmony. He was also always prepared to defend those of his friends who were accused of "modernism" or "formalism." Schnittke's archive is full of sketches for all sorts of speeches, talks, lectures, and letters (including letters that were never sent).

When he was teaching at the Moscow Conservatory (1961–1974) he wrote articles on Prokofiev's and Shostakovich's orchestration that were published in Russia in the 1960s and 1970s.

Some of Schnittke's writings on music are, in fact, summaries of his own analyses of Western music: he was constantly analyzing all sorts of music. In the early 1970s he wrote eleven analytical essays for a collection on the subject of the technique of modern composition. The purpose of this collection was to help students and listeners to gain a better understanding of the music of Ligeti, Berio, Stockhausen (at that time still very little known in the Soviet Union), as well as the music of Bartók, Stravinsky, and Webern. This collection, however, was never published. At the proof stage, officials at the Ministry of Culture decided to cancel the publication, which seemed to them too "avant-garde." Thus, these eleven essays are published for the first time ever in this volume. Some of them Schnittke used later for his research talks, in particular for his talks on Stockhausen and Berio at the Moscow Conservatory and at the Composers' Union in the 1970s.

One of his most important essays—on Stravinsky's paradoxical logic—was written for the collection *I. F. Stravinskii: Stat'i i materialy* [I. F. Stravinsky: Articles and Materials], published in Moscow in 1973. After Stravinsky's visit to Russia in 1962, a Russian translation of *Conversations with Igor Stravinsky* (written with Robert Craft) was published in the Soviet Union in 1971, but only in extensive excerpts. It was a time when Soviet officials were trying to change the official "image" of Stravinsky in Soviet Russia. Instead of being referred to as a "hooligan" and "composer with no musical talent whatsoever" (as he was frequently described in official Soviet textbooks on music history published in the 1950s), Stravinsky started to be called a truly Russian composer.

Schnittke was always interested in Stravinsky's music. His comments on Stravinsky's latest compositions (*The Flood*, *Threni*, Cantata) are particularly interesting. Schnittke was engaged in a search for a hidden tonality in Stravinsky's serial works, but he never published any results of this analysis.[1] Fortunately, his essay on Stravin-

---

1. Stravinsky's scores with Schnittke's remarks may be seen at the Schnittke collection at the Centre for Russian Music, University of London. —ed.

sky is published in the present volume. It shows not only Schnittke's ideas on Stravinsky but also the "paradoxical" principles that we can clearly detect in his own music.

Schnittke was a very good friend, with the ability to listen and to respond to other people's needs. His essays on Edison Denisov, Sofia Gubaidulina, and Giya Kancheli, and on various performers, speak for themselves. They show Schnittke's special gift for listening to his friends' works and finding the most essential features in their compositions. Giya Kancheli often says that Schnittke understood his music better that Kancheli himself.

Some of the texts published here were originally presented as talks. One of them, "Polystylistic Tendencies in Modern Music" (given at the Moscow International Music Congress in 1971), reflects Schnittke's own experience, as he was engaged in writing his "polystylistic" Symphony No. 1. Schnittke's address on Prokofiev (at the opening of the Prokofiev festival in Duisburg, Germany, 1990) was his last public address. In it he summarized some of his ideas on the development and progress of music (in which he did not believe!). Also included are personal recollections of Prokofiev's last public appearance at the première of his *Sinfonia Concertante*, and on Prokofiev's funeral in March 1953 (which coincided with Stalin's funeral).

This volume presents Schnittke's most important articles and talks, together with selections (in Chapter 1) from conversations we had between 1985 and 1994. (The complete book of these conversations was published in Russia in 1994, and in Germany in 1998.) When Schnittke talked about music, what he said was so nearly perfect that it could be published practically without any editing. He spoke as if he were writing! I tried to preserve the "presence" of his own "voice" and "intonation" in the text of our conversations.

I should like to express my sincere thanks to John Goodliffe for his wonderful translation of the often complex and difficult texts. And a very special "hero" of this publication is Professor Malcolm Hamrick Brown, founding editor of the series Russian Music Studies. Together with Jeffrey Ankrom (formerly music editor at Indiana University Press), Professor Brown has devoted an enormous amount of time and energy to editing this book, going far beyond what one might expect of any ordinary editor. Using his considerable skill, insight, and specialized musical knowledge, he has helped to produce the clearest and most expressive English equivalent of what Schnittke said or wrote. The editor would like to express deepest thanks to The Leverhulme Trust (UK) for sponsoring his research work at the Alfred Schnittke Archive, Goldsmiths College, University of London.

I hope that this book, the first to present Schnittke's own ideas in English, will help to promote a better understanding of his life and work, and that its readers will thus be enabled to share his many original and brilliant ideas on the development of culture.

Alexander Ivashkin
London, December 2000

CHRONOLOGY

1934

Alfred Garryevich Schnittke born 24 November in Engels (Boronsk), capital of the Autonomous Soviet Republic of the Volga Germans, established by Lenin after the Revolution of 1917. His German-speaking Jewish father, Harry (Garry) Viktorovich Schnittke (1914–1975), is a journalist and translator. His mother, Maria Iosifovna Vogel (1910–1972), a Volga German, teaches German at school and later edits the correspondence section of the German-language newspaper *Neues Leben,* published in Moscow. Alfred's grandfather, Viktor Mironovich Schnittke (1886–1956), and grandmother, Thea Abramovna Katz (1889–1970), are originally from Libava (now Liepaya) in Latvia, which was part of the Russian Empire from 1795 to 1918. Their ardent revolutionary Communism causes them to flee from Russia to Germany in 1910. Born and brought up in Frankfurt, Harry Viktorovich Schnittke speaks Russian with a strong German accent. In 1927 Alfred's grandparents return to the USSR and settle in Moscow. Alfred's first language is so-called Volga German, which was brought into Russia by the Germans in the eighteenth century. Stalin's terror increases in the Soviet Union. Writer Maxim Gorky declares new principles of so-called "socialist realism," hailing Stalin as a "Great Leader."

1941

April–May: Schnittke is sent to Moscow for auditions at the Central Music School for gifted children, a branch of the Moscow Conservatory. Germany invades the Soviet Union on 22 June. Schnittke returns to Engels, which he describes as "a city of fences and sheds," and remains there throughout the war. On 28 July Stalin orders the dissolution of the Republic of the Volga Germans. All Volga Germans go into exile, some to Siberia, others to Kazakhstan. Harry Schnittke is able to prove that he is a Jew, and he and his family are therefore permitted to stay in Engels.

1945

Harry Schnittke obtains a position in Vienna on the staff of the newspaper *Öster-reichische Zeitung,* published by the occupying Soviet forces in Austria. Coming back to Engels on holiday, Harry tells Alfred about Kurt Weill's *The Threepenny Opera.* Alfred hears Shostakovich's Symphony No. 7 on the radio.

1946

The Schnittke family moves to Vienna. Alfred plays an accordion given to his father. His enthusiasm for the instrument is later revealed in his first large-scale composition, the Concerto for Accordion and Orchestra (1948–1949). Alfred begins music theory and piano lessons. Writes his first composition, a piano piece in A major (reused in his music for film cartoons).

1946–1948

Attends numerous concerts in Vienna (especially Beethoven, Schubert, and Bruckner). Sees operas by Mozart, Wagner, Leoncavallo, and Mascagni. Vienna becomes Schnittke's primary cultural homeland. These two years in Vienna determine the basic criteria of his future tastes in music; the Viennese idioms of Mozart and Schubert will become an essential part of his musical language.

1948

The Schnittke family returns to Russia, settling in the small village of Valentinovka, near Moscow, where they rent a small ugly wooden house. Schnittke starts his Concerto for Accordion and Orchestra (lost). Andrei Zhdanov, Stalin's spokesman for "Communism in the Arts," accuses Prokofiev, Shostakovich, and others (such as the poet Anna Akhmatova and the satirist Mikhail Zoshchenko) of "formalism." Tikhon Khrennikov is appointed head of the Union of Soviet Composers by special decree of Stalin and retains this position for more than forty years. At the Union's first congress, Khrennikov declares, "Formalism went deeply into the music of Prokofiev, Shostakovich, and many other composers."

1949

In August Schnittke auditions for the October Revolution Music College in Moscow (now the Schnittke Music College and Institute). He becomes a student in the Choirmasters' Department. This is his only chance to study music; now almost fourteen, he has had very little performance and musical training. He reads Thomas Mann's *Doktor Faustus* for the first time, which is to have a major impact on his life and music.

1950–1952

Starts regular private lessons in music theory with Iosif Ryzhkin. Regular piano classes under Vassily Shaternikov, along with fellow students such as Rodion Shchedrin, Karen Khachaturian, and Yuri Butsko. Discussion of Skriabin, whose music is officially banned at the time. As a pianist Schnittke performs Haydn, Mozart, Chopin, and Grieg. LPs first appear in Soviet Union, and Schnittke borrows many records.

1952

Schnittke is present at the first performance of Prokofiev's *Sinfonia Concertante* in Moscow on 18 February—the last public performance at which Prokofiev was present. It is played by Mstislav Rostropovich and conducted by Sviatoslav Richter.

1953

Stalin and Prokofiev both die on 5 March. Schnittke is unable to attend Prokofiev's funeral because millions are thronging Red Square to say farewell to their dictator. While at college he completes his first orchestral score, *Poem* for piano and orchestra.

In September he commences his studies at the Moscow Conservatory, studying composition with Evgeni Golubev and orchestration with Nikolai Rakov. He attends the first performance of Shostakovich's Symphony No. 10 in Moscow on 28 December, which makes a strong and lasting impression.

1954–1955
Begins to study scores of Schoenberg, Webern, Berg, and Stravinsky, and later of Kodály, Hindemith, and Orff. Only now are scores by these composers available in the USSR. Among his first compositions at the Conservatory (which include chamber works, piano pieces, choruses, and songs) are a sonata for violin and piano, a sonata for piano, and a suite for string orchestra.

1956
Following its Moscow première on 4 February, Schnittke is greatly influenced by Shostakovich's Violin Concerto No. 1. Makes plans to write his own violin concerto. Later that month the twentieth congress of the Soviet Communist Party openly condemns Stalin's methods amid sensational disclosure of his crimes. In March Schnittke marries Galina Koltsina, a musicologist and fellow student at the Conservatory. Their marriage is to last three years. In October Soviet troops invade Hungary. Schnittke finishes a symphony (No. 0), a student effort in what was to become one of his favorite genres; it is greatly influenced by Stravinsky. Receives his first official commission (one of the very few he would be given): *Three Choruses*. One of the choruses is performed and recorded on LP, conducted by the Conservatory's traditionalist rector, Alexander Sveshnikov.

1957
Completes his Violin Concerto No. 1, the first of a long sequence of compositions for the violin. From this time on the most important ideas in Schnittke's music frequently appear in violin concertos or sonatas. He later revises his score twice (final version, 1963).

1958
Graduates from the Moscow Conservatory. His graduation piece—an oratorio, *Nagasaki*—is criticized by the Composers' Union for "modernism." Shostakovich writes in support of *Nagasaki*, which is recorded for radio transmission abroad, but not within the USSR. Schnittke starts postgraduate studies at the Moscow Conservatory, remaining there until 1961.

1959
Composes *Songs of War and Peace,* a cantata based on modern folk tunes that he found in the Conservatory's archives. This is to become his first published composition (in 1964).

1960

First performance of *Songs of War and Peace* in the Great Hall of the Conservatory. Afterward Shostakovich shakes Schnittke's hand, pronouncing the cantata "a remarkable work." Composes Piano Concerto No. 1 and a string quartet (unfinished).

1961

Enters the Composers' Union with *Poem about Space* (inspired by Yuri Gagarin's first space flight) for electronic instruments, including the theremin, an instrument invented in 1920 by Lev Theremin (1896–1993) and already used by composers such as Varèse and Ives. Shostakovich sharply criticizes the piece for its "old-fashioned modernism." After completing his postgraduate studies, Schnittke is invited to teach at the Moscow Conservatory (until 1971). On 4 February he marries the pianist Irina Katayeva, his former private student. In August a wall is built in Berlin to prevent defection from East to West.

1962

Schnittke is now on the verge of becoming an "official" composer as the Ministry of Culture commissions an opera, *The Eleventh Commandment,* for the Bolshoi Theater. It is played for the Board of the Bolshoi Opera, but is not accepted for performance. He is then blacklisted by the Composers' Union and remains so until the mid-1980s. In October the Cuban missile crisis brings the United States and the USSR to the brink of war. The "Khrushchev Thaw" results in the publication of Alexander Solzhenitsyn's *One Day in the Life of Ivan Denisovich,* which is praised even in the official newspaper *Pravda.* The film industry offers the only chance for Schnittke to make a living, and he writes the first of sixty-six film scores. Much of their material is also used in his serious compositions.

1963

Luigi Nono visits Russia as a member of the Italian Communist Party. He meets Schnittke, Edison Denisov, Sofia Gubaidulina, and other young Russian composers, and tells them about the most recent Western music. Schnittke begins his "serial" period. Dedicates Violin Sonata No. 1 to Mark Lubotsky.

1964

Serial compositions: *Music for Piano and Chamber Orchestra* and *Music for Chamber Orchestra.* End of the "thaw" following Khrushchev's dismissal as Head of the Communist Party. Beginning of "stagnation" (until 1985) under Leonid Brezhnev.

1965

First performances abroad. *Music for Piano and Chamber Orchestra* is played at the Warsaw Autumn International Festival in September. Universal Edition buys rights to the work and becomes one of Schnittke's two principal European publishers (the other being Hans Sikorski in Hamburg). *Music for Chamber Orchestra* is performed in Leipzig in November.

1966

First commission from abroad: Violin Concerto No. 2 is written for the Jyväskylä Festival in Finland, and performed by Mark Lubotsky on 12 July. From now on, performances of Schnittke's works at major European festivals become more numerous.

1967

First performance of String Quartet No. 1 by the Borodin Quartet on 7 May. In September he travels to Warsaw for the first performance of *Dialogue* for cello and chamber ensemble. Mikhail Bulgakov's novel *The Master and Margarita* (written in the late 1930s, and very important for generations of Soviet intelligentsia) is published for the first time in Moscow.

1968

Begins working with Andrei Khrzhanovsky, director of film cartoons, one of which, *Glass Harmonica,* marks the beginning of Schnittke's "polystylistic" period. Music from *Glass Harmonica* is used in *Quasi una Sonata* (Violin Sonata No. 2) and the *Serenade* for chamber ensemble (both 1968). The orchestral piece *Pianissimo* (based on Franz Kafka) is premièred at the Donaueschingen Festival. Publication of Solzhenitsyn's *Cancer Ward.*

1969

Starts work on Symphony No. 1 (completed 1972) while simultaneously working on a film documentary *The World Today* (music from the film is used in the Symphony). Between now and 1972 he writes thirteen other film scores. Alexander Solzhenitsyn is expelled from the Writers' Union.

1971

Composes Concerto for Oboe, Harp, and Strings (performed in Zagreb in 1972). The ballet *Labyrinths* is staged in Moscow. Writes analytical essays on the music of Bartók, Webern, Ligeti, Berio, Stockhausen, and Nono (never published in Russia). His paper "Polystylistic Tendencies in Modern Music" is presented at an international music congress in Moscow.

1972

Sudden death of his mother. Dedicates Piano Quintet (completed 1976) to her memory. Starts work on *Requiem.* A new, simpler style now prevails in his music.

1973

Schnittke's important article "Paradox as a Feature of Stravinsky's Musical Logic" is published. Mstislav Rostropovich leaves the USSR.

1974

World première of Symphony No. 1 in the closed city of Gorky (Nizhny Novgorod). Schnittke is not permitted to present the Symphony in Moscow (he must wait more than twelve years for this to happen). Khrennikov says that Schnittke obviously lacks all talent for writing music and should not compose. Schnittke composes *Der gelbe Klang,* a "scenic composition" for pantomime, soprano, chorus, and chamber ensemble. Its libretto, by Vassily Kandinsky, is based partly on Rudolf Steiner's anthroposophical ideas. Schnittke is not allowed to attend the world première in France (as with nearly twenty of his other works from the 1960s to the 1980s). The political atmosphere in Russia hardens when Solzhenitsyn is deported.

1975

Shostakovich dies in August. Schnittke composes *Prelude in Memory of D. Shostakovich* [*Prel'udiya pamyati D. D. Shostakovicha*], which is first performed on 5 December in Moscow. Writes important article, "Circles of Influence," describing how "for the past fifty years [Russian] music has been under the influence of Dmitri Shostakovich."

1976

Piano Quintet is premièred in Tbilisi in September. *Moz-Art* (after Mozart's sketches) is premièred in Vienna.

1977

At the request of Gidon Kremer, Schnittke composes Concerto Grosso No. 1. Its first performance (in Leningrad) is a sensational success. With the Lithuanian Chamber Orchestra, Schnittke makes his first trip to the West as a harpsichordist/pianist in his Concerto Grosso and Arvo Pärt's *Tabula Rasa*—he is allowed to travel only as a performer, not as a composer. In Vienna, Schnittke revisits his first piano teacher, Charlotte Ruber. Khrennikov's office spreads the lie that Schnittke has defected to the West. Beginning of international success. Kremer performs Beethoven's Violin Concerto with Schnittke's cadenza (which quotes from all the major violin concertos). One American critic advises performers "to keep the moustaches off the Mona Lisas."

1978

In an article reminiscent of its attack on Shostakovich's *Lady Macbeth of Mtsensk* (as ordered by Stalin in 1936), *Pravda* prints "Planning an Outrage," attacking an upcoming new production (in Paris) of Tchaikovsky's *Queen of Spades* in which Schnittke is involved, together with Gennadi Rozhdestvensky and producer Yury Liubimov. Composes Violin Concerto No. 3 and Cello Sonata No. 1.

1979

Interests himself in yoga, cabbala, the I Ching, and anthroposophy. Symphony No. 2 ("Invisible Mass") is inspired by his 1977 visit to Bruckner's burial place in the Austrian monastery of St. Florian. Composes *Four Hymns* (on old Russian church tunes), and Concerto for Piano and Strings.

1980

On 23 April Rozhdestvensky conducts the BBC Symphony Orchestra in the world première of Symphony No. 2 in London. Schnittke gives a series of lectures on twentieth-century music, at the Vienna Hochschule für Musik. Composes String Quartet No. 2 (based on Russian Orthodox church tunes) as a compulsory item for the International String Quartet Competition in Evian.

1981

Minnesang for fifty-two voices is performed in Graz on 21 October. On 5 November Schnittke is present in Leipzig at the triumphant première (under Kurt Masur) of Symphony No. 3, commissioned by the Gewandhaus Orchestra. Elected to the Presidium of the Union of Soviet Composers and also to membership in the Academy of Arts in West Berlin.

1982

Decides to be baptized in Vienna as a Roman Catholic, though he usually makes his confession to a Russian Orthodox priest. In September, Concerto Grosso No. 2 is first performed in Berlin with Oleg Kagan, Natalia Gutman, and the Berlin Philharmonic Orchestra.

1983

Schnittke's popularity in Russia reaches unprecedented heights. All his concerts sell out, and the crowds are comparable to those at large-scale pop concerts. Schnittke is present when the *Faust Cantata* is premièred in Vienna on 19 June under Rozhdestvensky. For the Moscow performance, the Russian pop star Alla Pugachova agrees to sing Mephisto but ultimately withdraws, thinking it would damage her image to depict the Devil.

1984

String Quartet No. 3 is first performed on 8 January, and Symphony No. 4 is first performed on 12 April, both in Moscow. Violin Concerto No. 4 (written for Kremer) is performed in Berlin in September.

1985

An extremely productive year. The ballet *Sketches* is staged in the "official" Bolshoi Theater on 16 January. Other premières are *Ritual* for orchestra in Novosibirsk on 15 March, Concerto Grosso No. 3 in Moscow on 20 April with Oleg Krysa and Tatiana Grindenko as soloists, String Trio in Moscow on 2 June, and *(K)ein Sommernachtstraum* for orchestra in Salzburg in August. Schnittke also completes Viola Concerto and Concerto for Mixed Choir (both performed in 1986). Suffers his first stroke on 19 July at the Black Sea resort of Pitsunda. Three times he is pronounced clinically dead, but he rallies. He gradually returns to work, and by the end of September resumes work on Cello Concerto No. 1.

1986

First year of Mikhail Gorbachov's *perestroika* and *glasnost'*. On 12 January Yuri Bashmet performs the Viola Concerto in Amsterdam, but Schnittke is not well enough to attend. Schnittke (from now on always accompanied by his wife) is present when Natalia Gutman gives the first performance of the Cello Concerto No. 1 in Munich with the conductor Eri Klas on 7 May. Completes the ballet *Peer Gynt*.

1987

Numerous performances of Schnittke's music in the West, as well as in Russia. The music from *Peer Gynt* is first performed by the Hamburg Symphony Orchestra in 1987, conducted by Rozhdestvensky. Schnittke resumes contact with Rostropovich, who asks him to write a cello concerto, a symphony, and an opera for him. More frequent visits to Germany, not only because of performances but also for discussions with the Sikorski publishing firm. Elected Member of the Royal Academy in Stockholm.

1988

Leaves VAAP (Soviet Agency for Authors' Rights). Première of Symphony No. 5 in Amsterdam with Concertgebouw Orchestra under Riccardo Chailly. In Boston for a festival of Soviet music.

1989

Back in America for the New York première of the Piano Sonata No. 1. Major festival of Schnittke's music in Stockholm. A special fellowship in Berlin enables Schnittke to reside there for a year. Berlin Wall is dismantled.

1990

Travels from Berlin to London for the two-week festival "Schnittke: A Celebration." Première of Cello Concerto No. 2 in Evian with Rostropovich, who later performs the work in Berlin. Unification of Germany in October. Schnittke moves to Hamburg, where he is offered a composition class at the Hamburg Hochschule für Musik.

1991

Première of Concerto Grosso No. 5 in Cleveland with Kremer as soloist. His music is now regularly heard in America. In July he suffers a second stroke. Refuses the Lenin Prize. Between 1991 and 1994, twenty-six new works are written and performed, including three operas, three symphonies, eight further compositions for orchestra, chamber music, works from choir, songs, and piano pieces. Dissolution of the USSR on 26 December.

1992

Schnittke is present in Amsterdam when Rostropovich conducts the opera *Life with an Idiot* in April. Together with his son, Andrei, composes his penultimate film score, *The Last Days of St. Petersburg*. Accepts Praernium Imperiale (Tokyo).

1993

Travels to Moscow to receive the first Triumph Prize from the Russian Independent Foundation on 7 January. Completes his final film score for *The Master and Margarita*. Attends the première in Moscow of Symphony No. 6 by the Washington National Symphony Orchestra under Rostropovich.

1994

Makes his last trip to America for the première of Symphony No. 7 under Masur in New York on 10 February. In June has third and fourth strokes within days of each other. On 19 October *Concerto for Three* is performed in Moscow at a festival of Schnittke's music. Symphony No. 8 is premièred in Stockholm under Rozhdestvensky on 10 November. Schnittke listens to a tape of this performance on 24 November, his sixtieth birthday, while in a Hamburg hospital. Numerous festivals and performances of Schnittke's music around the world.

1995

In January he makes his last trip to Moscow. Stays in hospital until September. The opera *Gesualdo* is premièred in Vienna on 26 May, conducted by Rostropovich. His last opera, *Historia von D. Johann Fausten*, is premièred in Hamburg on 22 June.

1996–1998

In Hamburg. Composes slowly with left hand. Produces Symphony No. 9, Piece for Viola and Orchestra, and a work (variations) for string quartet.

1998

Suffers his final stroke on 4 July and dies in the hospital in Hamburg on 3 August. Thousands attend his funeral in Moscow on 10 August.

Chronology compiled by
Alexander Ivashkin

I

SCHNITTKE SPEAKS ABOUT HIMSELF

FROM SCHNITTKE'S CONVERSATIONS WITH ALEXANDER IVASHKIN (1985–1994)

IVASHKIN: There is such a marked difference between twentieth-century culture and the cultures that preceded it that some commentators have been inclined to suggest that in the twentieth century a new, fourth age in the development of human civilization has begun. This idea was expressed in 1921 by the Russian poet Vyacheslav Ivanov. "If, according to Auguste Comte," he wrote, "there have been three ages of human development, the mythological, the theological, and the scientific, at the present time a new mythological age is beginning." Do you agree that in our day symbolism and irrationality are playing an ever-increasing role and that our age is in some ways opposed to the rationalism of the Age of Enlightenment and closer to the Middle Ages? Are you personally conscious of the boundaries of the modern age in the past, present, and future?

SCHNITTKE: I completely agree with this idea, and also for subjective reasons. I have already said that after my stroke[1] I find myself able to remember much less than before, but at the same time I am aware of much more. I have come to rely not on intellectual knowledge but on a kind of animal feeling. I know something and can explain why it is so, can find arguments to support it (I usually do), but somehow I am not concerned about whether they exist or not. But I still *know* it, even though no one has ever explained it to me. Before my stroke I had to remember things and work out how to give a correct reply to any question.

Another personal and subjective feeling I have concerns my relationship with my son. I have long been aware of a kind of barrier between different generations. Our generation still adopts an intellectual stance; we are a generation with a kind of intellectual leavening: everything has to be weighed and measured. But the younger generation seems to lack this "leaven" by which everything has to be worked out mentally. But a direct primordial awareness of something is immeasurably more penetrating than intellectual awareness. If you ask my son about something, he has his answer ready, even though he has never spoken of or thought about the subject before. That means there can be knowledge without any formal training, and it is not of literary origin. For our generation intellectual knowledge may gradually change into intuitive knowledge, but perhaps it is still intellectual knowledge that only appears to be intuitive. But in the case of my son it is not at all intellectual knowledge,

---

1. Schnittke's first stroke occurred on 19 July 1985. —ed.

but an intuitive feeling that is much more precise. Fiction interests him far less than his reading about what interests him at any given moment. Everything that I first took an interest in only in my forties—oriental literature, philosophy—has been of interest to him from the very beginning. And this sphere of knowledge opened up for him long ago of its own accord. He did not have to move into it or decipher its meaning; it was already open and ready for him. It is strange that he has been interested in the East from early childhood. He has always been passionately interested in China and Japan—things for which a formal education gave him no predisposition. China was generally rejected as an intellectual topic because of its strange and wonderful atmosphere, something that remains obscure to us even today. But my son was still interested in the world of the East, rather than our world. The whole development of what is both positive and negative in rock music, in modern art in general, is directed against the pronouncement of long monologues and explanations and toward the idea of providing solutions that may be paradoxical but are still natural, and which have not been painfully worked out.

So in this respect a change of times is undoubtedly taking place, but it is not happening all at once. It is taking place gradually, revealing itself in the way a certain thing comes to predominate over another. One might say that on the whole, while people are apparently getting used to the development of what is intuitive, they still incline to what has already passed away. There is still a certain lack of precision, but there is certainly a move toward the intuitive. A revival of interest in what was taking place a hundred years ago, an interest in Blavatskaya, for example.[2] In general I have the feeling that nothing in history has a definite end, nothing can be finally defined or quantified. From each successive present-day perspective we merely gain the impression that we have finally achieved absolute clarity. Then seventy years go by and everything changes completely and we see a reappearance of what seemed to have gone out of existence long ago.

IVASHKIN: Which events in the twentieth century do you see as the most important? And which event—cultural, scientific, social—has had the most influence on your work? Can such events influence art? The present century has developed new conceptions of time, space, and the theory of relativity. Are any of these reflected in your music?

SCHNITTKE: I find it hard to speak of a single influence from one thing in particular, but I can mention a number of things that had a powerful influence. One of the most powerful "impressions" (forgive my use of this word) was the atom bomb and all its consequences, especially moral consequences. After the first atomic explosion there seemed to be no way out—all the dangers and horrors, all the even more terrible

---

2. Helena Petrovna Blavatsky, *née* Hahn (1831–1891): Born in Ekaterinoslav, Ukraine, she went to the United States in 1873 and in 1875 helped found the Theosophical Society in New York City, later continuing her work in India. She gained a considerable following, and her psychic powers were widely acclaimed, though these abilities did not fare well when investigated by the Society for Psychical Research. —ed.

bombs and weapons. The power of these weapons seemed to reduce every value to nothing. That is true in a certain sense, but not everything was deprived of its value. The inescapable tragedy that hung over our existence twenty-five or thirty years ago now seems to be there no longer, in spite of the fact that the actual number of universal dangers has not decreased, but our moral tension has been somewhat reduced.

Something that made a great impression on me and continues to do so is my growing feeling that the same amount of time can vary in length. In human life—at any rate in my own case—time has two circles of development. The first, the longest, which seemed for me to come to an end in 1985, and the second, which began after that time. Now every day has a very long time span. It contains a great deal. This is once again a primordial feeling, seeming to originate from childhood (although I haven't yet entered my second childhood!). This new feeling that time is once again expanding has been of great benefit to me. Previously, I constantly felt tired, life seemed to be "wearing me down," everything grew wearisome, there was so much of everything, and it had all already been. But now I have regained my ability to evaluate various phenomena not merely in the way they are linked together, but each one separately. This lengthens the experience of every second. I do not feel that each second is a momentary grain of sand. It is a segment of time, something in itself. And I had long since lost this sense of its being something. Even now I often grow weary, quickly, and for many reasons, but it is not the weariness of the age or the decade. It is a weariness that is very powerful, it seems to cover everything. But I need only half an hour to forget all about it. This is why my attitude to time has completely changed.

I have begun to feel in particular that for different people, and for one person at different periods of life, the length and speed of time can differ greatly. This is a kind of time that is infinitely varied, even though it contains the same number of seconds. The seconds tick by in the same way, but the distance between them varies. This is why I have come closer to the Einsteinian view of time, that it is relative. I have begun to understand this better because my own experience shows me that in my own life seconds have varied in length. I have reached this idea of time without any technical experiments or space travel.

IVASHKIN: You will recall Lev Tolstoy's *Circle of Reading,* something he published in his lifetime that contained excerpts from books written by various philosophers and authors. What is your "circle of reading"? Do you ever copy down anything that you regard as essential for your work or life? Are there any texts, formulae, or rules that you constantly repeat to yourself or to which you constantly return? What kind of reading matter do you prefer, fiction or essays?

SCHNITTKE: In theory I would be in favor of trying to systematize life in every possible way, and this would include copying things down. But that's only in theory. In practice I've never been able to do that, and nowadays I wouldn't even want to, just as I don't want to do anything else I was so anxious to do earlier. I am now conscious—and this follows from what I was saying before—that knowledge is both finite and at the same time infinite. It is finite insofar as you apparently cannot put into it any more than a certain quantity. If you learn something new, you are bound to lose something else that you read or learned before, and this moves away into the shadows and ceases to have any profound significance. There is a kind of standard amount of knowledge. But of course it is only a relative amount, because it is well known that when people are dying, they re-experience everything they have seen, known, said, done, and heard. They remember everything, including what their conscious memory no longer recalls. Their subconscious remembers everything.

Irrespective of this, I have come to understand that to rely on systematized knowledge comprising quotations, names, books, and an inner world built up over a long period (like constructing a whole state or world inside yourself) would be wrong for me. The reason is that human knowledge has one special characteristic: the more of what human beings are aware of unconsciously is transferred into the area of what they know consciously, the more of what is known consciously comes to lose those elements that are invisible and imperceptible, those elements that are a kind of shadow of human thought, before it crystallizes. In a certain sense the very word "crystallizes" already imposes a limitation on this strange and infinite world. When crystallization takes place, the whole outer shell of the world vanishes, and with it an infinite number of undiscovered possibilities. That's the danger of crystallization. When knowledge comes to be crystallized, although it acquires something, it loses a great deal. The "crystal" may be something bright, sparkling, and solid, but it is still a crystal, not a living thing, organic, changeable. This is why my preference is not for encyclopedically systematized knowledge, but for the kind of knowledge a human being has without appearing to know it. This is the kind of knowledge I now regard as more important.

As for reading, strange as it may seem, I used to read less, and I needed to read less than I do now. I remember that I had a passion for ideas from the East, and the time came when I lost interest in literature. It all appeared second rate and trivial, apart from a few philosophical writings. I somehow lost all sense of fiction having any connection with real life. Reading, I lost the feeling that fiction always made sense. I found it lacking in the kind of knowledge that is crystallized, clear, and complete.

But now I have again returned to an earlier feeling, when my reading of philosophical writings brought continual disappointment. Like many people nowadays I subscribe to *Voprosy Filosofii* [Problems of Philosophy].[3] One day I open it and find myself bitterly disappointed in Nietzsche, who had previously produced a literally hypnotic effect on me (I have not read many of his works, just one or two), but now what he writes seems so trivial and superficial. I just cannot read it.

Nor does Solovyov now seem serious enough. His seriousness is the kind of seriousness that systematizes, greatly superior to Nietzsche. But I think even he is now out-of-date. He was to make striking revelations and in many respects did so, but his writings now produce an impression of tiredness and mental indigestion.

---

3. *Voprosy Filosofii* began monthly publication in August 1947 as the official organ of the Institute of Philosophy of the Academy of Science of the Soviet Union. Its stated main objectives were the scientific elaboration and discussion of questions concerning dialectical and historical materialism, and the history of philosophy, logic, ethics, aesthetics, and other branches of philosophy. In the Soviet period it had a clear Marxist bias. —ed.

I think my attitude to philosophy has now basically changed. The philosophy infused in the Bible, which contains everything, including philosophy, has not lost its meaning, but the kind of philosophy that creates a system, however lofty it may be, has to some degree lost any meaning for me or relevance for the present day. So I have renewed my interest in fiction. But of course I realize that our current fascination with what we were deprived of for decades is the fascination people feel for what they have been starved of. I now realize how much we were starved of it, and I have been reading for the past three years and have still not grown tired of it. But many of the things I previously pounced on no longer arouse my interest. I no longer get excited about the endless articles that appear in every newspaper about Akhmatova, Mandelshtam, or Pasternak. But when I opened the copy of *Novyi Mir* [New World], where they had started to publish extracts from *The Gulag Archipelago*, I was deeply shaken.[4] That was one of the most powerful sensations I have felt in recent times. I look forward to its continuation, and in one way I am pleased that I did not read it before. I had naturally read parts of it, but never in their proper sequence. So now I am keen to read it all.

IVASHKIN: Do you regard modern thought as too rational and materialistic? What is your attitude to magic, religion, signs, and omens? Do you think it essential for the maintenance of spiritual discipline to observe the feasts in the church calendar, to adhere to the formal requirements of religious faith? Which philosopher do you take the closest interest in? Is there any particular philosophical system that is consonant with your own view of things?

SCHNITTKE: I am unable to name any formally organized system that I could regard as decisive for me, one that would dictate my way of life, or my way of working. Of course, at various times I have yielded to what I was reading and found fascinating at that particular moment. But nowadays I have generally lost my capacity for being fascinated by reading a book or studying philosophy. I have lost it because it is as if I am continually aware of the total inadequacy of a philosophy of ideas. Even at its most subtle it still reveals its permanent shortcomings. It is for this reason that all those naive mystics who were disinclined to systematize and limit what they knew, simply expounding it, are now more important to me than those who erected a structured system of knowledge. If one starts with Jesus Christ and takes the Gospel of Saint John, the writings of Saint Augustine, Meister Eckhart, or Saint Francis, in every case we are dealing with a mystery that will always remain a mystery, even when it is manifested through the naive and sunny disposition of Saint Francis. It is a mystery you cannot explain. This for me is the highest form of literature.

Moreover as soon as the mystery is systematized, as soon as it becomes a question of mysticism being measured out, as in the case of Rudolf Steiner or anyone

---

4. Chapters from Solzhenitsyn's *The Gulag Archipelago* appeared in 1989 in *Novy Mir* (Nos. 8, 9, 10, and 11). This was its first official publication in Russia, possible only as a result of *perestroika* and *glasnost'*. —ed.

else, I lose interest completely.[5] I lose faith in it right away. As long as human beings hold on to the feeling that the mystery is truly limitless, they never reach the stage of relative systematization, and one can always place reliance on what they say. But as soon as they begin to systematize, they immediately fall into one of the many errors caused by knowledge that is relative only, and I'm no longer interested.

As for religion, all the formal routine of religious faith—constantly followed every day in a virtuously literal interpretation—has, for logical reasons, lost its value for me. I cannot defend the idea of people motivating everything they do and say in connection with their religious faith on such realistic grounds. For them it may still be a religious faith, but its daily ritual *seems* to have lost its foundation. *Seems*, I emphasize, because if I ever find peace in a kind of "zero" position, I am at once brought back to a naive and primitive sense of religious faith and find I can at once have faith in it all, in spite of the naiveté of religion and its rituals. At a religious service I experience not only the joy of being there but also a feeling of depression—from the fact that during a long ceremony there may be ten-minute periods that are exciting but also other ten-minute periods that are just empty, when one is present only in a formal way. But religious faith never loses its basic qualities. And these are to be found in the fact that you have a sense, through all the imprecise words, the numerous translations, all the explanations of ritual, all the unreliable stories about them, all the false and incorrect interpretations—through all of these you sense the original meaning, derived not from a limited conscious mind that creates systems but from something limitless, like the words of Saint Francis or Saint John. In the naiveté something infinite is preserved. In spite of the unconvincing words, there seems to remain something invisible, what is most important, what is basic. So I am ready to submit to any ritualistic discipline, since I detect shining through it not the precision of every moment but the very basis of religious belief.

IVASHKIN: Does a connection between art and the physical world exist for you, and how does it manifest itself? What is the connection between meaning and its expression in sound? In the language of music (assuming music is a language) is there a symbolic dimension, and what does it consist of? Are the sounds used in music symbolic in themselves, or do they become symbolic only in a particular stylistic context? And, generally speaking, do you believe culture contains symbols? Do you consider it necessary to "interpret" a work of art, to discover its deeply hidden "mythological" dimension, so to speak?

SCHNITTKE: I believe there is a connection between art and the physical world, but I have no way of proving it. Yet I still have the feeling that it is there. In particular, when I am listening to serious music, or even just to loud music, I have the impression that something is pressing down on me, not merely with its weight, but with a kind of invisible mass. I have the sensation that some physical influence is working on me. This is why my next-door neighbor can make me suffer. When my

---

5. Schnittke was influenced by Rudolf Steiner's anthroposophical ideas when he composed his *Der gelbe Klang* (on Vassily Kandinsky's libretto) in 1974. —ed.

brother and sister were small, we used to share the same room, and I remember that throughout my childhood, from about the age of fourteen, I inflicted torture on them with my domestic music making.

When we speak of something being physical we must surely consider not just what can be weighed physically but also what is invisible and yet can still have a physical effect on us. There can be no doubt that music has a physical effect on me. This effect can be a very subtle one, as it is in the music of Webern, or in Luigi Nono's composition for string quartet, *Fragmente-Stille, An Diotima*. This work produces the most powerful effect on me, even though the volume of sound is almost nonexistent. One has the feeling that there are extremely refined forms of such a physical effect. For now I deliberately choose two extremes, ignoring more normal examples. We are used to the normal effect of good music well played, but in these two extreme cases a definite physical quality makes itself felt.

One other thing: the effect of Bach's music. That was something I constantly experienced. Try to have a loud conversation when Bach's music is playing and you find you cannot. When the *Saint Matthew Passion* is being played, you have to make a conscious effort to talk loudly. I remember, when I was teaching at the Moscow Conservatory, Nodar Gabuniya was formally enrolled as one of my students. During one of our lessons a tape we had ordered was switched on. Without being conscious of what it was, we started talking in a whisper, because we were hearing Bach's music.

IVASHKIN: What if it had been some other music?

SCHNITTKE: I don't think it would have had the same effect. Bach's music produces its own form of physical effect, although not one of loudness or harshness. In fact, one could call it a spiritual effect. But in Bach's music one ceases to be conscious of the boundary between what is spiritual and what is physical, or, to be more precise, the spiritual is a continuation of the physical, not something quite distinct from it.

Music is, of course, a physical reality, because volume and pitch are measurable. But it is also unquestionably a language. Not that it can be translated into its equivalent in words—the latter is the most elementary and primitive idea imaginable. Music is a language that carries a message, but not one that can be retold in words. Every attempt to translate music into words inevitably leads to banality; of that I am quite convinced. There can be something like a translation of music into words when something connected with the world of music is somehow recreated. For example, K. Svasyan's writings[6] always make a great impression on me, especially what he writes about Mozart. It is as though one were reading not a description of music, but a literary work of art. One also experiences a musical feeling. And this is exactly the kind of literature about music that has no harmful effects. I could give other examples. Everything that Thomas Mann wrote about music in *Doctor Faustus* produces a most powerful impression—at any rate it once produced such an impression on me. I cannot say the same about descriptions of music written by

---

6. Konstantin Svasyan: Russian-Armenian writer and critic who published many philosophical essays, especially during the period of *perestroika* under Gorbachov (in the early 1980s). —ed.

musicologists. Hoffmann wrote some remarkable pages about music, but he was a composer, of course.

As for the symbolic dimension of music, I think it has two different origins. First, there is the kind of relative symbolism that attaches different meanings to the same things. For instance, in one tradition there is one meaning, and in another the opposite meaning, like the European and Chinese perceptions of black and white. There are no doubt similar differences in the ways musical signals and their meaning are interpreted, and this is the origin of relative symbolism in music. But music also involves the kind of symbolism that seems to give unity to all those things that are theoretically diverse. This symbolism is predetermined by the character of the sound. For example, a loud, harsh sound is a natural elemental phenomenon, something that evokes fear and alarm in the hearer. The same applies to another kind of sound that "turns you on" in some way, lifts your spirits, or simply calms you down. Furthermore a symbolic interpretation of sound is usually more noticeable in religious music or in what is connected with signals, like bells or the sound of hammers. Or the awesome mystical sounds in Buddhist music—all these are examples of the kind of symbolism that is not conventional. I don't know whether it is an absolute category, but it comes close to being one.

IVASHKIN: You mean the kind of symbolism that exists in any music from any period?

SCHNITTKE: In theory, yes, but there may be whole strata of music that are devoid of such symbolism. But this does not mean that it does not exist. It exists in the reality of sound of this segment of the human race, so to speak.

IVASHKIN: What about your own music? Very often themes or similar motifs seem to "wander" through various of your works. Is this done unconsciously, or do these themes signify for you particular symbols and "points of concentration"?

SCHNITTKE: No, I do not define them in words and am not now aware of any "points of concentration." It is more that every moment I have a feeling that they have to appear, and so I write them. But the fact that they have to appear does not depend on any kind of verbal proof. It is a question of each sound being linked with the sound that precedes or follows it. So the whole musical fabric is something in which all the sounds are linked, and one thing leads to another. But it would be fatal to define and try to explain all this in words.

IVASHKIN: But you are aware that you have composed the same thing before?

SCHNITTKE: Of course. There is a moment when I think, "I've used this before, and if I reproduce it precisely as it was, I am guilty of falsity because repetition is bad." But in reality I am wrong to think that because the truth has to be expressed in different ways at different moments, so there has to be this constant repetition. And I observe this kind of repetition in many composers, from Bach to Shostakovich. It is to be found not just in a single composer but in a whole group of composers living at the same period. This is not because they imitate each other or are careless of their own individuality. It is inevitable because it is part of the spiritual reality, the force field in which the composers are working. So when they do the same things it is because they are under the influence of the same forces. They are not stealing from each other. It is the effect of a kind of general sphere of influence that unites them all, not merely the way they influence one another.

IVASHKIN: Do you regard yourself as a man of nature or a man of culture? Do you see these two concepts as being in mutual opposition? Are you open to everything, even the base elements of life, or just to its upper layer? Is your art, and that of your colleagues, elitist? What do you see as the meaning of individual artistic creativity? Is it self-expression or is it the reflection of a world order, of a "higher" form of creativity?

SCHNITTKE: I cannot, of course, regard myself as a man of nature, because I do not live in the country, I do not plough or sow, I have no garden, I do not go fishing. In short there is nothing in my life that bears witness to nature, and I regard this as my own serious shortcoming. But I am still bold enough to insist that this situation will continue, and that is not just because I should now find it physically difficult to do any of those things. I shall continue not to do any of them, while being fully aware of my shortcomings.

   I am convinced that culture is important, but less important than nature. My own inadequate contact with nature was to some extent predetermined by the fact that by my origins I half belong to a milieu that had many links with nature! And it is as if I have still not forgotten that. The other half of me belongs not so much to a cultural milieu as to an urban one, and those are two very different things! So while I have a great respect for culture I would give priority to nature. Even when nature is as cruel as she is kind, even though in nature there is much that is good and much that is dangerous, she is still nature.

IVASHKIN: In connection with this, is the music itself, your own music, a reflection of certain phenomena that exist in nature, in the broad sense of the word, or of what comes from culture, that is, of what relates to human consciousness? Does your music reflect nature, or does it reflect you?

SCHNITTKE: Every attempt I might make to explain my music is inevitably doomed to fail, because when human beings have to talk about anything, they find themselves in chains. Are they expressing what they want to? All I can say, and that will be convincing enough, is that I have never had any preconceived ideas like those Beethoven had in his *Pastoral Symphony*. If I had any, they were brought to light in what was written about my music, and I have no recollection of them. I never had any intention of trying to depict a storm at sea, an earthquake, or laughter and tears. However, when I used an actual text, when I was writing my *Faust Cantata*, for instance, some things did come close to this. But they came into the music in conventional concert form, in the form, as it were, of music from the past. And in the music I did not try to convey the sound of wailing physiologically, but in a rather stylized way. If I had tried to express wailing as it is nowadays, I should have felt limited. Faust is a figure from the past, and in any case not a naturalistic one.

IVASHKIN: What about the C major triad, which occurs so frequently in your music? Is that a natural phenomenon or a cultural fact?

SCHNITTKE: For me it is a natural phenomenon. And not just the C major triad. For example, I believe that the overtone series has a basis in nature. I have heard it several times by the sea in the morning and in Ruza, too,[7] from somewhere in the distance. I can't explain it. It might have been a milking machine being started up that produced the sounds of a whole-tone scale, it might have been a mere accident, but I had the impression of something going on outside me.

IVASHKIN: Where do your ideas come from, and how are they realized? How do the conception of the form and meaning of the whole work come to you? Are you doing the writing, or is it some higher power writing through you? Do you make any conscious effort to ensure that an idea appears in a particular form?

SCHNITTKE: This is like so many other things. When you start talking about it, all your attempts to explain it in more or less precise terms are a complete failure. But you still have to try to explain, you still have to try to come closer to what you cannot actually grasp, in the hope that this time you might manage to get a little closer to it. Basically, if you have a pattern inside you that has formed irrationally, you have to divide yourself into two spheres. One of them is your self in the narrow sense, the other is what is revealed to you through your self—what is considerably larger than you are. And it is this larger sphere that is in control, not the narrow sphere of your self. In fact, a person's whole life is an attempt to be not oneself but an instrument of something outside the self. This is what dictates form, words, and your conditioned response to what is outside you. It is as if you do not belong to yourself. As long as you have this feeling, your work is never a burden. You are not the one prescribing, you are doing something prescribed for you by someone else. "Someone else" is to put it very crudely: it is something more important than you are. And once it begins to prescribe what you do, it basically predetermines the form of expression you use. So the ideal form of utterance that you are striving to achieve is predetermined by this initial feeling, and the whole of your work is an attempt to tune in more precisely to what is, what always has been, and will be. This tuning-in process can never be perfect; it may continue for an hour, even an hour and a half, but then it stops. Nevertheless, the

---

7. Rusa is a small place near Moscow where there was a "Composers' House" owned by the Union of Soviet Composers. Moscow composers used to meet there and write music. They lived for a month or two in separate village-style cottages and thus were able to see each other more often than was possible in Moscow itself. —ed.

whole of your work is not at all a putting together and carrying out of technical instructions; it is a kind of listening in to something that is already there. And this predetermines everything—the significance of the details and the rational interpretation of them. Of course there is a certain moment when the ideal conception has to be turned into reality, and then you have to resort to a rational explanation that simplifies the process. In this simplifying process you come down from a higher step onto a step that coarsens and distorts this truth you are aware of, but at least you have been given the opportunity to express it. Otherwise you have no right to use even words. Words are distortions of ideas. So you consciously accept the coarsening process merely because it enables you to say something. Words act as coarsening agents if you try to utter a thought, and so do the written notes, if you write music down. I have known attempts to go beyond these limitations, when I've heard recordings of musical improvisations. I mean genuine ones, not artificial quasi-improvisations.

For example, a remarkably handsome man once came to the Taganka Theater. He brought some photographs with him, which showed him sitting, a halo round his head, while worshipful young ladies surrounded him. But when he began his improvisations, my view of him changed. They were improvisations that could have lasted as long as a film. There was no feeble repetition or weak monotony of rhythm. No commonplace harmonies, no startlingly incomprehensible twists and turns. It was not a conscious performance of the unexpected, but an improvisation that was not concerned about how the audience responded to it, so in that moment it was transformed into something genuine.

Alemdar Karamanov could play like that when he sat down at a piano and improvised fugues.[8] They really were fugues, not sham polyphony. Naturally he did not attach great importance to this gift. In theory there is a lofty and more serious way of reaching this level of performance. But I regard it as a different kind of musical existence, superior to what we are used to in the European tradition of composed music. It reminds me of what one finds in serious oriental music, in Indian music.

IVASHKIN: Is there any such thing as "the spirit of the age" to define the character of an epoch, which may at present be unidentifiable but which in all probability becomes clear in the course of time?

SCHNITTKE: Yes, there is, and it is the manifestation of a certain universal force. Paradoxically there is a relationship between the work of Bach and Brahms. This is because they are in the grip of some sort of powerful energy source, a kind of general flow. The same applies to writers. A similar general force relates Kafka to Hesse, although they could not be more different as writers.

---

8. Alemdar Sabitovich Karamanov (born 1934): Russian composer; Schnittke's friend at the Moscow Conservatory. Schnittke called Karamanov a genius. Karamanov composed twenty-four symphonies, most of which have religious titles. For many years Karamanov lived in Simpheropol, in the Crimea. Since the 1980s he has lived in Sergiev Posad (formerly Zagorsk), about 100 km from Moscow. There is a Karamanov Society in London. —ed.

Whenever a new technique or a new set of ideas appears, it is not something that comes to the mind of a single individual, but something permeating the air. Hauer and Schoenberg, Golyshev and Obukhov.[9] And I do not attach any real importance to the question of who first discovered it.

No composer gains or loses anything from using or not using a new technique, because each of them is bound primarily to himself and only after that to every type of technique. The works of Hauer, Schoenberg, and even those of Berg, Webern, and Schoenberg are completely different. When Schoenberg was at his pre-twelve-tone stage, there was a short-lived resemblance to Webern—the same short forms, a certain enigmatic symbolism, as in his *Six Pieces*, his *Herzgewächse* for soprano, harmonium, harp, and celesta. But there is still a vast difference between Schoenberg and Webern, and between Berg and the other two.

The difference between Hauer and Schoenberg is even greater. And discussions about who was the first to use the twelve-tone system, which almost turn into legal arguments, in time become meaningless. In the same way Thomas Mann's fatuous comment given to *Doctor Faustus* that "the twelve-tone technique is the spiritual property of Arnold Schoenberg" now seems like nonsense. Also the fact that Wagner liked luxury, lived all his life deep in debt, and was far from a perfect human being. And the fact that Brahms, too, was far from perfect, but was perhaps guilty of fewer of the "deadly sins." And that Anton Bruckner's life was almost holy. With the passage of time, all this becomes completely meaningless!

There is, for example, a definite resemblance between Andrei Volkonsky's[10] *Shchaza's Laments* and Edison Denisov's[11] *Sun of the Incas*. Volkonsky's work was composed earlier, but this does not mean that *Sun of the Incas* is inferior. A long time ago Yuri Butsko[12] showed me his *Polyphonic Concerto*, a work unique of its kind. It is a composition for four keyboard instruments in every possible combination. It also has a strictly worked-out system based on the repetition of tetrachords, all formed in the same way. But, in addition, as the notes get higher, flats predominate; and as they get lower, sharps. A kind of endless arch is formed. So if you start with A, B, C, D, and

---

9. Efim Golyshev (1875–1970) and Nikolai Obukhov (1892–1954): Russian composers of the beginning of the twentieth century; both left Russia after the Revolution of 1917. They developed twelve-tone techniques as early as 1914 (String Trio by Golyshev, 1914; *Ten Psychological Tables* by Obukhov, 1915). —ed.

10. Andrei Volkonsky (born 1933 in Geneva): Russian composer and harpsichordist. Moved to Moscow in 1947. One of the leaders of Soviet avant-garde music in the 1950s and 1960s. Founder of Madrigal, the first modern group in Russia to perform music of the Renaissance and Baroque eras on period instruments in authentic style. Volkonsky left the Soviet Union in 1972. —ed.

11. Edison Denisov (1929–1996): Russian composer, very influential teacher, and the leader of the Soviet avant-garde (together with Schnittke, Volkonsky, and Gubaidulina). Founded ASM-2 (Association of Modern Music) in 1990. —ed.

12. Yuri Butsko (born 1938): Moscow composer, studied at Moscow Conservatory with Schnittke. Composed four operas, five symphonies, a number of instrumental concertos, cantatas, and chamber compositions, including four string quartets. He devoted many years to adapting the old Russian "chant" (*znamennyi rospev*) to modern times. He has constructed an original system which he describes as a kind of Russian dodecaphony, applying a twelve-tone row extracted from Russian material. In 1968–1969 he composed *Polyphonic Concerto* for four keyboard instruments, which inspired Schnittke in his own experiments with *znamennyi rospev,* especially in his Symphony No. 4. —ed.

move upward, you then get D, E, F, G; then G, A, B♭, C; C, D, E♭, F; and so on. The further you go, the more flats there are. And if you go down, there are more sharps.

In my Fourth Symphony, written many years later, I use four intonational systems organized in the same way, which interact. There are two tetrachords: one major, for Russian Orthodox music, the other minor, for Catholic music. Furthermore, for Jewish music there is a chain not of tetrachords but of trichords. For example, A♯, B, C; D♯, E, F; G♯, A, B♭; C♯, D, E♭. And for Lutheran music there is a six-step scale: B, C♯, D, then E♯, F♯, G♯, then the same sequence of six steps is repeated a seventh higher, starting from A. In short, roughly the same principle that Butsko used, but there are also a multitude of other things that have no connection with anything he used, because in the symphony there are many ideas apart from the intonational structure, ideas connected with the form or the style, to say nothing of the inner program or the fact that it is based on fifteen episodes—five, five, and five.

In making conscious use of this principle I took it further. We cannot say that Butsko was relying on something existing in reality. We may detect a tendency for sharps to increase as one goes lower and for flats to increase as one moves higher, but we cannot turn this into something so absolute that it becomes a system. It is entirely Butsko's contribution. And this does not mean that he used a technique that had long been in existence. What happened was what usually happens with all technological concepts: you look for natural premises to justify them.

IVASHKIN: But doesn't such a system already exist in Russian Orthodox church music?

SCHNITTKE: In Orthodox chant it doesn't work according to that system. In one case you get a natural, and in another a flat—the same step in the same octave. Every time there is a new technological idea, including Butsko's, we have something being built on what already exists but which has not yet become dogma. And in the process of becoming aware of it as a theory, we have to allow for a process of elimination of what is unsystematic from what is systematic—and the crystallization of what is systematic.

The same thing happens when we try to make sense of folk music and the intervals it uses. For hundreds of years there has been a continuous tendency to schematize it and remove its "inaccuracies." And what happens is that what was identified in the first interpretations of folk music as inaccurate a hundred and fifty years ago becomes precious for folklorists at the turn of the century and in the 1920s and 1930s. They go "chasing" after these "inaccuracies," these variants. In fact, and this is important, there is no such thing as a perfectly crystallized variant, and yet all theorizing tends to turn recognized concepts into crystallized ones and eliminate chance impurities. It is my own belief that what is random is as normal as what appears not to be random.

Nikolai Karetnikov showed me the music of his *Mystery of Paul the Apostle*.[13] There is a tango in it to accompany the hero's suicide. Later Karetnikov was absolutely

---

13. Nikolai Karetnikov (1930–1994): Russian Soviet composer, the most consistent in his use of twelve-tone technique up to the late 1980s. His major compositions include operas (*Mystery of Paul the Apostle, Til Eulenspiegel*), four symphonies, sacred choral music, and chamber compositions. —ed.

convinced that the tango I used in the First Concerto Grosso was there because of his influence. And when, even later, he heard the tango in my *Faust,* he regarded it as direct plagiarism. But long before the tango in Karetnikov's *Mystery,* which accompanies the death of Nero, there had been Kurt Weill's *Threepenny Opera,* in which a similarly cynically cruel tango was one of the best numbers. The music of *Threepenny Opera* had been in my head since 1949 because my father was crazy about it. When old records of it turned up in 1949, he immediately started playing them. And when he got to the GDR in 1955, he had with him a recording of the whole opera.

It is curious that even before that, Mayakovsky, in his poem *War and Peace,* written in 1915, included written music of the *Argentinian Death Tango.* And there are later examples, too. Remember Bernardo Bertolucci's famous film *Last Tango in Paris,* in which the tango still plays the same fateful role. It is as if this were an inevitable function of the tango at any time. So, with all due respect to Karetnikov, I cannot plead guilty to stealing something from him, because I was doing what people did before both of us—and are still doing afterward.

At the end of the 1950s, after Lev Mazel[14] described the harmonic phenomenon of "common mediants" (for example, between B major and C minor), many composers, myself included, made use of it. It was indeed Mazel who first identified it, but for some reason Yuri Kholopov still does not accept the relationship or even the expression used to describe it. But the examples given by Mazel in his analyses, from Beethoven to Liszt, are very convincing: in one of the *Valses Oubliées,* for example, where we have F-sharp major and G minor.

IVASHKIN: You find the same thing in Shostakovich.

SCHNITTKE: Of course. For instance, the finale of his Eighth Symphony starts in C major and then briefly moves into C-sharp minor. I am simply trying to make the point that this was "in the air" and made its appearance in many people's music, especially in the 1950s and 1960s.

Throughout the history of music there are vast numbers of such parallels: Stravinsky's *Rite of Spring* and Prokofiev's *Scythian Suite.* Or the neoclassicism of Stravinsky, Hindemith, and Honegger. All these are multiple manifestations of the same phenomenon. I think that if they really wanted to, each of these composers could accuse the others of plagiarism.

I recall Stockhausen in one of the first two volumes of his *Texts on Music*[15] referring indignantly to the disgraceful way Boulez had behaved. This was because when Stockhausen showed him his *Groups* [*Gruppen*], Boulez had reacted unfavorably to the idea behind the work, but then immediately wrote his own composition for two or three interacting orchestras.

---

14. Lev Mazel (1907–2000) and Yuri Kholopov (born 1932): Two leading Soviet musicologists, both professors at the Moscow Conservatory. —ed.

15. Karlheinz Stockhausen, *Texte zur Musik* (4 vols.) (Cologne: DuMont, 1963, 1964, 1971, 1978). —ed.

The same sort of thing happened to me at the Conservatory in 1956 or 1957, when I wrote my Symphony. The third movement, the Passacaglia, starts with pizzicato in the double basses. The work was performed by a student orchestra under the direction of Algis Zhyuraitis. Kabalevsky and Shostakovich were present. Now in Shostakovich's Eleventh Symphony the slow movement starts with pizzicato double basses, and I had the feeling that he was using what he had first heard from me. But that, of course, is nonsense, if only because the meaning of music is not merely a question of technical devices. What really matters is never passed on from one composer to another.

Another point. The phenomenon of "polystylistics" in music existed long before I started to use the word and thought about the interaction of musical material in different styles. The first twentieth-century composers to make use of it were Ives and Mahler. And among the serialists one of the first to use it was Bernd Alois Zimmermann. And Henri Pousseur was fascinated by it—in the general context of serial organization he employs a whole system of interacting styles from different periods. The tonal quotations were like fragmentary remnants of a tonal world that had been absorbed into atonal music. Then came Luciano Berio's Symphony and many other works that used musical quotations.

The fact that I began to use a polystylistic method was brought about, first, by everything these composers had done before me, which I naturally could not ignore. But there was a personal element too. The polystylistic method, the use of interacting styles, gave me a way out of the difficult situation in which I had been put by having to combine, over a long period, work for the cinema with work "at the desk." There was a time when I simply did not know what to do: I had to drop either one or the other.

My way out was not just on the surface, it lay at the heart of the problem, because what I did for the cinema was serious, not mere hack-work. In my early years as a composer I was even interested in writing real marches and waltzes, not stylized ones. It gave me a certain personal satisfaction. Then I reached a critical point when I no longer knew how to proceed. And the way out I found was the First Symphony, in which there is an interplay of film music and music written "at the desk."

IVASHKIN: It seems to me, as far as allusions are concerned, that it is your Third Symphony that more closely resembles Luciano Berio's Symphony, not your First.

SCHNITTKE: Yes and no. In Berio's Symphony, unlike my Third Symphony, all the quotations are genuine, and the composer's task was to join a vast number of them into a single whole so they seem to have developed by natural course of chance.

IVASHKIN: I believe Berio's starting point was literary texts, Lévi-Strauss and the structuralists, whereas in your First Symphony your starting point was the cinema. Apparently, when he was working on his symphony Berio was greatly assisted by Umberto Eco. In your First Symphony there is no mythological or structuralist layer.

SCHNITTKE: You are right, I derived a great deal from the cinema. As long ago as 1965–1967 I remember having many conversations with Elem Klimov[16] and Andrei Khrzhanovsky,[17] who at that time were attempting to use the polystylistic method, to use quotations in film. Khrzhanovsky's animated film *The Glass Harmonica* (*Steklyannaia garmonika*) uses a great number of quotations from painting. And this was in a film completed in 1968, that is, before Berio's symphony. And at the same time Klimov was talking about so-called "harmonic eclectics," in other words combining diverse elements into a single quality. Later he apparently gave up the idea. But a film he made in 1965—*The Adventures of a Dentist* (*Pokhozhdeniia zubnogo vracha*)—is based on that idea precisely.

IVASHKIN: Let's get back to what we were talking about before—the ways "the spirit of the time" reveals itself.

SCHNITTKE: Of course, the meaning of what in general is "hovering in the air" reveals itself in many people at one and the same time. We must not exaggerate this, but its importance must not be diminished either. The process largely depends on ideas that may not previously have been expressed clearly enough, but which were given utterance by someone for the first time. I don't know who is of more value to the history of music, the person who first discovers an idea but proves not to be a worthwhile composer, or the person who is not a pioneer but proves to be of worth in the actual process of turning the idea into reality.

In the history of music, one may continually observe pairs of competing originators. For example, in the history of Russian music, Tchaikovsky and Rimsky-Korsakov, Scriabin and Rakhmaninov, Prokofiev and Shostakovich. In the music of one member of the pair, one can actually detect more new technical devices. For instance, there are more such devices in Rimsky-Korsakov's music than in Tchaikovsky's, and far more in Scriabin's than in Rakhmaninov's. But when it comes to the question of making a final evaluation, we are on less definite ground. In the pair of Tchaikovsky and Rimsky-Korsakov, there can be no doubt that Tchaikovsky comes first. In the Rakhmaninov-Scriabin pair... Scriabin still comes first. The debate continues, as it were.

IVASHKIN: What do you feel you have in common with your fellow composers Denisov and Gubaidulina?[18] Today your music appears to be different, but in a hundred years' time all three of you will probably be put together on one branch of Russian music.

---

16. Elem Klimov (born 1933): Film producer, friend of Schnittke. —ed.

17. Andrei Khrzhanovsky (born 1939): Cartoon producer, for whom Schnittke wrote film scores. Their film *Glass Harmonica* (1968) was especially important for Schnittke's polystylistic compositions in the 1960s and 1970s. —ed.

18. Sofia Gubaidulina (born 1931): Leading Russian composer and friend of Schnittke. She lives in Hamburg. —ed.

SCHNITTKE: As soon as you put that question to me, I find myself in an awkward position. Of course I can refer to formal, technical matters: aleatoric elements, serialism, tonality, and so on. But I still cannot say anything about what is essential. I feel inhibited when people talk about what we have in common. It would be a different matter if you put the question somewhat differently and asked what the works of contemporary composers have in common. Then my thoughts would be less inhibited.

Apart from the question of a common school of rationalism—which we shall not discuss, although whole books could be written about it—there is a certain common feeling, dictated by the avoidance of the crude dynamics that once seemed to be quite inseparable from music. I have in mind the whole system of conventional dynamic structures. These now seem to be totally sham, and they are just what all composers avoid, in spite of their differences as composers. If they do touch it anywhere, it is in a kind of reflected form—the system is essentially alien to them.

To continue. The emphasis on everything that is irregular is expressed by avoiding geometrical squareness. Music has ceased to be crude verse and has turned into prose or subtle verse. It is the verse not of Lermontov and Pushkin, but of Rilke, Trakl, or Baudelaire. These are poets whose verse is verse "once again," but at a different level. And something like this has happened to music and all its rational techniques, regularity, and traditional forms—they have come back, but at a different level. There has been a return to all these things, and in recent years this return can be sensed more acutely than before, and in a great many composers: in Penderecki and Lutoslawski, and to a certain extent in Nono, Stockhausen, Berio, and others. It is a return to poetry—I mean to rhythmic elements, not in a literary but in a general sense. It is a return to an awareness of time that is ordered in the subtlest way, but which is still regular. What came before, what was linked with atonalism, dodecaphony, and the widespread use of these technical devices, all this had in it too much that was for show. It was as if the composer were showing off to himself, telling himself, "I am always different from everyone else, always new." Of course I am expressing this crudely. They were doing this in all honesty.

From a present-day perspective this was a time of rather naive avant-gardism, twenty or thirty years ago. Now we can speak of the next step. But in fact all history consists of a series of different consecutive steps, in which each successive step appears to be a further development of the preceding one, while we remain unaware of the way they overlap one another. Perhaps the next step from the present one will appear naive. This will come about as a consequence of that temporary deactivization of the new that operates when there is a change to what is newest of all. But this is only a temporary phenomenon. The period when serial music seemed hopelessly out of date is now coming to an end. Serial music is coming to life again, not all of it, just that part of it that deserves to come back to life. And this is why I believe that a final verdict on it still lies in the future.

IVASHKIN: Is Russian culture universal? Must its boundaries be preserved?

SCHNITTKE: Cultural boundaries must not be preserved. The idea is inadmissible. I regard as grossly mistaken all those attempts that have been made to preserve them throughout many centuries and decades, especially in the last hundred and twenty or thirty years. Of course there were outstanding people involved in this movement. But it should never exist as a principle, a theory, a general tendency. I am not arguing that it should not exist at all, but I am opposed to the idea of everything being unified and subordinated to this one idea. Everything should be looked at simultaneously—and there should be something identifiable as absolutely Russified—but it is important that it be genuine and natural, not just something being proclaimed in the press. I see a definite danger in *newspaper nationalism* and in particular in Russian culture at the present time, when everything that is important in it that had been lost or crushed for decades is coming back to life. It is wonderful that it is coming back to life. But the process carries with it the danger of a new overflow....

The earlier overflow, forcing out everything else, brought in a level of culture that was sham and empty show, loudly proclaimed as showy. Thank God we have finished with that. But now another danger looms: a desire to limit outside influences, an unwillingness to have contact with them. Personally I would never be in favor of this, although, in the end, it depends on the individual. Take a giant like Dostoevsky. I regard as mistaken the belief that it was Dostoevsky who strove to lay the foundations of this tendency to keep Russian culture separate from the rest of the world. Dostoevsky is all things at once. And if we merely focus on the Dostoevsky who asserts the autonomy and independence of his world from the world of the West, we are being grossly unfair to him. To say nothing of the fact that like any other person he had the individual right to say what he liked and to make what mistakes he liked. But we must not turn a personal point of view into a general principle. Applying individual points of view to everything will inevitably bring error and inexactitude. Every individual person is wrong. Wrong are those who now stand up against nationalism and national autonomy in favor of eliminating what is specifically national and establishing a kind of universality. But their mistake will become serious indeed if from a judgmental statement it turns into a firmly fixed dogma.

IVASHKIN: Is Russian culture closer to you personally than any other?

SCHNITTKE: If we talk about that side of things, I find myself in a situation that gives me no answer. I found a relative answer when I realized there was no answer.

I have spent my life mainly in Russia, and what this life has brought with it, not just musical impressions, but actual living experience, predetermines my belonging to *this* life and its problems. Whether I quote Russian folk songs or not is of no real significance. Only the death of Shostakovich led me to the realization that he was a real Russian composer—not merely outwardly (he used Russian songs in his work) but in every respect. In every detail of his work—however sharp and unusual his musical language—he remained a Russian composer. Of this there is no doubt, and for me Shostakovich is no less a Russian composer than Prokofiev, whose work outwardly shows far more signs of Russian music. I think the same sort of thing will happen in the future with the evaluation of the work of composers such as Denisov and Gubaidulina, and even of my own music. But for now I should like to talk about what contradicts this.

In the first place, I haven't a drop of Russian blood in me, even though I have lived here all my life. In the second place, I am constantly aware that I have a German half. This has nothing to do with how much German I know, or the fact that I spent two years of my childhood in Vienna. It is predetermined by the fact that my German forebears, who lived here for two hundred years, remained Germans. Not, in a certain sense, the kind of Germans who grew and flourished in the West, but the kind who seem to have preserved the psychological characteristics peculiar to Germans in an earlier time. It is indeed a fact that people who leave a certain kind of reality behind them conserve the reality they have brought away with them. For example, Ukrainians and Russians living in Canada have preserved more of their earlier traditions than those who live here.

Furthermore, I have in every respect experienced an enormous influence from German culture, German literature, and of course the strongest possible influence from German music. Given this, it is clear that without any effort on my part, the German side of my character remains a second powerful force. This second side of my being cannot be defined by answers to a questionnaire; it is predetermined by nature itself. So for me this interaction of Russian and German music is fundamental and final. It is what I came from and what I came to. For me there is no other solution to the whole of this problem. It is this that predetermines all my difficulties in trying to evaluate national or nationalistic preoccupations and passions from one side or the other.

IVASHKIN: What do you think of composers living in emigration?

SCHNITTKE: I think that in the final analysis where people live at a certain moment ceases to play any decisive role, but this is only if their change of place does not come too early, before they have formed properly. In other words, at the present moment where I live is of no significance; everything derives not from where I live but from the whole of my life. It seems to me that the life of such a powerful literary figure as Solzhenitsyn demonstrates this. In every respect he remains an absolutely Russian person, irrespective of the fact that he has lived outside Russia for so many years. In this respect I think there is a certain age when the question of where you live becomes irrelevant. At the same time I understand all the practical advantages enjoyed by someone living in conditions where there are no material problems of existence, no problems, if you'll pardon the expression, of "daily bread." Of course these problems have always existed, but now there are fewer of them. Life in the West offers definite advantages. But then I ask myself, "Do I want to live there?" I want to live both there and here, I want to live both here and there, I want to be able to decide for myself where I live and decide for myself when I can return here and when I need to leave. I don't want to be burdened by a predetermined situation dictated by temporary considerations. And unfortunately *temporarily* sometimes turns out to mean *for a very long time.*

IVASHKIN: Was the cultural climate here in Russia favorable to art, and if life in the future gets better in the social sense, will this be better for art?

SCHNITTKE: My answer to that would be as ambiguous as the meaning of your question. When I was writing mainly film music (although I liked writing it and much of the work was very interesting) for fifteen years, I naturally still felt it to be my secondary task, and I had too little time and opportunity for my main one. I would still argue that one depended directly on the other.

But what if I ask myself what it would be like for a composer whose career develops normally, one who has no connection with the cinema, who is free of such burdens, but who inevitably seems to have lost something by not having them? I believe that basically the balance of pluses and minuses in my life—since it hasn't altogether deflected me—has turned out to be beneficial. But if it had bent me and turned me into nothing but a composer of film music, then almost the same thing would have had a quite different significance. That's why I can't give a final answer. I can answer only for myself and for the present time.

IVASHKIN: There is something in your music that shocks some people—the stratum of banal pop music, the musical clichés you use in a number of your works. It is associated with images of what is evil and diabolical, and it appears in concealed, attractive, and, what is most important, accessible form. It seems to represent *entropy*, the destructive tendency existing in the world. I think that you are in fact interested in the *mechanism of the link* between good and evil, between creation and destruction. In the way evil manifests itself.

SCHNITTKE: Nowadays what is often called "pop culture" is the most direct manifestation of evil in art. Evil in a general sense. Because evil has a localized coloration. Every locality shares a common tendency of its people to stereotype thoughts and feelings, and set patterns are the symbol of this process. Rather like canned food or a pill with a guaranteed effect, these are part of pop culture. And this is the greatest evil: the paralysis of individuality, making everyone like everyone else. The product itself, the cause of all of this, is itself part of pop culture. There is a link going the opposite way between the origin of pop culture and its influence on the development of new pop elements and more stereotyping. Of course there is in pop culture a certain mechanical positive quality. People do aerobics to pop music, and this is surely a good thing. If they did it to Bach's music it would be a bad thing. But basically pop elements in the development of art are a symbol of evil.

To your next point. It is natural that evil should be attractive. It has to be nice and tempting, it has to take the form of something that can creep into your soul without difficulty, something pleasantly comfortable. Whatever it is, it must be fascinating. And pop culture is a good disguise for any kind of devilry, a way of creeping into your soul. So I can see no way of expressing evil in music other than by using elements of pop culture.

Depicting negative emotions—using broken textures, broken melodic lines to express a state of disintegration, tension, leaping thoughts—all this is of course a representation of a certain kind of evil, but not of absolute evil. This is the evil of broken good. Perhaps a soul torn to pieces is also good. But it has been torn to pieces, and this has made it turn bad. Expressing hysteria, agitation, spite, is to express the symptoms of a disease, not its cause. But pop culture comes close to being its cause. It is an evil projecting itself in the form of delusions and torment. It is difficult to fight against.

You refer to the pop elements in my music. This surprises me, because if I count these elements in chronological order, it turns out that there are not so many. But they "stick out" because they are vivid examples of "infection."

The question might be asked, Why don't I depict good instead of evil? The fact is that to express good directly and plainly in music is the most difficult of tasks, sometimes simply impossible. Remember Liszt's *Faust Symphony*. What is the least interesting part of it? The "heavenly" finale—it is sanctimonious and dogmatic. But maybe Liszt is a special case, a composer with leanings toward Satanism in music and the man who actually brought Satanism into music.

In modern music, too, the positive qualities have no connection with the brightest pages of the score. For example, if we take Shostakovich's Seventh or Eighth Symphonies, the relatively colorless positive passages do not outweigh the evil he depicts in them.

IVASHKIN: Why is this?

SCHNITTKE: Clearly there must be something objective behind it. It is a different matter to avoid contact with evil, to keep it out of art, to try and avoid it altogether. For example, a new way of coming close to what is good has emerged. This is to use music that is in every possible way meditative and expressive of weariness, music based on overtones, music that involves a long and slow progression into static harmony. This seems to "guarantee" the impression of something good. But I suspect that this might be a mere routine mask and seriously doubt whether it is really a genuine solution to the problem, because the negative side of reality still continues to exist. One might turn away from it, one might "go into a monastery," but I see no possibility of my doing so. And while not accepting the reality that gave rise to this cliché-ridden musical material, I am still obliged to deal with it all the time.

IVASHKIN: So there cannot be such a thing as a sphere of pure virtue, because it cannot exist in isolation from a human being—or on the basis of human imperfection? I realize that in Dante's *Divina Commedia* the part about Heaven is not at all the most interesting.

SCHNITTKE: No, the part about purgatory is more interesting. In the first place one must separate the problem of good and evil from the way they are expressed in music. In literature this is not necessary, because everything is expressed directly through ideas and words. But if a composer starts to analyze himself while he is composing, and to ponder over what he is writing "on the good side" and "on the evil side," he will give up composing altogether. In fact it often happens that the same thing has two faces (for example, in my Third Violin Concerto). Although good and evil exist as opposite poles and come from mutually hostile sources, there is a point where they unite, and somehow they share one nature. Augustine wrote that evil is an imperfect degree of good. There is in this, of course, an element of Manichaeism and inner duality. But I can grasp this. I understand that when Thomas Mann writes in his *Doktor Faustus* of an imagined oratorio on the Apocalypse in which the music of the righteous entering the Kingdom of Heaven and the music of Hell use the same notes, we have as it were the negative and the positive. This is important for me as a structural necessity: a work of art must have structural unity. This unity can be expressed in different ways, at different levels. For example, it can be expressed by means of a serial or polyphonic technique. Or it can be expressed in a less overt, ambivalent way, when the same material is turned round diametrically.

My starting point—not merely to enable me to compose music but also to enable me to exist—must be that the world is ordered, that the spiritual world is by its nature structured and formalized, that it contains its own patterns and laws. A great many things convince me that this is true, including the events of my own life where many things "rhyme," where there are reprises of various kinds, or certain punishments follow irrevocably for my deviations from what I ought to be doing. When I lose the feeling for what I ought to be doing and act according to a piece of advice or a rational idea—doing something that runs against the feeling implanted in me— what I conceive does not work out, and punishment follows.

IVASHKIN: Do you mean an artistic punishment?

SCHNITTKE: No, a purely practical one. I have the feeling that someone is constantly "leading" me, offering approval or chastisement—a kind of force, perhaps outside my own personality. And it is from this that I derive the feeling there is a kind of higher order. And everything that creates disharmony in our world, everything that is monstrous and inexplicable, terrible, or incomprehensible to us in the way it was incomprehensible to Ivan Karamazov, all this too is part of the order.

I am given further evidence that this order exists by my experience of inexplicable phenomena, when facts and phenomena, apparently from different sources, for some reason coincide as though they shared a single unified basis. I recall an example from the cinema. I was to write the music for a film made by Marlen Khutsiev.[19] At the beginning of the film the main character is sitting and watching a flying display on television. There are gliders in beautiful flight. Khutsiev looked at possible material and decided to add music—this usually has a beneficial effect on audience reaction, the "joins" don't show, and the inserted footage looks better. So he took the first music that came to mind: the first movement of Beethoven's *Moonlight Sonata*—the most obvious cliché imaginable. The result was amazing: the music seemed to have been made to measure. It was as if the *Moonlight Sonata* had been written as an accompaniment for the film. And I don't mean just the fact that the character and rhythm matched perfectly—the cuts matched too, the up and down movements—as if it were an animated film! One had the impression that,

---

19. Marlen Khutsiev (born 1925): Producer of many films that were very popular in the Soviet Union in the 1960s and 1970s. He completed Mikhail Romm's documentary *The World Today* (with Schnittke's music). —ed.

independently one of the other, the film and the music followed the same structural pattern, a pattern one could not express in concrete language. So patterns like that must exist somewhere. It is a different matter if we try to approach them rationally, use them and understand them rationally. But our consciousness is not the whole of our reason. It leads us along a false trail. It is only very rarely that we reach understanding by following the path of consciousness. More often we arrive at a correct solution not by means of reason, but empirically, through our feelings, by trial and error. And that is why the whole time people were preoccupied with the rationalization of technique, everything they were doing in the 1960s (which derived from the feeling that there was a basic structural law and from an attempt to discover that law), none of this could be successful for the simple reason that proper understanding is never revealed to reason. But I have no doubt whatever that there is in nature a basic structural law.

IVASHKIN: In other words, you think that this law is irrational?

SCHNITTKE: For me in the whole of life there is uninterrupted interaction between what is rational, or divinely preordained, and the uninterrupted flow of what is irrational, of what, so to speak, has not yet "germinated," of what is completely new. And it is on everything that is new that the Devil's attention is especially fixed (I use the word "Devil" as a convenient way of referring to the whole sphere of evil). I am convinced that there exists a dark irrational sphere, which, more than anything else, is always focused on the new. All the most terrible and monstrous events in human history are connected with what is *new*. I mean the Terror of the French Revolution, the October Revolution, and everything terrible that is linked with the reaction against the October Revolution in the guise of Fascism and what grew out of it. And all this revealed itself at its most terrible in its *first* manifestation. The Devil pounces on what he has not yet tried.

IVASHKIN: But doesn't the new in time become the old? And doesn't the Devil then leave it?

SCHNITTKE: It is as though he begins to take an interest in something else. The Crusades, the Inquisition—these were all a kind of *perversion of the truth*, not what was false. And it is precisely this sphere the Devil turns his attention to: it is here that the steps to inertia lie, leading to disaster.

IVASHKIN: Steps to inertia? But surely the impulse to the new is intrinsically a creative impulse?

SCHNITTKE: Any impulse to the new is always both creative and reactionary. We must not simply welcome it as a principle of what is new and therefore good in itself. What is new is both good and bad; which one it proves to be depends on the people who take hold of it. If scientists had foreseen the consequences of the invention of the nuclear bomb, they may well not have devised it. They didn't fully understand what they were doing. The whole of Andrei Sakharov's life is an endless attempt to overcome the utterly monstrous sin he took upon himself. Nothing in history ever finishes, and it may always bring an unexpected danger. For instance, at the moment I see great danger in computer madness....

IVASHKIN: What danger? The fact that the variants available to a computer are limited or the fact that they are notoriously schematized, although that is carefully concealed?

SCHNITTKE: The danger is always the same, and it is a very simple one. As soon as something new appears, there is a temptation to look at the whole of history through it. That is to look at the world with the eyes of the computer. Then the whole world is inevitably "trimmed" to fit the computer, and the computer itself (which has its own important place in the world) turns into the chief and only thing in the world. A computer that takes over the whole world. Just like the world being taken over by war, politics, drugs, vodka. At a particular moment, something turns into a dangerous substitute for the whole world, and this can lead to a catastrophe.

IVASHKIN: My own opinion is that the chief danger of a computer is that it tends to formalize our consciousness. The computer often seems to exercise an influence on our ideas, to "retune" our brains to accommodate it. No doubt you will say that this is the Devil tempting us again. But, in any case, what really is "the new"? Where does it come from? Is it somehow lodged in the everlasting memory of the world, as opposed to the memory of a computer? Or is the fundamental idea of "the new" false—and "the new" does not exist at all?

SCHNITTKE: In practice I take no account of the question of whether the idea of "the new" is false or not. Electric batteries existed at the time of Moses. In the Bible—I think it's in the book of Ezekiel—there is a description of something that has a wheel revolving every way at once.[20] And this something can turn in any direction in a moment. Something that still doesn't exist as a technical device is already described there. There is in the Bible, in the form of legends and echoes, evidence of knowledge that is now *returning* to us, and this is not the first time it has come to us, nor, consequently, the second. This is because life proceeds endlessly in a circle. Things return and then go away again.

The Devil is most of all aware that the way to deal with everything that is new has not been worked out in as much detail as the way to deal with what has long been known. So what is new may lead to exaggerations, and that's when the Devil can "play his tricks."

IVASHKIN: So how do we avoid this?

---

20. The reference is to the first chapter of Ezekiel. —ed.

SCHNITTKE: By being on the alert. And by adopting a skeptical attitude toward ourselves and our imperfect human natures. Human beings are always trying to distance themselves from their own personalities. And in so doing they run the risk of becoming like false angels.... In avoiding danger number one, you immediately fall into dangers two and three.

IVASHKIN: Still, the question remains: How does one define the reservoir from which humanity draws new ideas? Does the new exist, or is it merely the Devil trying to put us in a false position?

SCHNITTKE: I believe that there is another aspect to all this, apart from the one connected with the Devil. What happens is that certain total qualities increase or decrease. The whole of life—not my own personal life, not even human life over millions of years—has a total meaning, a totality that keeps changing. I hesitate to make this presupposition, but I think that if we divide everything into two worlds, the world of God and the world of the Devil, we cannot ultimately express everything we want to. We can express something only in a form comprehensible to us humans. I think that with regard to God and an understanding of His nature we fall into the same kind of error that we make with regard to the computer: in both cases we take something that is *particular*, turn it into something absolute, and use it as a universal measure. While the only thing that can give the right answer is irrational consciousness, some basic essence that directs our behavior, telling us whether we are acting well or badly. And, irrespective of the way we act, we ourselves know when we are right or wrong. In each one of us there is an ideal evaluator, and I believe there is one in both a saint and a sinner. This makes impossible the idea of a saint or a sinner in the absolute sense. It is an inescapable feature of every human being as a fragment or reflection of what is universal. Furthermore, not only is a human being this kind of reflection, so too are the animal and vegetable worlds. There is ample evidence of the existence of consciousness in those worlds and the possibility of contact between different levels of consciousness. Contact between human beings and plants is possible. Perhaps we have not yet discovered the ways to make contact with other areas of existence. Maybe there is contact—only a more remote kind—with air, clouds, and the objects around us in a room. All these things live.

IVASHKIN: Do you agree with Vladimir Vernadsky when he asserted that what is accurately demonstrated by science is initially revealed in art?

SCHNITTKE: You mention Vernadsky. But exactly the same idea was clearly expressed by Karlheinz Stockhausen, who naturally knew nothing of Vernadsky. Any scientific discovery reveals something that has been forgotten, something that turns out to exist already.

IVASHKIN: It is an interesting question whether science serves art, or vice versa.

SCHNITTKE: Everything is important. At a given moment one thing becomes decisive, then the emphasis shifts to something else and the first thing goes into hibernation for millions of years. It is as though there were an endless process of correction going on forever. Generally speaking, human beings have always made and continue to make the same mistake: they are all intuitively convinced (although they never admit it to themselves) that their generation has reached the highest level of attainment and that there is no further to go.

IVASHKIN: You said that Fascism was a reaction to the October Revolution. But are all revolutions, like all new developments, false steps taken by humanity at the inspiration of the Devil?

SCHNITTKE: Of course they are. I am a conservative, of course, as you know. I think that the Pugachov rebellion, the Razin rebellion, the slave rebellion in ancient Rome, and the endless series of remarkable revolutions of this kind—all of them are a piling-up of nightmarish horrors, endlessly repeated.

IVASHKIN: And what about mythology, particularly in the case of Wagner? In mythology there is always an element of revolution....

SCHNITTKE: In Wagner something was hidden that was to develop fifty years later: Fascism. Fascism basically derived from two things. First from an exaggerated, absolute interpretation of what is mythological. This is what emerged in Fascism, by way of Wagner. That is one side of it. And on the other, there is a monstrous profanation of everything achieved by the modern age. All these things were profaned by Fascism and Communism!

IVASHKIN: How should we react to the idea of "a hero," a heroic figure? Russian Orthodoxy has saints, not heroes. Is heroism an attribute of revolutionary consciousness?

SCHNITTKE: What about Alexander of Macedon?

IVASHKIN: But he wasn't from God....

SCHNITTKE: True... and what is especially irritating is the fact that more than two thousand years have gone by and his image is still idealized.

IVASHKIN: This is true for other "heroes" who are patently negative. Napoleon, for instance, is still revered as a great figure.

SCHNITTKE: That's another example of the power of the Devil. In the case of Napoleon, I would simply count up how many hundreds of thousands, not to say millions, of people died because of him.

IVASHKIN: But his tomb is still a place of worship.... Or take Faust, who also strove to make revolutionary transformations, perhaps only inside his own personality. What about Faust?

SCHNITTKE: Which one do you have in mind? There are many Fausts.

IVASHKIN: Goethe's, of course.

SCHNITTKE: I am not concerned with Goethe's Faust. Goethe idealized him. But in the original Faust there revealed itself precisely that duality of the human and the diabolical in which the diabolical predominates. If we take the whole history of Faust, it becomes obvious that what was human about him reveals itself only when he, beginning to understand where it is all leading, starts to lament, to weep, to grieve. In his last days he became a human being who realized what he had really done.

What is important in Faust is the way his character has been loaded by the future. The human race needed an ideal image it could invest with all its insatiable thirst for knowledge—and, looking back, it directed this onto Faust. The original Faust dabbled in magic, of course, and loved to travel, but his thirst for knowledge was not the dominant force in his life that it became in Goethe's Faust. Goethe's character came as close as possible to what human consciousness was heading for, but he failed to reach it. Generally speaking, Faust is like a mirror reflecting the changes in human beings in recent centuries. You know, when you start to evaluate the events of most recent history, beginning with the Renaissance, you fail to grasp why they occurred. The most striking example is the monstrously rapid diabolical process that began with the First World War in 1914. Before the war there had been no preliminary indications of this.

IVASHKIN: On the contrary, it was a time of blossoming....

SCHNITTKE: Indeed! And suddenly there was all this hideous nightmare.... Of course we might mention the Russo-Japanese War [1904–1905]. But who could have imagined that as the result of the assassination of an Austrian archduke a nightmare would begin, lasting until the present day. One gets the impression that there was *something* controlling all these events, simply because they could not derive from the general insanity of millions. There must be some underlying causes that are hidden from us.

IVASHKIN: We've been talking about the irrational—in history, in life, in art. Do you think the irrational dominates in your music?

SCHNITTKE: I am glad you asked that question—perhaps my definition was imprecise. There is the irrational that preserves its *infernal* irrationality. For example, humanity will never get an answer to the question of why the First World War began, because it does not lie in politics, economics, or religion. But there is a different sort of irrationalism—the sort that can be grasped intuitively. This is when we don't know the question, but we still know the answer. This is what is called the human conscience: the ability to evaluate one's own and other people's actions. The irrational is not what lies outside reason; it is what has not been decoded by reason.

IVASHKIN: The Faust theme in the broad sense—the theme of journeying through circles of doubt and a subsequent return—this is actually the theme of any one of your latest works. Take *Peer Gynt*, for example.

SCHNITTKE: Of course. The Faust theme is not as all-encompassing for me as you imagined. Naturally I have been in contact with this theme for many years, and I include indirect contact, in such subjects as *Peer Gynt*. But still I have had little *direct* contact with it. In itself this theme is endless and can be realized in thousands of ways by different people. It can never be exhausted. It has many layers. Layers of time, layers of content. But particularly important for me is what I have heard about it from the priest who regularly visits me, Father Nikolai.[21] I first heard from him the idea that when human beings die there is a certain eternal, moral reckoning connected with their lives that does not die. Not just in the sense that all the good they have done continues to exist in the life of others, although they themselves are dead. But the bad they have done also continues to exist, and not merely in the bad that continues to develop. Life can turn that in another direction—even in the direction of what is good. And this may happen long after the physical death of a particular human being. The moral reckoning that concerns every deed and every word contains a hope, not a guarantee, but a hope of possible salvation (speaking from the point of view of a religious person), even for a character like Faust. Not, of course, a hope for the instantaneous salvation available to a person who has not made such improbable mistakes and committed so many sins.

For me this was completely new and unexpected. I began to look at the character of Faust in a new way: he was no longer stigmatized as an utter sinner, cursed forever. This is because his destiny—I don't mean his physical but his moral destiny, which continues to exist—is not finally decided and contains this new potential, which is decided by the way people react to him and his posthumous fate.

IVASHKIN: In light of this, then, do you mean that music is not bound to be in the realm of what is sacred but can also reflect what is sinful? I ask this because certain people see in your music the incarnation of something sinful that is incompatible with its religious feeling. We have often discussed this, and you have always argued that it is essential to concentrate on evil, because then a human being can more readily identify and eradicate it.

SCHNITTKE: It is my belief that throughout their lives—from the first moment to the last—human beings cannot count on the fact that they have been cleansed of sin and can regard themselves, therefore, as saved. They must fight for their salvation throughout their lives. But this fight must be genuine, brought about by contact with real dangers, not with something that only appears dangerous on the surface. And its genuineness involves a new situation and a new danger every second. Those who

---

21. Father Nikolai (Vedernikov): Russian Orthodox priest to whom Schnittke used to confess (at home). Father Nikolai conducted the church service at Schnittke's funeral on 10 August 1998 in Moscow. —ed.

throughout their lives remain conscious of danger at their back and struggle against it have, in my opinion, a greater chance of overcoming total danger than do those who labor under the delusion that they have rid themselves of danger and can live the rest of their lives in demonstrably ideal fashion. I don't believe in such a model and demonstrably ideal life because as soon as I start to believe in it, I lose the ability to regard myself critically. This is one of the temptations that human beings put in front of themselves, but they must never give way to it.

IVASHKIN: If you wrote church music, what would it be like?

SCHNITTKE: When I included episodes of church music in various of my works, I was quite serious about what I was doing. I believe that in this respect using genuine or pseudo-quotations that limit one stylistically is something *obligatory*. This is not because it involves a hypocritical demonstration of one's own humility, but because in essence it means that one understands the necessity of moral limitations that one is obliged to impose on oneself. You have no right to anything very much, although you may imagine that you have. You must constantly rise above yourself. That reminds me of an old illustration from Tolstoy, when he was talking about people crossing a river. To land where you want, you have to row upstream—because you will be carried downstream no matter what. Only by aiming *higher* can you land where you want.

IVASHKIN: Have you ever had the idea that church music is the only real music that has to be written?

SCHNITTKE: No, never. And I think that that is one of the temptations human beings have to face.

IVASHKIN: Vladimir Martynov, for instance, believes that to find true and pure music one must look to music written for the church.[22] He has expressed this viewpoint many times—for instance, in his book about the history of Russian church choral singing.

SCHNITTKE: When I hear such things, I feel very imperfect. So all of a sudden what I regard as true turns out to be false.... For example, I am to meet a false Christ. I may be completely wrong in my beliefs.

A viewpoint like Martynov's is a defensive one. It is defensive because it is aimed high. And this is why it offers many solutions: the height acts as a kind of defense. Perhaps that way is acceptable for him. But not for me. I know that the Devil

---

22. Vladimir Martynov (born 1946): One of the most original Russian composers. Martynov started as an avant-garde composer in the 1970s and taught music at various church schools. Many compositions for church services, as well as cantatas and oratorios in the style of Russian Orthodox music, with elements of a kind of minimalism. Author of three books on the theory and history of Russian church music. —ed.

is everywhere, and you can't defend yourself against him just by taking yourself off into something pure; you'll find him there, too. The essential thing is not to try to escape into some kind of purified space but to live with the Devil and engage in a constant struggle against him.

IVASHKIN: You once spoke of your attempt to look into the future by consulting the I Ching. As you worked on *Faust* over a long period, did you ever resort to using any occult systems? Did you make any contact with the cabbala?

SCHNITTKE: For no apparent reason I once received a present from Luigi Nono—a book about the logic of the cabbala. The author—Jewish, a highly perceptive and intelligent man—simply gave free rein to his imagination, which had cabbalistic features. His imagination seemed to be fatally, finally, and soullessly enclosed. The world of the cabbala reminds me of a psychic illness, which is in essence a continual and critical accumulation of negative experiences. And I am very much afraid of plunging into this world. It is an area that is potentially dangerous.

Are you familiar with the analysis of Bach's duet made by Ulrich Siegele,[23] a German music critic? I read his article sometime in 1979; Alexander Goehr gave it to me. There are four Bach duets written for harpsichord. When Siegele analyzed the second one, he drew attention to the fact that if you express the length of the musical phrases by counting the bars, you get a completely inexplicable sequence of numbers, which constantly changes. This sequence does not fit into any known numerical progression, but its changes are so complicated that they cannot be arbitrary. He struggled to decipher it for a long time until it occurred to him to apply a cabbalistic method. The cabbala makes use of the fact that in ancient Hebrew the letters and numbers are expressed by the same signs. 'A' is one, 'B' is two, and so on. Siegele translated this into Latin and found a prayer, the absolutely precise text of a prayer! We know that according to Albert Schweitzer the whole of Bach's intonational structure is predetermined semantically. Many things are concealed in it—the prayers of Golgotha, of Christ raised on the Cross, of his Agony.... But even at this level, it turned out that everything was structured! Having completed this particular analysis, Siegele decided never to use that method again....

There are many occasions when we run the risk of taking a dangerous path. I was once watching a television program about Midsummer Night. I was horrified by the fact that they showed film of a hypnosis session. An extremely vulgar and forceful young man was putting dozens of people under hypnosis. They were weeping, trying to say something.... It induced a monstrous feeling of hellish anguish. I had a sense of evil, of devil's horns.... Two intelligent, eloquent people were trying to prove that there is no boundary between good and evil.... It was the kind of Manichaeism that immediately reveals the Devil at work. A hand held out to the Devil. And there is no way I want to hold out my hand to the Devil. I am a freethinker, unattached to any church, but I still have a sense of where that boundary is!

---

23. See also Ruth Tatlow, *Bach and the Riddle of the Number Alphabet* (Cambridge and New York: Cambridge University Press, 1991). —ed.

IVASHKIN: You have on your bookshelf the writings of Johann Faust. Do you have similar feelings when you read that?

SCHNITTKE: Of course I do! That's like playing a game with the same world of the Devil. And I am afraid of missing the moment when it becomes dangerous—for me! Every decision I make has been confirmed in a much more important sphere. And, without being aware of it myself, I make a decision that has already been made. Until now that has saved me and, I hope, brought me closer to the truth. But the danger remains....

IVASHKIN: Has your work on your opera *Faust*, in that sense, been an act of struggle?

SCHNITTKE: That's how it has turned out.

IVASHKIN: As I understand it, *Faust* is one of your main compositions, isn't it?

SCHNITTKE: Yes. But at the same time my work on it reminds me of the subject of Henri Pousseur's *Votre Faust*—an endless process that is almost impossible to complete. As I work on *Faust*, I am struck by how much I feel this style of composition, without concerning myself especially about it. Where does that feeling come from? I don't know! And I don't know why! That surprises me and makes me suspect that I am being guided by the Devil, who is instructing me. Because the opera is about Faust.

IVASHKIN: But surely you don't think that merely by writing this opera you are putting yourself in the hands of the Devil?

SCHNITTKE: No, but the critical questionable situation remains. Whether I like it or not, I am making negative contact with a world that is *always* dangerous. It can never be otherwise.

IVASHKIN: You spoke about your attempts in the past to write rock music. But apparently in your opera *Faust* there are scenes linked with rock music, aren't there?

SCHNITTKE: I want the whole of the section of the opera that is connected with the period when Faust bought happiness from the Devil—twenty-three years of loathsome happiness, for which he later had to pay—to be accompanied by music that is increasingly fateful in character. Not fateful in the literal sense: it must be music that uses the distortions and transformations of sound peculiar to rock music. I asked my son, Andrei, to help me with this.

IVASHKIN: And there must be no trace of Goethe's *Faust*?

SCHNITTKE: No, no Goethe at all. Everything that happens was three hundred years before Goethe's time. A pop-literature [*Volksbuch*] version of the Faust story appeared in 1587, two hundred years before Goethe. Nor do I concern myself with the later Fausts: I treat them as though they never existed. Not even Margarita is there—her name does not appear in the early version.... There are, it is true, female characters we also find in Goethe, for example, La Belle Hélène. There are even two Walpurgis Nights. But Margarita first appeared only in Goethe. He seems to have felt some personal guilt, similar to Faust's. His biographers sometimes make semi-hypotheses about this—Werther, Charlotta—there is something connected with this in Goethe's own life, something that continued to operate in his consciousness.

I have no criticism at all of what Goethe did. But I feel what happened four hundred years ago as if I had actually experienced it. The furniture, the clothes of that time are closer to me than those that existed two hundred years ago. This may be because my forebears, who came to Russia at the time of Catherine II, knew nothing of Goethe's milieu. But they did know the milieu of the "Ur-Faust."

Faust is really an enigma for me, like *Peer Gynt*, and like another of my ideas— the ballet *John the Baptist,* on the subject of Salome. I once had a plan (now almost abandoned) to write a one-act ballet for the Salzburg Festival as a companion piece to *The Soldier's Tale (L'Histoire du soldat).* John the Baptist is a very enigmatic character. He is more difficult and inscrutable than Jesus Christ. The character of Christ is somehow inexhaustible: you can do what you like with it, and further variations will still remain. Whereas John the Baptist is a character whose entire significance is in the sphere of what is unknown. I know that many people will see this idea as having something in common with the so-called near-Christian heresies. I've also come across the following idea: that Christ is the power of fire, an enormous power for one occasion only, whereas John the Baptist is the power of water, long-lasting and acting gradually....

Peer Gynt is a strange character, having no key, perhaps even stranger than Faust. Talk about *Peer Gynt* began a long time ago. When I first met John Neumeier,[24] he told me he wanted a ballet written and suggested two subjects: something from Chekhov or *Peer Gynt.* And I immediately said *Peer Gynt....* Somehow I have no feeling for Chekhov in this particular musical world. But *Peer Gynt* caught my interest at once, and I will tell you why. There are some subjects that seem to have only one possible realization, and once realized, are at once exhausted. And there are other subjects with an endless number of realizations, and none of them is ever completely exhausted. In this sense the subject of *Peer Gynt* reminds me of Faust— it is something with a limitless periphery. And it seems to exist at any point on that periphery, even though it's the periphery and not the whole thing.

I have the feeling that Pushkin, too, has no single final definition. So much has been written about him, and yet he continues to reveal more and more that is new, without having to be distorted. But can the same be said of Lermontov, for example?

---

24. John Neumeier (born 1942 in Milwaukee): Ballet dancer, choreographer, and artistic director. Danced with the Stuttgart Ballet (1963–1969) before assuming leadership of the Frankfurt Ballet (1969– 1973) and the Hamburg Ballet (since 1973). Known for acrobatically expressive contemporary ballets. Staged Schnittke's *Peer Gynt* in 1989. —ed.

Definitely not! Different interpretations are still possible, but only within narrow limits. One can imagine two or three different views of Lermontov. But it is impossible to imagine the endless number of views that there could be of Pushkin.

It was something like this in the case of *Peer Gynt*. Perhaps this "something" is repeated in different characters in world literature. Peer Gynt is a character who generally gained nothing, achieved nothing, and ended as the zero he was when he began. All his life he made mistakes and was wrong. In this respect he reminds me of Feuchtwanger's[25] book about Josephus Flavius, in which Josephus always remained indeterminate, never occupying a definite and final position—and was always condemned by his opponents primarily for this reason. But it turned out that this indeterminate and incomplete person—by very virtue of his indeterminacy— embodies more of life than certain characters who are complete and purified. That's an inexplicable paradox, but it certainly exists. And it is this that links Peer Gynt with Faust. So I naturally seized on the subject.

IVASHKIN: Had you read *Peer Gynt* before then?

SCHNITTKE: Yes, but I had only a rather vague impression of it. Of course I reread it several times. And even now, when I open it, I keep finding endlessly new material in it—I shall never grasp all of it, just as I shall never grasp *Faust*. I have read Thomas Mann's *Doctor Faustus* at least five times. The first time—in 1949–1950—it had only just come out, and somehow my father had acquired it, not permanently, but just to read. Since then, although I read it all the time, I've never fully grasped it.

IVASHKIN: Do you read it in Russian?

SCHNITTKE: No, I can't read it in Russian. I now have a copy of it in Russian, but somehow something I can't explain is lost as soon as I try to read the Russian translation. The magic, the dark magic of the book, which intensifies as you read it, seems artificial in the Russian version. In German it's not artificial at all! There is something fundamental in the German, not at all bookish, which is completely lost in the Russian translation. This is not the case with all German writers. For instance, for a long time I had the feeling that Kafka lost very little in translation. But now, when I reread the translation of *The Castle*, it seems to me that he too loses something, but not so definitely. Whereas Thomas Mann loses what is most important— something infinite.

IVASHKIN: Let's get back to *Peer Gynt*.

---

25. Lion Feuchtwanger (1884–1958): German poet, novelist, dramatist, and short story writer. He left Germany in 1933 and settled in California in 1941. His best-known novel is *Jud Süss* (1925). The book about Josephus Flavius is called in English *Josephus and the Emperor* (published in 1942), translated from the German *Der Tag wird kommen* (1936). Josephus Flavius (Joseph ben Mathias), born circa the year 37, was a Jewish historian, priest, and soldier who eventually settled in Rome and became a Roman citizen. —ed.

SCHNITTKE: In Neumeier's production there are several different ways in which the musical elements interact with the elements of physical movement. There is the kind of interaction that is standard and normal—here everything is clear. But at the beginning of the third act everything changes. The whole production contains, as it were, three circles of reality. There is the lowest one, the childish one; then there is the one to do with outward show—starting in the theater and ending in the madhouse, the climax of the second act. And finally, the third act marks a return to a new level of reality. But now there is no longer any synchronic interaction of the musical numbers with the physical movements; there is a different kind of interaction. And the music is different—not in separate numbers, but continuous.

IVASHKIN: Did Neumeier himself want separate musical numbers for the first two acts?

SCHNITTKE: Yes, of course. The first two acts represent two realities that are similar. And the Epilogue at the end of the third act is a fourth kind of reality. Everything that has happened is repeated, re-experienced, but at a new level. But I can't explain that either, just as I can't explain the idea of a fourth dimension that constantly "flickers into view." The idea of a fourth dimension momentarily breaks through into clear consciousness and immediately vanishes again. Our present life can give me no more than that. But I have a Utopian sense of the fourth dimension. And the Epilogue in *Peer Gynt* is an attempt to express the shadows of the fourth dimension given to us in our present lives. This is not surrealism, but a realism that is not of this earth: a kind of beginning of a new circuit of existence. And I have tried to put this new idea into the music.

In music I have come across things that I cannot define in words, although I can speak of my feeling for their quality. Here is one: The choral music in *Peer Gynt* is, in fact, repetitive (the same eight bars repeated fifty times or more). But it doesn't seem like repetition of the same thing: the static material is "charged" by what is living and visually changing. And because the music of the orchestra is constantly changing, the illusion is created that the music of the choir is changing too. The choral music is colored by the orchestral.

In the Epilogue, the physical rhythmic movements of the ballet are so slow that we do not perceive them as movements taking place to orchestral accompaniment. We have the illusion that they correspond to the sounds of the choral music. It is that *other-world* tempo. The orchestral music, by contrast, is more real, but the introduction of each new theme is marked by some visual or auditory emphasis. For example, Solveig, old and blind, seemingly after death, sees a crowd of shadows. And among the many faces of the crowd she recognizes Peer's. This cannot be explained. He is wearing the same hat, the same suit, the same tie as everyone else, like something in a Magritte painting. But she still recognizes him and drops the stick she is leaning on....

Compared to the first three acts, there is no new music at all in the Epilogue. What you hear are all the themes of the previous scenes. But now you hear them not in succession, but piled one on top of the other—like clouds. While one theme is still being played, you can hear another one. And it is this ignoring of the boundaries of the numerous themes that creates a picture beyond reality, no matter how loudly the orchestra plays. It is still something beyond reality.

From interviews conducted between 1985 and 1994. The full text of these conversations was published in Russian as Chapters 5 and 6 of *Besedy s Al'fredom Shnitke* [Conversations with Alfred Schnittke], compiled and edited by A. V. Ivashkin (Moscow: Kul'tura, 1994), pp. 127–173. A German edition was published as *Alfred Schnittke: Über das Leben und die Musik. Gespräche mit Alexander Iwaschkin* (Munich and Düsseldorf: Econ Verlag, 1998).

II

SCHNITTKE ON THE LENIN PRIZE

LETTER TO THE
LENIN PRIZE COMMITTEE (1990)

The introduction of a multiparty system in our country has completely changed material and spiritual reality. From uniformity and centralization of values to real mutability and flexibility is a giant leap. Thus from day to day the function of everything has changed, and this also applies to historical figures. Whereas in former times they served to sum up history and peoples, acting as symbols of an epoch, nowadays they are losing this generalizing role. Their role in history is no longer one of centralization, but a concrete and historical one. No longer are they symbols—once again they have become real people.

Until recently the figure of Lenin still had a generalizing historical role. He was a man who undoubtedly had the strongest possible influence on the twentieth century and the history of our country, and was therefore its symbol in the long period of centralism, irrespective of one's personal attitude toward him. But today, in a pluralist climate of opinion, he is losing this generalizing role and needs more precise evaluation, more especially in the personal judgment of each one of us. It is thus impossible to approve the retention of the name of a man who, in spite of his enormous importance, expressed the interests of but *one* party, albeit the most authoritative, in the official title of an important state prize, one intended to express the *complete* and varied picture of our present reality.

I can see no possibility of my accepting this prize, were it awarded to me, if only because I am a man of faith, while Lenin was an atheist. For more than seventy years, and still recently, we looked upon the figure of Lenin as the expression of the centralism of the time—but today we look upon this figure in the context of the whole of historical reality with all its contradictions. In the conditions which, although they have only just arisen, are new in principle, the former function of Lenin's name—which until recently was the absolute and undisputed symbol of the age—becomes untenable, and his name regains its true role in history as that of the leader of a proletarian revolution in the early twentieth century. This role is diametrically opposed to the real historical significance of Grigor Narekatsi, the Armenian monk and thinker who lived a thousand years ago and who in his *Book of Sorrow* expressed purely Christian ideas. For me to accept the prize in these circumstances (not a month ago, but at this actual moment!) would be to compromise my principles, both in relation to the role of a twentieth-century communist leader and to that of a tenth-century Christian philosopher.

I am very grateful to the Lenin Prize Committee for retaining me as a candidate for a prize. I regard this as in the highest degree an expression of trust and goodwill.

All the more so because it has been the highest award for a whole group of figures of our time whose greatness and supremacy are indisputable.

But that time was different; it left one with no choice in the matter: in the world of officialdom almost everything good was rejected, and, when this proved impossible, it was distorted. So let anyone nowadays dare to cast a stone at Prokofiev, Shostakovich, Khachaturian, Karaev, Oistrakh, Mravinsky, Gilels, Richter, Rostropovich, Rozhdestvensky, and other Lenin Prize winners (this is just to speak of music)— let them dare nowadays, when to each one of us it also seems "easy and pleasant to tell the truth" (much easier than it was to keep silent twenty or thirty years ago, with destructive effects on one's heart, blood pressure, nerves, life...)!

I trust that I shall be understood and not blamed for asking that my name be removed from the list of candidates.

Alfred Schnittke

Russian text published in *Besedy s Al'fredom Shnitke*, compiled and edited by A. V. Ivashkin (Moscow: Kul'tura, 1994), p. 233.

III

SCHNITTKE ON HIS OWN
COMPOSITIONS

3

ON CONCERTO GROSSO NO. 1
(LATE 1970s)

In May 1976 Gidon Kremer and Tatiana Grindenko asked me to compose a work for them and the Lithuanian Chamber Orchestra under the conductor Saulius Sondetskis. Had anyone told me then that during the next year this would be performed several times and recorded, I would not have believed them, since for the most part I work very slowly, write many versions of a work, and never complete the first version.

But the score was ready by the end of 1976, and when I gave it to Gidon Kremer for his thirtieth birthday on 26 February 1977, his intention was to perform it at the earliest opportunity, that is, in Leningrad on 20 March. I thought that was impossible, but Gidon Kremer always gets what he wants, and in the course of ten days the whole work was copied into parts, and after three rehearsals the first performance was given under the baton of our mutual friend Eri Klas (from Tallinn). Afterward I made several cuts, and Kremer and Grindenko played it in Vilnius, Moscow, Riga, Tallinn, Budapest. During the Salzburg Festival in August they recorded it with the London Symphony Orchestra under Gennadi Rozhdestvensky.

For several years I experienced an inward urge to write music for the cinema and theater. At first I enjoyed doing this, then it became a burden, and then it dawned on me: my lifelong task would be to bridge the gap between serious music and music for entertainment, even if I broke my neck in the process. I have this dream of a unified style where fragments of serious music and fragments of music for entertainment would not just be scattered about in a frivolous way, but would be the elements of a diverse musical reality: elements that are real in the way they are expressed, but that can be used to manipulate—be they jazz, pop, rock, or serial music (since even avant-garde music has become a commodity). An artist has only one possible way of avoiding manipulation—he must use his own individual efforts to rise above materials that are taboo, materials used for external manipulation. In this way he will gain the right to give an individual reflection of the musical situation that is free of sectarian prejudice, as, for example, in the case of Mahler and Charles Ives.

So into the framework of a neoclassical Concerto Grosso I introduced some fragments not consonant with its general style, which had earlier been fragments of cinema music: a lively children's chorale (at the beginning of the first movement and at the climax of the fifth, and also as a refrain in the other movements), a nostalgically atonal serenade—a trio (in the second movement) guaranteed as genuine Corelli, "made in the USSR," and my grandmother's favorite tango (in the fifth movement), which her great-grandmother used to play on a harpsichord.... But all these themes are perfectly consonant with each other (a falling sixth, the sighs of seconds), and I take them all completely seriously. The form of the work is as follows: (1) Prelude, (2) Toccata, (3) Recitative, (4) Cadenza, (5) Rondo, (6) Postlude.

Written in the late 1970s. Russian text published in *Besedy s Al'fredom Shnitke*, compiled and edited by A. V. Ivashkin (Moscow: Kul'tura, 1994), pp. 243–244.

4

ON THE FOURTH SYMPHONY (1984)

The idea of the universality of culture and its unity seems to me very relevant, particularly nowadays in connection with the change in our perceptions of time and space. Today we have an image of the world different, let us say, from what we had twenty or thirty years ago. This relates to the acoustic side of our sensations. Just think, for example, of the synthetic sound image we get from an ordinary radio! In our day there is also a different conception of space: in three hours one can reach practically any point on the surface of the globe. But, in spite of the exceptionally dynamic character of the twentieth century—its drive for the future—in recent years in art, especially in music, there has been a sharp rise of interest in the past. Thanks to enthusiastic performers who have carried out vast amounts of research, we can now be familiar with examples of music from which we are separated by seven hundred, even a thousand years.... By making contact with the creative work of our distant ancestors we have a different sense of time, of time as an unbroken line, almost as a "simultaneous chord."

I wanted to bring together different layers of culture in one of my latest works— my Fourth Symphony, which recently had its première in Moscow, in the Great Hall of the Conservatory.

In this work I adopted the approach of stylizing the ritual music of three religions: the Orthodox, the Catholic, and the Protestant. In the symphony there are elements of Orthodox processional singing, Lutheran chorales, and triumphal hymns recalling Gregorian chant. I also included synagogue singing, wanting to show, together with the differences, a certain basic underlying unity.

To give form to my idea I chose three intonational systems that are characteristic of the ritual music of each of these religions. Common to all the harmonies is the fact that in their use of intervals we find constant variant alterations of the same steps in different registers. As a result there are diminished or augmented octaves. The whole work is sustained in this "distorted intonational space." "Corrected" pure octaves appear only in the coda, where all the themes are combined and a diatonic scale is established. The development of the musical action is slow, by way of variation on a "melodic cell" and repetition of rhythmic motifs. Outwardly everything is static in a way that is so typical of a religious ritual. My initial idea was that this would be a chamber symphony with solo piano. But as the work proceeded I found it essential to add two more solo instruments—a harpsichord and a celesta. The reason for this was that the musical material required its own special "varied canon," a continuous imitation of the piano part using related timbres. I also introduced a choir and soloists into the score. Furthermore there are two variants for performance: one for chamber orchestra and four soloists (soprano, alto, tenor, bass) and one for large orchestra with a choir and two soloists (alto and tenor) who sing in the episodes where the character of the intonation requires greater individualization. The symphony is not divided into movements but comprises three cycles of variations united through a composed continuous form. I developed the themes according to their character, trying to achieve the restrained austerity of a religious rite. In the final episode, when the choir is introduced, as I have already mentioned, the basic themes, so far heard separately, come together contrapuntally.

Written in 1984 and published in *Muzyka v SSSR* [Music in the USSR], October–December 1984, p. 82; Russian text reprinted in *Besedy s Al'fredom Shnitke*, compiled and edited by A. V. Ivashkin (Moscow: Kul'tura, 1994), pp. 71–72.

ON FILM AND FILM MUSIC
(1972, 1984, 1989)

I can count on my fingers the number of times I met Mikhail Il'ich Romm—perhaps five, perhaps seven—in the process of his work on *The World Today,* when there was still a long time to go before my direct involvement in the project of composing and recording the music.[1] Alone among the whole group of us, as we watched the rushes, I was a mere spectator. Comparing what we saw then with the final result, after the self-sacrificing efforts of E. Klimov and M. Khutsiev, I like all the other participants can only regret the impossibility of also reproducing the sound of Romm's voice, which we all had heard after the rushes, when he commented on what he had tried to do. Although what he said then contained no global philosophical generalizations, there was in it—not so much in the actual words and their meaning as in his intonation—a kind of indescribable eccentric humanity, despite the irony. There was something comforting and encouraging about an old man, as he watched the insane chronicle of our century, talking about it in plain words, calmly and skeptically with no hint of the tragic. While speaking intently and soberly about the calamities of the age, Romm never sought to inspire fear. He categorized the improbable, terrible evils of the century as though they were mundane events, although not without their imbecility, as though they were a stage in the process of history, and so the evil lost its apocalyptic quality of fantasy, and an unrealized hope emerged that now— given the fact that all-seeing old age could talk with such equanimity about all this— that *this* time the world would be healed (although Socrates would again have to drink poison and Archimedes' calculations would again be interrupted by the sword). Of course none of this was actually said in words, only in the intonation of an ironic stoicism, but it caused the infernal circle to break open and expose the banal, ordinary nature of evil as the consequence of the baseness of the human soul and the impotence of the human mind.

Romm's intonation ("None of this is new" and "All this has happened before") could not have been faked. It was the product of real conviction—to acquire it one needed to have lived seventy years of twentieth-century history, a history that momentarily raised up idols and antichrists and cast them down again, building a thousand-year heaven for the chosen few that proved to be a twelve-year hell for everyone. This faith based on skepticism, this negative optimism had in it an

---

1. Mikhail Ilyich Romm (1901–1971): Soviet film producer and leading figure initiating intellectual trends in the Soviet film industry. His documentary *The World Today* inspired Schnittke to write his Symphony No. 1. —ed.

unformulated confidence that evil was doomed to extinction because of its lack of talent. So the need for direct condemnation of recidivism and demonstrative support of progress simply faded away.

But there were times, and these were moving in their silent purity, when Romm said nothing. The opening of the film was one of these, when for several minutes the screen was filled with children running out of a school in Paris toward the camera that unexpectedly blocked their way. The living quicksilver of a crowd of children, its noisy showing-off demonstrating to the camera the fact that it was alive, made one continually conscious of the idea that the sea of life is eternal, that it casts onto the shore one new wave after another, only to be broken by those that follow. Here too Romm allowed himself no universal statements—but they came to the mind of the audience anyway.

There is none of this in the finished film. The changing shots on the screens can not recapture the eloquence of Romm's spoken ideas, which were eloquent through their very lack of eloquence. No tape recording of his commentary survives—Romm did not wish to immortalize words that were impromptu.

Written in 1972. Russian text published in *Besedy s Al'fredom Shnitke*, compiled and edited by A. V. Ivashkin (Moscow: Kul'tura, 1994), p. 123–124.

[II.]

From the musical point of view I found myself with a split personality. I had my own interests—an interest in modern musical techniques, in new compositions; I studied all this and made use of it in my music. But life saw to it that for about seventeen years I worked in the cinema much more and more often than I ought to have done, and by no means only in films that I found interesting. Eventually I began to feel uncomfortable, as though I were divided in half. At first the situation was that what I was doing in the cinema had no connection with what I was doing in my own compositions. Then I realized that this would not do: I was responsible for everything I wrote. This kind of split was inadmissible, and somehow I had to revise my views of both kinds of music. And apart from that, I gained no satisfaction from—speaking frankly—producing music by calculation. I am simplifying, of course; there was more to it than mere calculation. I realized that there was something radically abnormal in the split that exists in modern musical language, in the vast gap between the laboratory "top" and the commercial "bottom." This gap had to be bridged, not only by me in my own personal situation, but also as a general principle. The language of music has to be unified, as it always has been; it has to be universal. It may lean one way or the other, but there cannot be two musical languages. And yet the growth of an avant-garde in music has led to a conscious split and the discovery of a new elitist musical language. So I began to look for a universal musical language. From the musical point of view, this was what my evolution appeared to be.

A composer working in the cinema inevitably runs risks. There are good reasons for the fact that in America one has the profession of composer and the profession of

Hollywood composer—something quite different. In the West at the present time not one decent self-respecting composer is working in the cinema. The cinema cannot but dictate its terms to a composer. The case of the collaboration between Eisenstein and Prokofiev is perhaps the only exception; maybe there are others. But even Shostakovich had to submit to the dictates of the film director. There is nothing you can do about that—it is not so much the dictates of the director as the specifics of the medium in which one must work. Being aware of this it is possible—and this is what I have tried to do in recent years—to work with those directors in whose films interesting musical tasks arise of their own accord. When I complain about the excesses of my own work in the cinema, I have in mind not everything I have done and not everyone with whom I have worked, but those cases forced on me by practical considerations, when I was compelled to write absolute rubbish. From the outset, my work in certain films was experimental: one day I would write something, the next day listen to the orchestra play it, not like it, change it on the spot, although I might have tried out a certain device, an orchestral technique, or something else. In this respect, I gained a great deal from the cinema. Then too, the actual treatment of the inferior material inevitably dictated by the cinema may prove useful for a composer (I can't remember how many marches for brass band and banal waltz tunes, how much chase music, gunfight music, landscape music I wrote). I can transfer one or another of the themes into another composition, and by contrast with the other material in that composition, it acquires a new role. For example, my Concerto Grosso No. 1 includes a tango taken from the film *The Agony*, about Rasputin. In the film it is a fashionable dance of the day. I took it from the film and by giving it a contrasting context and a different development tried to give it a different meaning.

From a 1984 conversation with N. Shakhnazarova and G. Golovinsky, published in *Novaya zhizn' traditsii v sovetskoi muzyke: stat'i i interv'yu* [New Life for Traditions in Soviet Music: Articles and an Interview] (Moscow: Sovetskii Kompozitor, 1989), pp. 332–349. Reprinted in *Besedy s Al'fredom Shnitke*, compiled and edited by A. V. Ivashkin (Moscow: Kul'tura, 1994), p. 124.

[III.]

As may be seen in the work of such masters as Tarkovsky and Bergman, the cinema has become an area where all the arts combine, in which the director is the synthesizing author. That used to be the case in the theater, but after the cinema was introduced, interesting changes took place in the theater too. The modern theater also belongs to the director, and here we can see a parallel with film. I repeat that in the cinema the composer is working in conditions different from those of the opera, in which the musical element is the main thing. In film much of what is in the music—its form, its dynamics—is defined by the director. And cinema provides more new audio-visual possibilities than the theater. For all these reasons the cinema as an art form now occupies first place. Naturally this has its dangers. The influence of a film is short-lived: in five years it is out of date, and in ten years it has become hopelessly old-fashioned. It has a powerful effect, but a brief one, by contrast with the theater, which can create productions much less prone to aging.

The exceptions to this are the films in which the kinetics of the plot are subordinate to what is purely poetic—those of Tarkovsky or Bergman, for instance. I shall not forget the shattering impression Fellini's *8½* made on me twenty years ago. But years later, the film seemed old-fashioned. This did not happen in the case of Tarkovsky and Bergman, with their cinema poetry. It is difficult to express this—you have to experience it. As an art the cinema continues to develop and will go on doing so. Perhaps there will be stereoscopic films. For example, Coppola's *Apocalypse Now* is a breakthrough in this direction.

There are striking things in the theater too. I saw a production of Shakespeare's *Henry IV* by the French director Ariane Mnouchkine. In it the actors did not simply run out onto the stage; they literally shot out onto it, and the performance continued at this frenetic pace for six hours, with just one intermission. The intensity of this endless climax was unbelievable. The production had a stylistic totality that combined the European and Oriental theaters, the visual and aural elements. This was made apparent visually—the characters were dressed in costumes that were simultaneously European and Oriental, modern and authentically historical, thereby bringing different ages together. An incredible range of devices, including not merely the traditional theatrical forms connected with the spoken word but also things previously hardly ever touched by the theater. For instance, one long episode has no words or dialogue in the usual sense—the actors convey what is happening by using sounds and interjections. Especially striking is the fact that the words sound as if in French translation from English, although you cannot identify a particular language. The action loses its typicality, the spoken word loses its dominance—the heightened state of the whole presentation "crushes" the words. This may have been the most powerful theatrical experience in my life.

Something similar to this is found in cinema that does not go out of date, in which there is a quest for poetry, along with the traditional lyricism, which may be comprised in the strict basics of film. Some things in the cinema I would never try to narrate in words: *Solyaris* [Solaris], *Stalker* [Stalker], *Andrei Rublyov*, *Zerkalo* [The Mirror].[2] From the beginning of his career, something in Tarkovsky made people call him a mystic. The same is true of Bergman. For me the highest achievements in cinema are linked with these two names. Their films, with little dialogue, contain an enormous compressed power.

---

2. These are all films directed by Andrei Tarkovsky (1932–1986), recognized as one of the cinema's true poets. Born in Moscow, he spent his final years in exile in Paris. *Solaris* (1972) and *Stalker* (1979) offer bleak visions of the future. *Andrei Rublyov* (1966, banned in the USSR until 1971) is about the famous fifteenth-century Russian icon-painter. —ed.

ON STAGING TCHAIKOVSKY'S
THE QUEEN OF SPADES (1977)

Like any other art, opera, in its endless striving for realism and authenticity, rejects—as it develops—one convention after another. But it is precisely the earlier achievements of realism, derived from real life and so true to life, which now always prove to be more false than those conventional devices long hallowed in practice. The reason is that with them art falls prey to the danger of naturalism, that is, external realism.

Operatic realism developed only comparatively recently, just a hundred years ago, seeking to overcome what was false and artificial in "grand opera." But today these singers with their true-to-life gestures and "realistically" motley chorus crowds are intolerable. Nowadays *The Magic Flute* and *Orpheus* are more true to life (and consequently more realistic in the genuine sense of the word) than *Carmen* and *Aïda*.

Tchaikovsky's *The Queen of Spades* is a work of genius in the way its characters are psychologically authentic. In it everything is true—except for the superficial elements of realism.[1] Exactly what in it relates to superficial realism but has no connection with the truth? It is primarily and almost without exception the crowd:

1. the crowd that is falsely neutral—the crowd of strollers in the first scene, the nurses, children, governesses, and other superfluous characters;
2. the crowd that is falsely *interested*—the maidservants' chorus in Liza's room, the chorus of people visiting the Summer Gardens frightened by a thunderstorm;
3. the crowd that is falsely *false*—the guests at the ball, the chorus of shepherds and shepherdesses in the pastoral scene.

In the first two cases, (1) and (2), supporting the background superfluity of the characters is a corresponding stereotyped form of music. These musical numbers are not among the best pages of the score; they are a genre tribute to operatic realism inside a psychological drama. They could simply be omitted with no detriment to the music—and to the advantage of the drama. This is what we did (the conductor, director, designer, and I), with two exceptions: the chorus of people caught in the storm in the first scene and the chorus of singers in the third. Here we kept the music, but changed the libretto: the chorus sings not about the weather and ballroom

---

1. No one objects to realism in the broad sense, in the sense of a correspondence to reality. What is meant here is realism in the narrow sense, the realism that bases itself on a literal trueness to life to the detriment of the truth of the work as a whole. —A.Sch.

etiquette, but about playing cards, a subject that is really exciting to all the characters in the opera.

But in the third example—the intermezzo, "The True Shepherdess" from Scene 3—the music is delightful. And yet this pastoral scene is completely unnecessary to the opera. Rather, it fulfils the traditional function of a ballet divertissement in Act II of an opera, nothing more than that. At best, it is an idyllic distraction from the drama, having no dramaturgical or thematic motivation.

You know, everything that happens has not one, but *several* motivations, and it is only when these intersect that what transpires can be convincing. There might be some supplementary motivation if the pastoral interlude somehow contained in itself the entire formula of the whole work (like "The Mousetrap" in *Hamlet*) or at least if there were some thematic analogy. But there is none—it is impossible to identify German with Milovzor! For such an identification the pastoral scene needed to be reinterpreted, its wonderfully naive music had to acquire a supplementary allegorical meaning. To achieve this we had to

1. pass the scene through German's abnormal consciousness, turn it into a hallucination, a presentiment;
2. while preserving all the musical themes of the pastoral scene, put them in a parallel montage with the ominous themes of Scene 4; and
3. transfer the roles in the pastoral scene to the main characters of the opera (Liza-Prilepa; the countess-Milovzor; Yeletsky-Zlatogor).[2]

Of course, while the genre numbers we omitted are also less attractive musically, they had a specific and beneficial dramatic function in the opera—they effected an essential lowering of tension. By omitting them, thereby increasing the tension, we ran the risk of overburdening the audience. But their function is taken over by the textual interludes introduced by the director: the reading of extracts from Pushkin's story in Merimée's translation, accompanied by themes from the opera played on the harpsichord. This brings about a lowering of the tension, but not one that is artistically distracting. Rather it is graphically austere, involving an instantaneous switch from the incandescent sound-world of voice and orchestra to the cold informational world of the spoken word and the harpsichord.

An indirect consequence of this is a sharpening of contrasts in the sound-pattern of the work as a whole. Usually the relatively uniform sound of the full orchestra in nineteenth-century opera reminds one of a kind of lava flow, its white-hot evenness removing the possibility of the kind of variation in the sound-pattern that is so wonderful in seventeenth- and eighteenth-century operas, when the numbers for voice and orchestra alternate with *recitativo secco* or simply with ordinary speech. The efforts by contemporary opera composers to introduce chamber-music details

---

2. Here it is particularly important to substitute the Countess, not German, for Milovzor. German is no longer himself: he is possessed by the evil spirit of the card game, the spirit of the "old witch." In his subconscious there is an inevitable identification with the Countess, a feeling that his own personality has been replaced by a kind of werewolf. —A.Sch.

into their scores leads in the same way to a pointing-up of the sound pattern, which is now more like the zigzag pattern of an oscillogram than an even wave-like flow. We tried to achieve the same result, not by tampering with the actual score but by contrasting the full-blooded orchestral sound of Tchaikovsky's music with quotations from it played on a harpsichord.

To point up the sound pattern of the opera we are also introducing a system of microphones set out among the chorus, allowing separate voices to be picked out from the unified choral sound. This should eliminate the ludicrous unison spontaneity of the crowd. The more a composer tries to make the choral outbursts spontaneous and natural, the more improbable they appear.

The statuesque oratorio style of the choruses in Stravinsky's *Oedipus Rex* does not appear artificial—here we have an up-front device derived from the chorus in Greek drama. Neither do the characters briefly emerging from the chorus in *Boris Godunov* seem absurd. It is the middle course that is unconvincing—when a whole mass of people with false spontaneity utter synchronized banalities about their lives and the weather.

Of course, it would be inadmissible to rework completely the musical text left to us by a great composer. But it is permissible to interpret this text in different ways, and that includes using a different sound. From time to time doubts arise about the vitality of a certain artistic phenomenon. We recently attended a discussion in which the novel had to defend its right to survive. Tonality, harmony, even rhythm (in the traditional way of understanding them) and likewise the sonata and symphony forms, even music itself as an art intended solely for a listener (that is, without any spatial acoustics or any visual component)—all these were seen as no longer viable in the recent age of the avant-garde. It was only ten years ago that Pierre Boulez called for opera houses to be demolished, and yet several years later he took his place on the podium at Bayreuth.

Today the danger from leftist nihilistic attacks on opera has already passed, but all the more real is the danger of a return to outmoded operatic canons and the nostalgic dogmatism of some of the absurd conventions of "realistic" opera. It is now, when no one is trying to kill opera, that it stands in need of new developments and a critical reassessment of some of the results of its previous history.

Written in 1977 but first published as a note to a production of *The Queen of Spades* in Karlsruhe, November 1990; subsequently published in *Muzykal'naia Zhizn'* [Musical Life], 1991, No. 6, p. 8; Russian text reprinted in *Besedy s Al'fredom Shnitke*, compiled and edited by A. V. Ivashkin (Moscow: Kul'tura, 1994), pp. 202–204.

IV

SCHNITTKE ON CREATIVE ARTISTS

7

ON SHOSTAKOVICH

Circles of Influence

(1975)

For the past fifty years, music has been under the influence of Dmitri Shostakovich. During that time his style has been continually evolving, and this has given rise to ever-new types of influence. One could name dozens of composers whose individual characteristics were formed under the hypnotic influence of Shostakovich, but one could equally divide these pupils (whether they formally attended his classes or not) into generations, according to the debt they owe their teacher. One group, formed as long ago as the 1930s, adopted the biting sharpness and paradoxical naiveté of his early works. Another, which grew up in the 1940s and 1950s, adopted the neoclassical austerity of expression characteristic of works such as Symphonies Nos. 5 through 10, or the first five string quartets. Finally, in the 1960s and 1970s, a group of composers appeared who further developed the unique "late" philosophical lyricism of Shostakovich.

So we find that different composers—completely individual, with quite distinct features, at almost opposite poles, like Sviridov and Peiko, Weinberg and Levitin, Ustvol'skaya and Boris Tchaikovsky, Galynin and Meerovich, Denisov and Nikolaev, Tishchenko and Banshchikov, and many more besides, branched out in their own musical ways from the trunk of Shostakovich's music, while the trunk itself kept growing and putting out new branches.

As time went on, so the "angle of radiation" widened too. Initially it was the composer's brilliant orchestral style that exerted the most powerful influence. Then the main focus shifted to the chamber-music linearity of his musical texture. Next came the influence of Shostakovich's dramaturgical ideas, which created new forms. And today it is the composer's creative stance, the philosophical and ethical elements in his music, that serve as a model for musicians of different generations.

It is just as interesting to examine the way in which Shostakovich, as he developed, came under the influence of other composers of his time. It may be that the unique quality of an artist reveals itself most clearly in the fearless way he opens himself to alien influences, when he makes everything coming from outside his own, as he absorbs it into the immeasurable and unidentifiable substance of his own individual genius, which adorns everything it touches. In the twentieth century only Stravinsky had the same magical power to make his own everything that came into his field of vision.

Shostakovich's career as a creative artist is remarkable in the way it has constantly renewed itself and continued every spring to flower anew. The composer has transformed and fused a wealth of influences, but his music has always been uniquely his own, his musical cast of thought an organic element of every bar he writes. Even the collages of musical quotations, so characteristic of the [music of the] 1920s and 1930s, and of the present, are heard by the listener, surprisingly, as Shostakovich's own material. And this is not merely because of the intonational, rhythmic, and timbral links with the basic text of his music; it is also because, once the alien material comes into Shostakovich's magnetic field, it acquires colorations that are distinctive to him.

But, last and most important, all his life Shostakovich has been under the influence of Shostakovich. And here I have in mind not the unbroken thread of continuity linking all his works, but the reprises, the self-quotations, the returns to the thematic imagery and material of his earlier works which are so characteristic of the composer, and how he rethinks them and develops them in a new way. String Quartets Nos. 8 and 14 and Symphony No. 15, are, in their way, the most distinctive crossroads in time, where the past enters into new relationships with the present, and, like the ghost of Hamlet's father, intrudes into the reality of the music and actually forms it. In Shostakovich's music, when thematic material from his earlier personal musical career intermingles in collages with thematic material borrowed from the earlier history of music, a striking effect is created: one of objectivization, of an assimilation of what is individual with what is universal. And it is precisely this that determines the purpose of an artist's life—to influence the world by merging with it.

Not everyone is given time to achieve this purpose, nor can everyone find in himself the power to achieve it. A special kind of power is required—not the mere physical ability to maintain constant activity, but that inner determination that is an essential part of any artist's being. It is this, sometimes independently of the artist's conscious will, that irrevocably guides him along a single path and inevitably returns him to it. And in this respect, too, Shostakovich will be a model not only for the present but also for the future, and will exert his most significant and strongest influence on the destiny of music.

Written in 1975 and first published in *D. Shostakovich: Stat'i i materialy* [D. Shostakovich: Articles and Materials], compiled and edited by G. M. Shneerson (Moscow: Sovetskii Kompozitor, 1976), p. 225. Russian text reprinted in *Besedy s Al'fredom Shnitke*, compiled and edited by A. V. Ivashkin (Moscow: Kul'tura, 1994), pp. 89–90.

CHAPTER
8

ON PROKOFIEV (1990)

The history of humankind has never known progress from worse to better. But if there were no hopes of improvement, life itself would cease to be. Every generation has striven—not cold-heartedly, but with the greatest passion—to bring a secret dream into being. Sometimes the impression was created that this had really happened. And then once again it all proved to be merely an illusion. But if what was inaccessible in the reality of the horizon of history did not constantly shift into the future, life could not continue.

The First World War rattled the all-embracing 100-percent-guaranteed optimism of the Silver Age for the twentieth century—so passionately anticipated. Yet hope still remained. Who could anticipate at that time another historical catastrophe that would take many more millions of lives, the destructive power of the atomic bomb, and much more besides? If we consider the sum total of human victims, there is no doubt that our own century has surpassed all the previous ones. But are the Forces of Evil yet satisfied?

And yet the beginning of the twentieth century promised humankind the long-awaited stability of historical progress. Wars, large-scale wars at least, no longer seemed possible. Science had taken the place of religious faith. All insurmountable obstacles were soon to disappear. So among young people the aim of life came to be cool and sporty, directed at what was most useful and most inspiring. Prokofiev was one of them. Theirs was a natural optimism—not ideologically inspired, but genuine in its own right. The many different ways of identifying with the period and all its features were reflected in the habits of Prokofiev's life—the express trains, the motor vehicles, the aircraft, the telegraph, the radio, and the like—all these enabled him to organize time in a soberingly ecstatic way, extremely precise, perfected once and for all. And this is why the terrifying experiences still to come, the worst in history, were for a long time seen merely as a tragic misunderstanding. This is also why the optimism, which had become a way of life, survived what lay in the future, albeit with the inescapable correctives supplied by everyday experience. The unwillingness to acknowledge the surrealistic horrors of true reality, the ability to remain inflexible, to suppress inner grief, to ignore venomous attacks—all these seemed to be a way of surviving. Alas, they proved illusory. Once that part of Prokofiev's (outwardly sporty and business-like) character—which, although invisible, was more important and the most essential—once it had encountered falsity, it was grievously wounded, but still was able to hide the wounds so deep that they could not be healed. They brought the composer's life to an end in his sixty-second year.

Yet Prokofiev was not the sort of person to bend beneath the weight of his time. It is true that there are no instances in his life of any open resistance to the ritual theater of destruction. On the other hand there are no compromises made with it. Prokofiev was one of those people who preserved his human values in the most dreadful circumstances, who did not surrender at the discretion of the outwardly all-powerful daily regime.[1] The resistance he offered to it was peaceful, but no less sturdy. His behavior in various circumstances gives the impression of a man who is cold and calculating, very precise, protected from the deceptive mirages of contemporary life by his ironic rationality. This is confirmed by what we hear from those who knew him, Nikolai Nabokov, for example.[2] There is ample evidence of Prokofiev's genius for organizing his time. The most convincing is his actual legacy, which would hardly have been as vast and of such high quality had his life been that of a so-called normal composer who regards the opportunity to work as a rare gift. Prokofiev must have been keenly aware of the dynamic interaction between his creative nature and his business-like working habits. Think, for example, of the shortness of his letters, the time-saving way he had of writing in the Old Russian style with the vowels omitted, his mastering of his own complexes, for which there were more than enough reasons, from both outside and inside. Or his self-control, his refusal to offer ordinary human excuses like "I was sick" or "I didn't feel like working." In fact he was still working on the very last day of his life, 5 March 1953.

But, of course, he knew the whole truth. And he knew full well that he was ill and could not hope for a long life. That is why, as time went on, he refused to perform as a pianist, or later as a conductor, so that he could have more time to compose. And it was this capacity for constant self-denial, this ability to set aside the routine false problems of public life, this refusal to allow external actuality to intrude into his home and heart, even perhaps into his music, this avoidance of social activity, which produced such impressive results: a creative legacy of 131 opuses, nearly all of them high-quality music. This kind of productivity was more usual in the eighteenth century, when life may have been harder, but incomparably more natural than it is in the tangled confusion of our modern times, with their interminable demagogic presentations. That apparently long-vanished reality which could be recreated only in the stylized or idealized reconstructions of neoclassicism appears, in the case of Prokofiev, natural and capriciously alive, as though the dark night of the present did not even exist! He saw the world differently, even heard it differently. No doubt nature had endowed him with fundamental gifts, means of perception, which were different from those of the vast majority of human beings. For him the dark depths of real life were always bathed in sunlight. This is completely unique. There is no one with whom to compare him. Prokofiev's last composition, his Seventh Symphony, seems to have been written by a young man. It is full of spontaneity and the inexhaustible force of life.

This ability to focus on the eternal at the expense of the present was not an exclusively intellectual achievement, although there is something intellectual in it. It is an all-embracing resolution of life's problems, a particular conception of how to live. It is obvious that all human beings remain the same at all stages of their life as

---

1. Schnittke is, of course, referring here to Russia under the Soviet regime. —ed.
2. Nikolas [Nikolai] Nabokov: American composer; brother of Vladimir Nabokov. —ed.

they were at the beginning and that time has no effect. But one must make the proviso that Prokofiev was likewise aware of the darker depths of human existence. We have only to recall the auto-da-fé scene in *The Fiery Angel*, or Andrei's death scene in *War and Peace*, together with the numerous tragic and dramatic moments in, for example, the Sixth Symphony, the Eighth Piano Sonata, or the First Violin Sonata. Likewise, the double suicide scene in *Romeo and Juliet*. For too long this extremely serious music has been judged only for its bold outward form, while its deeply felt inner essence has been ignored. Only the carnival glitter of the outer shell was noticed, and no attention was paid to the austere seriousness inside it, which ensured that the suffering did not flood out and swamp everything. And there was a serious element in Prokofiev from the very beginning. One has only to think of the Second Piano Concerto, of its world of sound, filled with harsh severity, about which there is still critical debate. Or of the *Scythian Suite*, "Ala and Lolli," this highly original "shadow version" of Stravinsky's *Sacre du printemps*. Of the Second or Third Piano Sonatas, and of much more besides.

Prokofiev, of course, knew the awful truth about the time in which he lived. It was merely that he refused to allow it to crush him. His musical ideas remained within a classical framework, but the tragic power of what he was expressing was all the more heightened in all those gavottes, minuets, waltzes, and marches. He was, in the literal sense, "a gentleman wearing collar and tie." Thus, when in 1948 he turned up wearing ski clothes at Zhdanov's quasi-intellectual performance of destruction at the Party Central Committee, it had a much deeper significance than mere outward appearance. Its deeper importance may be seen in what happened later: essentially this unsentimental man could not tolerate the idle chatter of the so-called responsible party workers. It broke him and shortened his life.

And yet his life began so marvelously! A happy, if by no means idyllic childhood, studying with Glière, Rimsky-Korsakov, Liadov, Esipova, and Nikolai Cherepnin. A happy youth—that is to say a youth rich in conflicts, giving concerts very early in his career, and composing non-stop. But then came war and revolution, and he made the decision to go abroad to wait for the situation to improve, which he did, like so many others, with the help of Lunacharsky. Then came the decision to return—a decision taken by very few. It was as if Prokofiev refused in principle to accept the apocalyptic upheaval into the history of the twentieth century, which had begun in such a blaze of enthusiasm. He tried to see it through with the cool relaxation of a sportsman, as if he neither heard nor saw the approach of carnage and destruction unprecedented in history. More precisely, he did not want to see or hear it. To a degree this puts him on common ground with his great contemporary and rival Igor Stravinsky, as distinct from his friend Nikolai Miaskovsky, slightly older than he was, who had a clear but naive sense of the unavoidable approach of the inferno. Dmitri Shostakovich felt it all much more strongly, recording almost with the accuracy of a seismograph the most destructive earthquake in human history.

Obviously Prokofiev's return to Russia can be looked at in different ways. It might have been a miscalculation. Had he stayed in the West, he would certainly have lived longer. But, had he done so, it is highly likely that he would not have composed such important works as the Fifth, Sixth, and Seventh Symphonies, the operas *War and Peace* and *Betrothal in a Monastery,* the ballets *Romeo and Juliet* and *Cinderella,* the Second Violin Concerto and the *Symphony-Concerto for Cello and Orchestra,* the Sixth through Ninth Piano Sonatas, the First and Second Violin Sonatas, and a whole series of other works. Or they would have sounded quite different.

As it was for Shostakovich, the Second World War for Prokofiev was the most difficult, and yet the most important, period in his life. He continued to compose symphonies and piano sonatas, went on working on *War and Peace* and *Cinderella.* In those days there was simply no time for distracting official speeches and the curse of official interference. But as soon as the war was over, the usual pantomime began again. Then came a decisive attack, such as earlier had been made on only a single composer, on Shostakovich, and which had wounded him grievously more than once. But now new victims were needed, and it was the turn of Prokofiev, Aram Khachaturian, Miaskovsky, Shebalin, Popov, plus the makeweight figure of Vano Muradeli, who was singled out as ringleader. In January 1948, Stalin's loyal hatchet man Zhdanov made his speech, and everyone pretended to be as stupid as he was; his colleagues were somehow inspired to make a hysterical demonstration of irrational personal loyalty. And there was a greater and more dangerous consequence: almost everyone fell prey to a spiritual despair that provoked the selfish desire to save one's own skin at any cost. Whereas in fact only those who did not care at all about their own skins were really able to survive.

This ideological farce of self-destruction, the worst in history, had dire and multiple consequences for our music, and they have still not been remedied. Artists affected by the Central Committee Resolution soon felt its influence. Prokofiev felt it, too. And the fact that he did not bow to it is explained by the paradox of his situation. He survived thanks to his determination to preserve order in his life in circumstances that had completely changed, an ability that had become second nature during his years of emigration. The true tragedy of Prokofiev's life lies in the fact that he refused to accept the tragic as one of life's highest criteria, because the consequence of such a refusal is that the tragic becomes twice as powerful, twice as cogent. Consequently, the only recourse left to him was to try to overcome the enormous and complex catastrophic problems of his personal life by adopting a consciously worked-out approach to the forms and concepts of the so-called objective conditions of the time and to attempt to ease the tragic situation with an objectivity of external habits and forms of expression. The only way left to him was to pay attention to fine details, to everything that could be defined temporally and spatially, and which could help him overcome the real tragedy of life—to try to ignore what was bad, to eliminate constantly all that was dark from his daily existence.

Prokofiev shows us how a human being can remain human in a situation when that is almost unthinkable, how, in order to achieve an ideal humanity, you can make your purpose in life the conquest of what is part of the day-to-day routine of humanity. But Prokofiev's life, like that of Shostakovich, teaches us something else: that even isolated concessions lead to wrong decisions. Neither *The Stone Flower* nor *The Story of a Real Man* were genuine creative successes—and probably never will be.

The individual works that appeared in the last years of his life (that is, after 1948) provide documentary evidence of the self-destruction forced upon a great artist, an artist who in fact tried to write more simply in order to come closer to the people. But here the very idea of "the people" is false, since in actual fact it covers everything—the highest and the lowest. So any attempt to adapt to what is supposed to be the single taste of one people is false. It was merely one step in the direction of the official false idea of "the taste of the people," but it entailed a whole series of steps away from the individual taste of one of the greatest composers in the history of Russian music.

But, in spite of this, there were many other things that enabled Prokofiev to conquer his day-by-day attachment to the time in which he lived: things that were the result of the pitiful brevity of his life. For example, his many contacts with artists of various ages. These began in his early childhood—Taneev, Glière, Rimsky-Korsakov, Esipova, Nikolai Cherepnin—and continued as he grew to maturity—Miaskovsky, Stravinsky, Diaghilev, Koussevitsky, Balanchine, Meyerhold, Eisenstein, Tairov, Lavrovsky, Ulanova, Oistrakh, Gilels, Richter, Rostropovich, Samosud, Mravinsky—and went on developing even after his death. In particular, it was thanks to Gennadi Rozhdestvensky that seven of Prokofiev's compositions were heard in public for the first time after 1953....

I had the good fortune to be present at the first performance of his *Symphony-Concerto for Cello and Orchestra* in the Great Hall of the Moscow Conservatory on 18 February 1952. It was in many respects a unique occasion and will always remain one. At any rate, two important features were never to occur again: Sviatoslav Richter appearing as a conductor and Prokofiev coming out to acknowledge the applause. It is not for me to pass judgment now on the way Richter conducted. At all events, he made a powerful impression, and it was thus a great shame that, as he mounted the podium, he tripped, and this bad omen apparently dissuaded him from trying his hand as a conductor at any future performances. After the performance Prokofiev came out to take a bow, but from the floor, clearly being too weak to get up onto the stage. I can see to this day his tall thin figure wearing dark glasses. Rostropovich's playing was lively and full of wit, and my impression of that première remains unsurpassed.

Soon afterward Prokofiev was dead—and fate decreed that his death was to be on 5 March 1953, the day Stalin died.

It is now difficult to describe how everything happened on the day of the funeral—everyone present has his own picture of it and has every right to defend his picture as the genuine one. But one thing is indisputable: along an almost deserted street that ran parallel to the street carrying a seething mass hysterically mourning the passing of Stalin, there moved in the opposite direction a small group of people, bearing on their shoulders the coffin of the greatest Russian composer of the time. Unfortunately I am unable to give the names of all those who were present, although I have tried to obtain as much information as possible. As far as I can tell, apart from Prokofiev's family, the following took part: Dmitri Shostakovich, Nina Dorliak, Andrei Volkonsky, Evgeniia Miaskovskaya, Karen Khachaturian, Olga Lamm, Levon Atovmian, Andrei Babaev, Semyon Shlifshtein, Alexei Nikolaev, Vladimir Rubin, Mikhail Marutaev, Tomas Korganov, Edison Denisov, Alexandr Pirumov,

Izrail Nestiev, Marina Sabinina, Gennadi Rozhdestvensky, Lazar Berman, Lev Lebedinsky, Sergei Arababov. Obviously, there are missing from this list several names that one would have expected, almost certainly, to find. It is clear that they are those of people prevented from attending for some reason or forced to take part in the other official funeral ceremony—either of their own free will or from fear or compulsion. And it is thus that history preserves the picture of this small, special group of people moving in one direction, their purpose and their goal different from those in the other procession. I regard this picture as symbolic. To move against the tide in those days was completely hopeless. Yet even then there was—just as in earlier ages—the possibility of a choice between two decisions, only one of which was right. So it was that this movement against the tide, once begun, gradually broadened, was joined by similar streams flowing from other places and turned into the flood we see today—a flood fateful in its scope, stormy in its potential, often threatening danger, but inevitably linked with the turn of events of which there was a vague presentiment on the day of Prokofiev's funeral. A turn of events leading to a new and hopeful road in the history of this great and restless country.

Written in October 1990 as notes on a German recording; published by N. Zeyfas in *Sovetskaya Muzyka* [Soviet Music], 1990, No. 11, pp. 1–3. Russian text reprinted in *Besedy s Al'fredom Shnitke*, compiled and edited by A. V. Ivashkin (Moscow: Kul'tura, 1994), pp. 210–215.

9

ON GUBAIDULINA (1970s)

Carl Jung believes that men have a female soul (the anima) and women have a male soul (the animus). I am not sure about the first, but have no doubts about the second. This is borne out by examples from the history of art and the recent past: Akhmatova and Yudina, for instance. An example from the present day is Sofia Gubaidulina. In our time (indeed at any time previously) problems of creativity are inevitably problems of morality. The establishing, the assertion, the preservation of one's creative individuality is connected with the day-to-day answer to the question "To be or not to be," the day-to-day choice of direction—to the right, to the left, or to the center—and the day-to-day inner struggle to resolve the conflict not only between concepts that are not homogeneous (sincerity and form, for instance) but also between the true basic concepts themselves and their opposites (sincerity and sham, form and design, for example). This struggle requires male fortitude; its victories and defeats are not always visible to outside observers, who see in the artistic outcome only what has emerged victorious and who have no way of working out what might have emerged victorious but was lost.

In her very first compositions Gubaidulina impresses one with the remarkable integrity of her creative personality—providing evidence of a unique inner world and an indomitable artistic will. Her stylistic evolution may have sharpened the expressive qualities of her music, but it has not changed its character at all.

If we compare the two song cycles *Fatselia* and *The Rubaiyat*, separated by two decades, in both cases we observe the same qualities: there is a delicacy of vocal intonation that is both simple and somewhat recherché, a tense economy of texture, each sound having a precise function, and also that invisible thread of unity of form and meaning that unfailingly runs through all her works. As a result of her inflexible insistence on maximalism she is compelled to spend a long time putting careful finishing touches to the finest details. The consequence of this is not superficial elegance, but severe asceticism. Both her music and her life are integrated and equally uncompromising. She has shown herself incapable of making concessions to authority in either her creative or everyday life. She places the utmost demands on herself, combining this with benevolence and active generosity in her dealings with people, and a breadth of perspective and tolerance toward "alien" musical worlds and languages.

Written in the late 1970s. Russian text published in *Besedy s Al'fredom Shnitke*, compiled and edited by A. V. Ivashkin (Moscow: Kul'tura, 1994), p. 97.

CHAPTER

10

ON KANCHELI (1982, 1991)

[On the Third and Sixth Symphonies]

In Giya Kancheli's symphonies it is as though in a comparatively short time (twenty to thirty minutes of slow music) we experience an entire life or an entire history. But we have no sense of the jolts of time, we seem to be in an aircraft, not conscious of speed, soaring over musical space—that is, over time. In the Third Symphony, as in all his others, the composer avoids the stereotypical forms and typologies of the genre—there is no sonata form, no multiplicity of movements, no precise dramatic development. The symphony's distinctive "lack of drama" is based on contrasts of thematic images that in themselves hardly develop but which keep forming new relationships. There is the refrain of the voice based on the intonations of the traditional funeral chant from Svanetia,[1] which suffuses the whole work from beginning to end like an incarnation of the eternal spiritual principle. There are the heroic syllabic "choral" exclamations from the brass. There is the subdued pulsing of the strings (the sound produced by tapping them, *senza arco*, with the fingers of the left hand). There are the distant sounds of a bell. There are the quiet, incorporeal sounds of a solo violin soaring above an unchanging chord. There are the sudden sharp breaks in the rhythm, the lightning-like interjections by the tutti, the endlessly drawn-out echoes. All these elements are presented to us only as brief motifs or simply as flashes of orchestral color. But there is no kaleidoscopic quality. The infrequent eruptions of related motifs leave a prolonged acoustic residue in the consciousness, and between them stretch intonational links heard as a stream of dotted lines that create a fluctuating polyphony of timbral layers. It is precisely this cinematic montage–like inconclusiveness, framelessness, that creates the impression of multidimensional space.

Running through the whole of the Sixth Symphony like an image of unchanging nature, the timbral refrain of the two solo violas acts as a link in the chain of contrasting episodes: now there is broken and gasping breathing, now concentrated meditation, now an unexpected spasm, now a tragic funeral procession, now blows struck by an unknown evil power, now a lyrical revelation, now frenzied violence, now the proud stoicism of humility—all this passes before us in sequence (and sometimes simultaneously in multidimensional counterpoint), and we do not know when and where these events, separated by centuries, took place. They are presented to us not in exhausting fullness, but in "dotted" incompleteness (just as, incidentally, everything happens in life). We cannot help believing in the reality of this world, revealed to us in its wonderful "formlessness," and we long to visit it

---

1. Svanetia: An area in the hilly part of Georgia. —ed.

once more and to come to understand what we failed to understand the first time, to listen properly to what we failed to hear....

From the notes to the recording of Kancheli's Third and Sixth Symphonies, Melodiya (C 10 20843000), 1982. Russian text reprinted in *Besedy s Al'fredom Shnitke*, compiled and edited by A. V. Ivashkin (Moscow: Kul'tura, 1994), p. 95.

[On *Oplakannye vetrom* (Mournings of the Wind)]

This work is simultaneously complex and simple, but nowhere does it become a repetition of something that has already been said. It is as though we feel the interaction of three layers of time: time that is metrically dramatic (unexpected, surprising flashes of history), time that is nonmetrically eternal (soaring like the clouds of an uplifted lowland), and time that sums up and is total (in which the islands of humankind's eternal drama and the eternal space of its low-level tranquility find a resolution that is both personal and superpersonal, both subjective and objective).

This feeling of form, for all its novelty, is perceived as objective and is deeply convincing—we feel it momentarily as something that has existed for all eternity, but that for some reason has not been noticed by anyone before Kancheli. And all earlier arguments about form and dynamics, about what is traditional and what is new, lose their meaning: all this appears in a new light, and we shall be conscious for a long time of the uncontrived novelty of this remarkable composer.

From the notes to the recording of Kancheli's *Oplakannye vetrom* [Mournings of the Wind], Melodiya (A 10 00777006), 1991. Russian text reprinted in *Besedy s Al'fredom Shnitke*, compiled and edited by A. V. Ivashkin (Moscow: Kul'tura, 1994), pp. 95–96.

IN MEMORY OF
FILIP MOISEEVICH GERSHKOVICH
(1988)

It is hard to find anyone who so strongly influenced several generations of compos-ers. Many people (who were later to become well known) passed through his hands, but they were not trained by him in the usual sense. Gershkovich merely had to tell his pupils what Webern had once told him about Beethoven's sonatas, and from his lips this was explanation enough of the history, pre-history, and future history of the most important of musical forms. But he was never a professor of music or even a teacher at any institution.

Nor has there ever been a musical scholar who made such an impact on musicologists. Irrespective of whether they later agreed or disagreed with him, they had contact with him and felt his influence. Their views (generally different from his) had to pass his test. But he never held academic rank or had any official position.

A number of our most outstanding musical performers studied "harmony and form" with him; that is, they learned to recognize Mozart and Beethoven in them-selves. But he rarely attended concerts and never wrote reviews.

He wrote, and in part published (in Tartus miscellanies on semiotics), his articles on Bach, Mozart, Beethoven, Wagner, Mahler, Schoenberg, Webern.[1] They are re-markable and radically different from most other descriptive works in musicology. But few people know of them.

He wrote a small number of talented musical compositions, performed occa-sionally by leading players. But he had no real ambition for them to be performed frequently and placed such high demands on the quality of their performance that rarely could anyone satisfy them.

Among musicians it is impossible to recall a person whose life was so disorga-nized. All the things that one might fancy—an apartment, work, money, fame, health, a homeland—he almost never possessed. They may have concerned him, but he could never be a slave to them.

---

1. In fact only two articles by Gershkovich appeared in *Trudy po znakovym sistemam* [Studies in Semiotics], a series of miscellanies published once or twice a year by the University of Tartus, Estonia. The articles were "Tonal'nye istoki shenbergovoi dodekafonii" [The Tonal Sources of Schoenberg's Dodecaphony], 1973, No. 6, pp. 344–379, and "Ob odnoi investii J. S. Bach'a" [On One of Bach's Inventions], 1979, No. 11, pp. 44–70. At that time, the Tartus miscellanies were a useful outlet for articles on the arts unlikely to be approved for publication in the USSR. Gershkovich's other articles were published much later. See his *O muzyke*, 3 vols. (Moscow, 1991–1993). —ed.

Only a year ago he was able to go to Vienna at the invitation of the Austrian Alban Berg Foundation and the music publishers Universal Edition to do research work and give lectures. For many years previously he had been invited but could never go.

Filip Moiseevich Gershkovich was a difficult person. Dealing with him sometimes led to misunderstandings. But the spiritual level of his personality was so high that it overcame everyday inconveniences. The impression of his deep involvement in the world of lofty musical and intellectual ideas and, above all, the impression of his restless, fiery, agitated heart, which only recently stopped beating, remains in our memories.

The attitude of the leadership of the Composers' Union toward Gershkovich was always negative, and it remains so even now. In spite of his apparent isolation, throughout his life invisible threads stretched to Gershkovich from the most diverse parts of the country. He had little interest in official music, but everything that was vital and gifted in our art aroused his most immediate interest. Many composers came to Moscow especially to show him their works and to hear his sometimes paradoxical, but always precise, opinions about them. His influence on the positive developments in our music has still not been evaluated. Filip Moiseevich Gershkovich was a vivid and inimitable personality, and his place in music unique.

Schnittke wrote the text of this obituary in 1988 and tried to obtain signatures from many important writers, composers, and performers. It was published, in Russian, in *Besedy s Al'fredom Shnitke*, compiled and edited by A. V. Ivashkin (Moscow: Kul'tura, 1994), pp. 215–216.

ON SVIATOSLAV RICHTER (1985)

For many people of my generation Sviatoslav Richter represents a certain peak of achievement, where the reality of music becomes its history. The idea that Richter is our contemporary, that we can actually see and hear him, cannot even for a moment make him usual and ordinary. For decades now he has been in the same category as historical figures such as Chopin, Paganini, Liszt, Rakhmaninov, and Chaliapin. He is a link between the present and the eternal.

For almost fifty years Richter, though outwardly private and unapproachable, has been the center of gravity of the musical life of Moscow—as a performer, as an organizer of festivals, as the first one to recognize and encourage talented young musicians and artists, as a connoisseur of literature, theater, and cinema, as one who collects paintings and attends private viewings, as an artist in his own right, as a producer and director. When an idea takes possession of him, he has the temperament to sweep aside all obstacles, whether the idea concerns a thematic cycle of concertos, an arts festival, an exhibition, or a private concert.

The demands Richter imposes on himself are legendary. He gives an outstanding concert, ecstatically received by both press and public, providing fruit for wholesale musicological researches, but then agonizes over the failure of some small detail, which only he has noticed. We must not regard this as some strange kind of pretentiousness: Richter has a different scale of values than the rest of us. Only he knows what the original concept behind his performance was, and only he can judge whether this concept has been realized in performance. We cannot tell what perfection of sound reaches his inner ear, and so we cannot judge what a performance might be in the ideal form he might have conceived it. We can only be grateful to him for that part of his conception that has emerged, and which goes far beyond everything we are capable of imagining.

I have been listening to Richter and worshipping him for more than thirty-five years. I still remember his concerts in the early 1950s—sonatas by Beethoven, Prokofiev, Liszt, Tchaikovsky; Mussorgsky's *Pictures at an Exhibition*; the études of Rakhmaninov and Scriabin; the waltzes and mazurkas of Chopin; the concertos of Beethoven, Rachmaninov, Liszt, Schumann, Rimsky-Korsakov, Glazunov, Saint-Saëns, Ravel, and many others. At that time I was able to attend every single one of his concerts. I heard about them in advance and went and booked my seat on the very first day tickets came available. I was fifteen or sixteen years old and trying unsuccessfully to make up for lost time and become a concert pianist....

Most of all I loved him in music itself—more than in the actual music he was performing. I was struck by the way he combined temperament with willpower, amazed at the way he "went beyond" technique (he seemed to be playing for himself, as if that were easy), idolized his touch (especially his *piano)*, and found his unfettered movements hard to accept, thinking they were mere affectation. I cut his photograph out of a newspaper and carried it about with me like a talisman, along with one of Shostakovich. I had no interest in other pianists and considered it blasphemous to compare anyone with Richter. And I listened, with a mixture of envy and contempt, to what the few people who knew him personally had to say about him. How could they call him "Slava," when he was so far above them? How could they even say in the same breath, "Richter told me (*him*?!)... I told Richter (HIM?!)"?

Then his popularity grew so enormously that for years I could not get to any of his concerts. It was only eight or nine years ago that I had the chance to hear him again. I was surprised at the change. The "affectation" had gone. At the keyboard sat an ascetic, a philosopher, a sage, who knew about something of which music was only part. The sense of his unattainability was even stronger, although in conversation he had proved to be the most modest and refined of men. By now even I had blasphemously "made his acquaintance."

His repertoire had changed, had become strictly thematic, its romantic base had receded into the background. There were more ensemble works—[by] Shostakovich, Hindemith, Berg, Janáček, Dvořák, Franck. There was still the same powerful temperament, but it was of a different quality, not subjectively romantic, but elementally objective. But this objectivity was not that of a classicist; it was not retrospective, but original, new. Still the same high level of qualities (but now purified of the conventional and "artificial"), monumentality and greatness without the slightest hint of a pose, as majestic and powerful as one who has renounced authority and ambition. The works he chose to perform were often "unrewarding"—the most modest pieces by Tchaikovsky or the Viola Sonata by Shostakovich, utopian in its evanescent ethereal character. In everything there was something of Beethoven's late quartets, where remains only the rarefied air of a mountain peak.

Before his seventieth birthday Richter rewarded us with one of his regular festivals—Masterpieces of Twentieth-Century Music, in which we were once again astounded by the power of his talent as a performer (in Shostakovich's Trio, with Oleg Kagan and Natalya Gutman). His talent was also revealed in a new dimension—as a producer of opera. In a tiny space that could not be called a stage, he put on an extremely difficult opera by Britten, *The Turn of the Screw*, making use of the simplest but completely original devices. One has only to recall the spine-tingling spatial separation of the voices and "bodies" of the ghosts. We should like to see more of Richter's work as a producer, but are afraid that this might mean he would play less.

Richter, of course, has an all-round versatility, and in evaluating him as a pianist we cannot ignore his other activities. It may be that he is a great pianist precisely because he is more than a pianist—the problems he deals with are at a level higher than the purely musical. These problems arise and are solved at a point where art, science, and philosophy meet, at a point where a single truth, not yet embodied in concrete words and images, may be expressed in a universal and all-embracing way. An ordinary mind usually seeks the solution to a problem on the surface of the problem itself, blindly groping its way over that surface until, more or less fortuitously, by a process of trial and error, it finds a way out. The mind of a genius seeks the solution to a problem by transferring it to a universal level, from which it can gain a bird's-eye view and at once see the right way to take. This is why those who confine themselves to a single activity achieve less than those who take an interest in contiguous spheres of activity. The latter add an extra dimension to their aesthetic vision, they see more—more accurately and more deeply....

But all attempts at discovering a rational key to the mysterious nature of genius are pointless. We can never find a formula for its gifts, and can never reproduce this Great Master who lives among us. Long may he live!

Written in 1985 and published in *Muzyka v SSSR* [Music in the USSR], July–September 1985. Russian text reprinted in *Besedy s Al'fredom Shnitke,* compiled and edited by A. V. Ivashkin (Moscow: Kul'tura, 1994), pp. 222–224.

ON GENNADI ROZHDESTVENSKY (1991)

I think the first time I had any experience of Gennadi Rozhdestvensky as a conductor was when I saw him give a performance of Andrei Volkonsky's Concerto Grosso. I believe this was in the Great Hall of the Moscow Conservatory in 1954 or 1955. But my first real contact with him was at the beginning of the 1960s. On that occasion, to celebrate the centenary of the Conservatory, the professors and teachers in the Department of Composition wrote a collective work. Like many of my colleagues, I took part in this. We all wrote variations on a theme by Miaskovsky. The results were extremely mixed, both stylistically and technically. I find it hard to name all those who contributed, but they included Dmitri Borisovich Kabalevsky, Evgeni Kirillovich Golubev, Mikhail Ivanovich Chulaki, Vladimir Georgievich Fere, Anatoli Nikolaevich Alexandrov, and many young composers—Nikolai Nikolaevich Sidelnikov, Alexandr Ivanovich Pirumov, Alexei Alexandrovich Nikolaev....[1] Naturally, the first problem facing any conductor in this case was whether the work could be performed at all, and then how to give it unity. In fact this was not so much a conductor's problem, more a compositional one: to turn completely heterogeneous material into something acceptable as a unified whole. But even this proved no problem at all for Rozhdestvensky. He arranged the material in such a way that, when at a certain moment the variations written by the professors ended and those written by the younger teachers began, from the different streams of music there emerged something that really was unified. Rozhdestvensky carried out the task of an invisible composer with the utmost simplicity and conviction. This was the first occasion when one of my own scores, along with the others, came into his hands.

Gradually we came to know each other better. He conducted a performance of my First Violin Concerto in 1963, with Mark Lubotsky as soloist. This was a very important occasion for me, because I had not yet had any contact with musicians of such stature, and I could not imagine a conductor with whom you did not have to spend a long time discussing various details, as I had done before. Here in Rozhdestvensky was a man who seemed to see and hear a work immediately. Certain questions of detail came up incidentally, but they were always derived from his original integrated conception of the work.

---

1. Schnittke's list of the contributing composers is not quite correct. *Collective Variations on the Themes from the Sixteenth Symphony of Miaskovsky* were written by Mikhail Chulaki, Anatoli Alexandrov, Evgeni Golubev, Sergei Balasanian, Vladimir Fere, Dmitri Kabalevsky, Alexei Nikolaev, Nikolai Sidelnikov, Andrei Eshpai, Rodion Shchedrin, and Alfred Schnittke. The work was first performed in the Great Hall of Moscow Conservatory on 15 October 1966 by the All-Union Radio Symphony Orchestra, conducted by Gennadi Rozhdestvensky. —ed.

Our contacts continued. In Leningrad he conducted such works of mine as Music for Piano and Chamber Orchestra and my Second Violin Concerto, again with Mark Lubotsky as soloist. And eventually in 1972 I completed the work I dedicated to him—the First Symphony. I worked on it for four years. This was not just because at that time I had to devote a good deal of energy to music for the cinema. There were other reasons, too. The task I faced was of great importance to me and, at the same time, highly appropriate to the character of the conductor who was to direct the performance. I am referring to the interplay of different elements: on the one hand, absolutely and utterly serious ones, and, on the other, highly playful, almost trivial ones. This interplay was to be found not only in the notated music but also in visual presentation of the work on stage. I wanted to write a work that could never be fully described in precise terms—just as a phenomenon like Rozhdestvensky cannot be summed up in any one word. I should never dream of trying to find such a word. In fact, I believe the idea of using a word in a situation like this to be quite out of place. Any verbal approximations to true reality cannot fully encompass that reality, they can merely bring us a little closer to an understanding of it.

In Rozhdestvensky I found someone who took a lively interest in this, as it were, extramusical component, which was not at all some kind of trendy addition to the score, but which had a function related to the essence of the work itself.

The fate of the symphony was complicated. It was performed only with great difficulty, and then not in Moscow, where Rozhdestvensky had been forced to leave the All-Union Radio Symphony Orchestra, but in Gorky. The combination of the Gorky Philharmonic with the Melodiya group under the direction of the trumpet-player Vladimir Chizhik and the saxophonist Georgi Garanian was a completely new and surprising experience for me. And this too was Rozhdestvensky's idea. My score included improvised episodes and approximate plans for their execution, but of course I had in mind a performance by "an orchestra," not one "from another world." And suddenly Rozhdestvensky made this suggestion, which proved ideal: to combine two highly professional, but completely different, musical worlds. And for both of them it turned out to be a completely novel and interesting experience. This is to say nothing of the extreme interest the composer himself took in how it would all turn out.

So this idea—simply to take the strict realization of the work to another level, from which it gained a great deal—this idea was Rozhdestvensky's. There is something else, too. My symphony ends with a quiet coda, with the sound of the orchestra dying away. As in Haydn's *Farewell Symphony,* this is connected with the idea that the music is going off somewhere, the musicians taking their music with them. Suddenly Rozhdestvensky asked a simple question: "But how are we going to take our bow?!" And he gave his own answer: "Why after all this shouldn't the orchestra—precisely as it came out onto the concert platform at the beginning—unexpectedly do the same thing at the end?" This is what was done, and it turned out to be absolutely right. It was a kind of final return from a very serious level to one that was outwardly less serious. As a result the whole work was lifted to a higher plane of abstraction. Only a person for whom the serious and non-serious are equally significant could have recognized the problem, formulated it, and solved it.

For me this was incontrovertible proof that a so-called improvisation, an instantaneous answer to a question, is by no means a decision lightly taken—it is a precise one. By this, of course, I do not in any way intend to cast doubt on the need for long periods of formulation and contemplation. But there is a time for everything. The work of an orchestral conductor combines years of hard work and moments of unexpected precise answers to questions. Both are essential for a real musician.

And both are equally serious. This departure from an academic position of "high priest" and the adopting of one that belongs almost to the circus—at once broadens the circle of influence and extends the scope of that influence.

Rozhdestvensky's famous "preambles" are in the same category. I remember many of his concerts not only from the way they were performed but also from his brilliant commentaries, full of unexpected shafts of wit, absolutely devoid of any sort of "pedantic tedium." How he can talk in such a lively and apparently spontaneous way seems incomprehensible. I know, however, that it results from deep thought and long study, not at a table in a library, at set times, but continuing through every moment of life. Rozhdestvensky has an immense thirst for knowledge and expresses it in extremely serious and extremely non-serious ways.

The vast range of different qualities in Rozhdestvensky interact with each other in such unexpected combinations, always with apparent simplicity. And yet, paradoxically, a conversation with him is for the most part not the kind of conversation in which people exchange ideas on an equal footing. You start putting a question to him and, at the very moment you open your mouth, he has not only answered your question but has already agreed or disagreed with you. So a conversation with him is something essentially very deep and... serious, although on the surface it may not seem like that at all....

I once calculated that there are now some forty compositions written for Rozhdestvensky—either derived from his ideas or else he was the first to conduct them. I could not believe it, but it really is so. I could even say that nearly all my own work as a composer depended on contact with him and on the many talks we had. It was in these talks that I conceived the idea for many of my compositions. I count that as one of the luckiest circumstances of my life. My work has brought me into contact with many outstanding musicians: Gidon Kremer, Oleg Kagan, Natalya Gutman, Eri Klas, Vladimir Krainev, Yuri Bashmet... Kurt Masur and Mstislav Rostropovich... and I could name many more from different countries. This has always been my great good fortune. And yet perhaps among all these people Gennadi Rozhdestvensky holds pride of place. The work we have done together for so many years is of the greatest importance for me. It has determined much of what I have done and have not done (what I have not done is also important). He has had an enormous influence on me.

But I must add that among his acquaintances there are many people like that; I am by no means the only one. I can recall hundreds of compositions by Soviet composers that were first conducted by Rozhdestvensky, and many of them recorded and performed many times in various places.

And think of all the remarkable ideas he has had for theatrical performances! And not just when he was working at the Bolshoi Theater or the Moscow Chamber

Music Theater. So many unexpected programs, so many tickets sold! A year ago he gave a series of subscription concerts with five of my symphonies along with works by other composers from other eras. The idea behind this was fascinating, and not at all insignificant. I am particularly grateful that works by Stravinsky and Gesualdo were included.... Then there were such brilliant ideas as that of recording all Bruckner's symphonies with detailed commentaries on them. It was not the mere fact that these works were performed—it was a way of generating general interest in Bruckner's music. Or, for instance, performing works by Walton, a wholly novel idea in Russia, or Martinu's symphonies.... And then there is his constant interest in works other than those that are staples of the concert repertoire, an interest in works that are quite fascinating, but sometimes forgotten, by both contemporary and long-established classical composers. All this has created the impression of a vast panorama of musical time and space. It is an enormous world (very difficult to measure or systematize) in which the interaction of one work with another, in a context outside the usual stereotypes, breathes surprising new life into our experiences. Every performance has brought new life, by its resolute avoidance of the systematization foisted on us by routine concerts or books. I hope that the very existence of this vast musical world in concert performances will continue and succeed in penetrating the consciousness of audiences. People do not go to concerts by accident. They go so that they can also hear the music again later on and think about it.... This is, in its own way, a kind of conservatory or university, much more serious and important than one that awards diplomas or degrees.

Rozhdestvensky and I naturally have plans for the future. In particular, we have agreed that my Eighth Symphony will be written for him and the Stockholm Philharmonic, which he now conducts. I also take a keen interest in other ideas we have discussed, and would be delighted if our collaboration were to continue in the way it has gone so far.

Muzykal'naia Zhizn' [Musical Life], 1991, Nos. 13–14. Russian text reprinted in *Besedy s Al'fredom Shnitke*, compiled and edited by A. V. Ivashkin (Moscow: Kul'tura, 1994), pp. 224–228.

SUBJECTIVE NOTES ON
AN OBJECTIVE PERFORMANCE
(ON ALEXEI LIUBIMOV) (1973)

A pianist or theorist of pianism would probably have written more objectively about the Mozart concert given by Alexei Liubimov[1] on 19 September 1973 in the Small Hall of the Moscow Conservatory, but the impression it made on the writer of these lines was so profound that it was difficult to resist the temptation to share them. The concert was not simply an event in the art of performance but also a demonstration of a definite creative position, interesting from more than the narrowly professional point of view.

First and foremost the concert was brilliantly *composed* by the performer as a perfectly integrated musical form. The two contrasting sections embodied two characteristics of Mozart's music—naive joie de vivre and tragic wisdom. Without taking into account the chronological order in which the works were composed, the pianist arranged them in an order that reflected the composer's evolution.

The first work on the program—the little-known Prelude and Fugue in C Major (K392, 1782)—served to remind us that it was from Bach that a living thread of music stretched to Mozart. The last work (a dramaturgically prepared encore!)—the extremely popular Fantasy in C Minor—already contained the whole of Beethoven; not only the Beethoven of the dramatic sonatas and symphonies, but also the introspective Beethoven of the late quartets. These two monumental works served another function in shaping the program: the youthful freshness of the major key in the "exposition" section of the recital and the mature bitterness of the minor key in the "reprise" section. In fact one can speak of the whole concert as having a Mozartian plan.

The works within this "arch" were also arranged in a harmonious fashion:

First section:
   Prelude and Fugue in C Major (K. 392, 1782)
   Allegro in G Minor (K. 312, 1774)
   Allegro in B-flat Major (K. 400, 1786)
   Sonata in C Major (K. 330, 1778)

---

1. Alexei Liubimov (born 1944): Russian pianist, outstanding performer of modern music and Baroque compositions. —ed.

Second section:
> Adagio in B Minor (K. 540, 1788)
> Rondo in D Major (K. 485, 1786)
> Sonata in A Minor (K. 310, 1778)

A whole series of analogies is possible here. Each section in itself comprises a completed form. The first is a four-part cycle, consisting of the strict polyphonic Prelude and Fugue in C Major, the scherzo-like Allegro in G Minor, the Allegro in B-flat Major, and the Sonata in C Major (once again a reprise of key!). The whole section may be joined together as the first movement of the broad cycle of the whole concert, and in that case the Adagio in B Minor naturally becomes its slow movement. The Rondo in D Major is its scherzo, the Sonata in A Minor the finale, and the Fantasy in C Minor the epilogue. Also clear is the rondo form of the concert, expressed by the constant return to the keys of the refrain: C major, the relative key of A minor, and the parallel C minor. The keys of the other pieces also have a harmonious form: two relative flat keys (G minor and B-flat major) in the first section and two relative sharp keys (B minor and D major) in the second. Naturally, the twice-repeated combination of relative keys leads to the displacement in the final work of the basic key of the concert (C major) by its relative key (A minor). And naturally after this the only way to restore the dislodged C is by its parallel minor (the Fantasy in C Minor). And so on and so forth.

Probably one could find many more formal connections ("thesis—antithesis—synthesis," "spiral," "concentric circles," etc.)—a perfect form always appears at the point where different logical "dimensions" intersect (even when the way to this point may be "multidimensional"). I do not know if the performer thought about all this consciously, but this is how it turned out, and this is what is most important, since it is connected not only with Liubimov's innate professional culture, but first and foremost with his characteristic high level of *spiritual* discipline. The vast amount of musical, literary, and philosophical knowledge that he has absorbed and that has passed through the individuality of this musician (a man who is extremely strict with himself, without any excessive ambition or "superstar" mannerisms)—all this is fused into a precious amalgam of depth and simplicity.

Liubimov's playing is romantically expressive and classically balanced; the listener experiences the double enjoyment of excited response and calm understanding. On the one hand, one is struck by the multiplicity of details brought to life beneath his fingers, details permeated with subjective expressivity (which usually pass unnoticed in a safe "neutral" performance). On the other hand, one is surprised by the objective harmoniousness of the created whole, for not only the "spirit," but also the "letter" of the style is observed—all the subtleties (yet again, for the millionth time!) which are already present in the musical text. All that is needed to bring them out is a fresh approach and a way of thinking that is not preconceived.

This combination of individual refinement and objective perfection was apparent in everything Liubimov did, both in his sense of form—not of course merely in the "macro-form" of the concert or of each separate item in it, but also in the "microform" of themes and motifs, in the way each individual phrase with its own expressivity was a "word" in the long "sentence" of the whole work; and the whole work, as we have seen, was a "word" in the even longer "sentence" of the whole concert—and in his strict adherence to the basic tempi of the movements, even with the numerous deviations from tempi in individual phrases of the music. It was apparent, too, in the combination of virtuoso skill (in Mozart it is more difficult to hide inaccuracies than, for example, in Rakhmaninov) with the illusion of spontaneous music making. One cannot but be envious of the culture of the pianist's sound, the wide variety of dynamic and timbral gradations at his disposal, but all this is kept within the bounds of the natural unforced sonority of the instrument. Like no other performer, Liubimov is at great pains to avoid the illustrative orchestral effects of "grand-scale" piano playing. Nevertheless at every step there are associations with an orchestra—a Mozart orchestra! Here we find *tutti* accentuation with the lingering "shadow" of strings in unison (the first bar of the Fantasy in C Minor), the quiet chordal sighs of woodwinds (the second bar of the Fantasy in C Minor), the stormy *tirati* of string basses (eighteenth and nineteenth bars), the discreetly pulsing repetitions of violas (the sixteenth bar of the Andantino of the Fantasy), the bouncy galant *spiccato* ("on tiptoe") of violins (the fifteenth and sixteenth bars of the second movement of the Sonata in A Minor), and the "horn fifths" of natural horns (in the same bar).

However, Liubimov's timbral palette evokes analogies not merely with Mozart's orchestra. One is reminded, for example, of the incredibly refined dynamic timbral shadings of Webern (Liubimov would undoubtedly have played Mozart less well had he not in recent years played and replayed so many works from the New Viennese School). Stylistic sterility ("What, nothing but Mozart?") would in principle have been impossible for Liubimov, as was evident in the "evolution" concept behind the whole concert. Mozart carried within himself the "genes" of composers later than Beethoven. Schubert is already immanent in the slow movement of the Sonata in C Major, and Brahms in its first movement. Incidentally, the artist V. Yankilevsky, who was sitting next to me, saw in the Prelude and Fugue in C Major a resemblance to Shostakovich's Preludes and Fugues, and he was right. Liubimov thus plays Mozart not as preserved in the eighteenth century but as alive today, as coming through the history of music and making it fertile. As a "reverse link," there were reflected in his performance of Mozart, as already noted, both the microshadings of Webern and the infinite structural variety (with uniformity of material) of Brahms. Incidentally, Liubimov scrupulously played all the repetitions within the movements, but always with timbral and dynamic variation.

And even with the complete perfection of its form, Liubimov's concert may be perceived as part of some endless cycle, reflecting the "open form" of musical history. Perhaps we shall soon hear the next "movement" (Beethoven? Schubert?) or the previous one (Bach?). Indeed in musical time, chronology is neither true nor obligatory. From this point of view, Liubimov's performance of Mozart is in the highest sense objective—not the static museum objectivity of dogma and piety, but the living objectivity of understanding and continuity.

P.S. Rereading this article I am surprised to discover that it is not so much about Liubimov's concert as about Mozart's music. But had there been no such performance, the audience could not have had so many thoughts about the music. And undoubtedly the supreme virtue in a performer is to assert the music he is playing, not himself.

Written in 1973 and published in *Sovetskaya muzyka* [Soviet Music], 1974, No. 2, pp. 63–65. Russian text reprinted in *Besedy s Al'fredom Shnitke*, compiled and edited by A. V. Ivashkin (Moscow: Kul'tura, 1994), pp. 219–222.

ON VIKTOR YEROFEEV (1988)

Reading Viktor Yerofeev's[1] book *Telo Anny, ili konets russkogo avangarda* [Anna's Body, or The End of the Russian Avant-Garde], you experience the dual effect of making contact with something that is both long familiar and yet completely novel. You experience the shock that we have all felt of simultaneously encountering Heaven and Hell, and you become aware of the utter incomprehensibility of what is apparently utterly hackneyed and banal. You cannot tell exactly what it is that makes you gasp. Is it your disgust at the blasphemous elements in the plot and characters ("Death and the Maiden")?[2] Or is it the rarefied atmosphere of an agonizing sanctity that is clearly felt, without actually being described ("The Parakeet")? Yet this unsolved mystery leaves you with an impression of absolute clarity in every particular. You recognize from the first moment that you have known this all your life, without ever realizing it, and are reading about it for the first time. Every stereotype assimilated from your reading immediately withers away in the astringent air of this cruelty, this almost sadistic truth, which has its own brand of verisimilitude that avoids both the usual crudity associated with verisimilitude and that opposition to dilettantism that is itself dilettantish. What is the meaning of all this? The author does not know. He formulates no meaning. He is a writer, not someone providing literary illustrations to eternal mathematical and moral principles that he has worked out. Neither to historical and philosophical questions. It is true that he is known to readers in a role that is diametrically opposite to this, one in which he knows everything and formulates it in precise terms. This is when he is a critic. A real critic, that is, not one who composes envious denunciations to do with the reality that is not always frightened away by history. It is a long time since two such extremes have coexisted in one individual. Artists like Viktor Yerofeev are rare indeed.

Written in 1988 as an introductory note to a book of short stories by Viktor Yerofeev, *Telo Anny, ili konets russkogo avangarda* [Anna's Body, or The End of the Russian Avant-Garde]; also published in *Knizhnoe Obozrenie* [Book Review], 15 December 1989, p. 9. Russian text reprinted in *Besedy s Al'fredom Shnitke*, compiled and edited by A. V. Ivashkin (Moscow: Kul'tura, 1994), p. 185.

---

1. Viktor Vladimirovich Yerofeev (born 1947): In 1978 Yerofeev began organizing, with the cooperation of Vasilii Aksenov, the literary almanac *Metropol* [Metropolis], which aimed "to provide a roof" for "outcast literature." As a result he was expelled from the Union of Soviet Writers, and his work was not officially published in Russia until 1988. He wrote the libretto for Schnittke's opera *Zhizn' s idiotom* [Life with an Idiot], based on one of his own stories, published in Moscow in 1991. "Popugai-chik" [The Parakeet] was first published in *Ogonyok* in December 1988. Its full version is in *Telo Anny, ili konets russkogo avangarda* [Anna's Body, or The End of the Russian Avant-Garde], published in Moscow in the following year. —ed.

2. "Devushka i smert" [Death and the Maiden]: In 1931 Stalin declared this poem by Maxim Gorky to be "more perfect than Goethe's *Faust*." —ed.

CHAPTER
16

ON THE PAINTINGS OF
VLADIMIR YANKILEVSKY (1987)

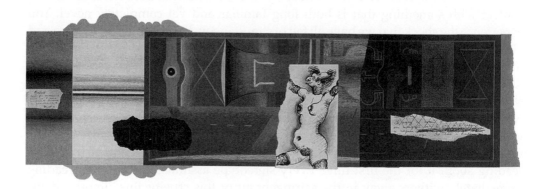

"City" (1966) from a painting by Vladimir Yankilevsky.

The impression made on me by the art of Vladimir Yankilevsky is of something that is, above all, inexhaustibly *profound*, but also of something powerful. Many of his individual paintings were already long familiar to me as parts of collective exhibitions. But now that they have been put together, his works reinforce each other, and the earlier ones acquire a new meaning that is more powerful. There is a remarkable unity—primarily of the artist's *world* (what he sees), but also of *meaning* (how he interprets it). There is a remarkable sense of the *multidimensionality* of time, in which *eternity* and *the moment* are one and the same thing, with the multiple facets of reality lying between them. The remarkable culminating point of this is the white, the burst of white in *Sodom and Gomorrah*, out of which streams something formless (surrounded by what is ugly). Remarkable too is the black burst in the center—a mystery within a mystery. We could have seen all this twenty-five years before... but this is not detrimental to it, because this is not the kind of art that is submerged in the actuality of a single day. Thank God for this—it was only the artist who suffered, not his world. The artist made the only correct choice—he was willing to use himself as payment for what he could see with his inner vision. But there is still time and hope. Hope that there will be more personal exhibitions of Yankilevsky's works.

Written in May 1987 and published in Russian in *Besedy s Al'fredom Shnitke*, compiled and edited by A. V. Ivashkin (Moscow: Kul'tura, 1994), p. 260.

V

SCHNITTKE ON
TWENTIETH-CENTURY MUSIC

17

POLYSTYLISTIC TENDENCIES IN MODERN MUSIC (c. 1971)

It is not possible in a short space to cover all the problems of such a vast and unfamiliar subject as the polystylistic method in modern music. I shall therefore be obliged to confine my comments merely to the exposition of certain questions arising in connection with it, and shall refrain from making any premature artistic evaluations.

By the polystylistic method I mean not merely the "collage wave" in contemporary music but also more subtle ways of using elements of another's style. And here it is essential at once to distinguish two different principles: the principle of quotation and the principle of allusion.

The principle of quotation manifests itself in a whole series of devices, ranging from the quoting of stereotypical micro-elements of an alien style, belonging to another age or another national tradition (characteristic melodic intonations, harmonic sequences, cadential formulae), to exact or reworked quotations or pseudo-quotations.

Here are some examples, deliberately taken from composers whose aesthetic approach differs radically:

Shostakovich, Piano Trio—the neoclassical passacaglia theme, which quotes the style of eighteenth-century music with its succession of tonic–dominant motion and diminished seventh chords.

Berg, Violin Concerto—the direct quotation of a Bach chorale, which has thematic links with the musical material of the work (there is an analogous quotation of a classical theme from Mozart in Boris Tchaikovsky's Second Symphony).

Penderecki, *Stabat Mater*—a pseudo-quotation from a Gregorian hymn, which forms the intonational basis for the whole work.

Stockhausen, *Hymns*—a "super-collage" mosaic of the modern world.

Pärt, *Pro and contra*—based on parodied baroque cadential formulae, which regulate the form of the work.

In the same category may be placed the technique of *adaptation*—the retelling of an alien musical text in one's own musical language (analogous to modern literary adaptations of ancient subjects) or a free development of alien material in one's own style:

Stravinsky, *Pulcinella* or *Canticum sacrum.*

Webern, *Fuga (Ricercata)*—Bach's music reinterpreted in a variety of timbres.

Pärt, *Credo*—Bach's notes, but Pärt's music in the way the notes are rhythmically and texturally transformed.

Jan Klusak, *Variations on a Theme of Mahler*—"How Mahler might have written, had he been Klusak."

Shchedrin, the ballet *Carmen*—on Bizet's music.

And finally, to this category belongs the quotation not of musical fragments but of the technique of an alien style. For example, the reproduction of the form, rhythm, and texture of music of the seventeenth and eighteenth centuries, and earlier periods, by the neoclassicists (Stravinsky, Shostakovich, Orff, Penderecki) or devices taken from choral polyphony of the fourteenth through sixteenth centuries (isorhythm, hocket, antiphony) in serial and postserial music:

Webern, starting with Opus 21
Stockhausen, *Gruppen, Momente*
Henze, *Antiphone*
Slonimsky, *Antiphons*
Tishchenko, Sonata No. 3, 1st Movement
Denisov, *Solntse inkov* [Sun of the Incas], *Ital'ianskie pesni* [Italian Songs]
Volkonsky, *Siuita zerkal* [Suite of Mirrors]

In addition there are what might be called *polystylistic* hybrids, containing elements not just of two styles, but of three, four, or more. For example, Stravinsky's *Apollo Musagetes*, where the quasi-antique neoclassicism conjures up clearly defined associations (as the composer himself acknowledges) with Lully, Gluck, Délibes, Strauss, Tchaikovsky, and Debussy. Or take the carefully controlled technique that (unlike Stravinsky's practice) uses stylistic modulations and polyphony in the cybernetic "game of Patience" in Pousseur's opera *Votre Faust*.

Sometimes the interpenetration of elements from styles of an individual composer and an alien style may be so organic (as, for example, in Stravinsky's *Apollo Musagetes*) that it crosses the boundary between quotation and allusion.

The principle of allusion manifests itself in the use of subtle hints and unfulfilled promises that hover on the brink of quotation but do not actually cross it. In this case it is not possible to give a precise classification; one can only give examples. Allusion is characteristic of the neoclassicism of the 1920s and the present day. We have only to recall Stravinsky or Henze, in whose music the texts quoted are almost all subtly decorated with stylistic devices from the past (allowing for the vivid individuality of the former and the undoubted eclecticism of the latter). I prefer to say nothing further about Stravinsky, whose paradoxical quality wholly derives from the way he plays with associations and deliberately mixes musical times and spaces. I would instead prefer to focus my attention on the widespread use of stylistic hints and allusions in the "instrumental theater" (Mauricio Kagel) or the subtle polystylistic emanations—the scents and shadows of other times in music—in the works of such widely differing composers as Boulez and Ligeti.

But should one use the term *polystylistic* in connection with the fantastic play of temporal and spatial associations inevitably evoked by *any* music? The polystylistic tendency has always existed in concealed form in music, and continues to do so, because music that is stylistically sterile would be dead. So is it worth even discussing the subject? I believe it is essential to do so, because in recent times the polystylistic method has become a conscious device. Even without making direct quotations, a composer often plans a polystylistic effect in advance, whether it be the shock effect of a clashing collage of music from different times, a flexible glide through phases of musical history, or the use of allusions so subtle that they seem accidental.

There are important preconditions for this widespread use of a consciously polystylistic approach to musical composition. These are both technological (the neo-academic crisis of the 1950s and the purist tendencies of serialism, aleatoric music, and sonoristics) and psychological (the increase in international contacts and mutual influences, the change in our conception of time and space, the "poly-phonization" of human consciousness connected with the constantly growing stream of information and the polyphonization of art—we have only to remind ourselves of terms such as *stereophony, split-screen, multimedia,* etc.).

Polystylistic elements have long existed in European music—not just overtly in parodies, fantasies, and variations but also at the heart of monostylistic genres (if only in the contrast between the idea of musical theater and the concept of a dramatic symphony). But the conscious adoption of the polystylistic method never went beyond the idea of "variations on someone's theme" or "imitations of some-one." The breakthrough into the polystylistic method proper originated in the particular development in European music of a tendency to widen musical space. The tendency toward organic unity of form, which supplemented this dialectically, revealed laws by which one could conquer this new musical space. What is special about the present situation is the fact that another dimension of music has been discovered—but its laws are unknown.

We do not know how many levels of stylistic polyphony the listener can perceive simultaneously. Neither do we know the laws of collage montage and gradual stylistic modulation—do they in fact exist? We do not know where the boundary lies between an eclectic and a polystylistic method, or between the polystylistic method and direct plagiarism. The question of authorship becomes more complicated both legally and in the sense of whether the composer is able to preserve his individual and national identity. It is presumed that his individuality will inevitably reveal itself in his choice of quoted material and its montage, as well as in the overall conception of the work. Whatever the case, Berio's super-collage symphony is an adequate demonstration of both the individual and national identity of the com-poser (the richness of the collage polyphony in this work is similar to the mixing of street sounds we hear on the soundtracks of Italian neorealistic films). Furthermore, the elements of an alien style usually serve merely as a modulated space, a kind of periphery that throws the composer's own style into relief. And there are other complications: it may be that the adoption of a polystylistic method reduces the absolute, non-associative value of the work, creating the danger of self-consciously striving for effect. There are also greater demands placed on the general cultural knowledge of the listener, who must be able to recognize the interplay of styles as something done deliberately.

But in spite of all the complications and possible dangers of the polystylistic method, its merits are now obvious. It widens the range of expressive possibilities, it allows for the integration of "low" and "high" styles, of the "banal" and the "recherché"—that is, it creates a wider musical world and a general democratization of style. In it we find the documentary objectivity of musical reality, presented not just as something reflected individually but as an actual quotation (in the third part of Berio's symphony we hear an ominous apocalyptic reminder of our generation's responsibility for the fate of the world, expressed by means of a collage of quotations, of musical "documents" from various ages—reminding one of cinema advertising in the 1970s). And finally it creates new possibilities for the musical dramatization of "eternal" questions—of war and peace, life and death.

Thus, in Zimmerman's opera *Die Soldaten* [The Soldiers] the polystylistic method emphasizes the relevance to all times of the basic theme of the work—it is a protest, not just against the actual German war machine of the eighteenth century that destroyed the characters in Lenz's play, but also against militarism anywhere at any time. And it is precisely the multiplicity of styles used in the music (the composer's own individual style is interwoven with Gregorian and Protestant hymns, polyphonic devices of the fourteenth and fifteenth centuries, jazz, musique concrète, and so on) that make the situations depicted in the opera characteristic of times other than when they actually took place.

The polystylistic method employed in Slonimsky's oratorio *Golos iz khora* [A Voice from the Chorus] similarly lifts us philosophically out of the time of the story. In it the inspired and anxious reflections of Blok about the fate of the world are expressed by various means, from the choral episode in the spirit of the sixteenth century to serial and aleatoric devices from the twentieth century.

It is doubtful whether one could find another musical approach that expresses as convincingly as the polystylistic method the philosophical idea of "the links between the ages."

Written c. 1971 and published in *Muzyka v SSSR* [Music in the USSR], April–June 1988, pp. 22–24. Reprinted in Russian in *Besedy s Al'fredom Shnitke*, compiled and edited by A. V. Ivashkin (Moscow: Kul'tura, 1994), pp. 143–146; the text as presented here also includes a portion of an interview in *Besedy s Al'fredom Shnitke*, pp. 143–146.

THE ORCHESTRA AND THE NEW MUSIC
(EARLY 1970s)

The source of many of the achievements of the New Music is the orchestra. The orchestra comprises most of its sound combinations, and their possibilities have by no means been exhausted. Insofar as the orchestra is a model of human society and the universe, its potential for allusion is extremely rich, if not limitless. It can present every relationship one can imagine between what is individual and what is general. There is nothing to replace this powerful field of energy, with its interweaving and multiplying streams. And thanks to the effects created by electronic estrangement, the sound possibilities of an orchestra can be extended to infinity.

The structures of the orchestra, however, must undergo definite changes for it to be able to adapt to the changing musical situation. What is dubious and off-putting in present-day music making with an orchestra is the naive obviousness of its imitation of events that are supposed to have taken place, the pseudo-dynamism of battlefields and guaranteed victories, the official pathos and hypocritical tears. Audiences have long since learned to see through these tricks, and the vast gap between them and "serious" (that is, also "new") music has been created by the psychological inadequacy of the latter. And this gap can be bridged only by investigating new, more convincing ways of representing actual events in art, not at all by inventing newer, shallow tricks. As long as music making remains for orchestra players nothing more than reconstruction work, it will remain unworthy of the audience's attention.

The structures of an orchestra ought to be changed. An orchestra should not be seen merely as a leveling association or as an arena where there are clashes between individuality and the mass. It should be seen first and foremost as a vast theater of universal individualization. Contact between the musicians should be fostered not just by their working from one score under the guidance of one conductor; between the players there should be more subtle, unplanned, spontaneous connections (as in jazz, for example). The arbitrary hierarchy created by the functions of the instruments in an orchestral score, like the different rates of pay for the players, should be supplemented and modified by a flexible hierarchy created by spiritual and intuitive differences. In addition, the current negative subconscious manifestations of collectivity (such as jealousy, competitiveness, passivity, mass psychology, and so on) might be exploited in a positive way. For instance, a composer could redirect these energies to making *music*, by writing a work in which the driving force would be found not on the surface of the sound but on the battlefield of instrumental and psychological rivalries, in a musical war of nerves, in striving acoustically to gain the audience's attention and to support one's fellow players. This would require a consequent inward transformation of the orchestra not merely into an Instrumental Theater, subject to the highest degree of manipulation, but also into something beyond that—into an Instrumental Sports Stadium that cannot be manipulated. A sports stadium seems to be the best reflection of present-day actuality. But the orchestra might also turn into an Instrumental Church, an Instrumental Parliament, an Instrumental Market (only not an Instrumental Cinema or Supermarket)—in short, it might turn into an Instrumental Life, but not an Instrumental Parade.

The education of musicians (composers too!) should change and broaden in the following ways:

1. Every musician should learn to master everything. Not only traditional avant-garde techniques but also what is psychologically alien—for example, jazz, beat music, folk improvisation, Asian musical meditation, the primitivism of magic ritual, and so on.

2. Inasmuch as these techniques cannot be acquired by traditional rational methods, ways should be found of awakening "intuitive" possibilities for learning. All musical training should change fundamentally in the sense that it becomes de-schematized, returning to a childlike, "unconscious" way of acquiring new skills and knowledge. This is not a specifically musical problem, it is a universal one—consciousness should emerge from a larva and learn to fly. But for learning to fly, the "step-by-step" method is unsuitable; one must have the courage to leap.

Musicians trained in the traditional way might learn from jazz, pop music, and folk music. This might lead to a change in the traditional method of notation, which is based on a division into schematic elements, and the adoption of a notational system based on ideograms. Like hieroglyphics, this would immediately give us a complete musical image, not merely its separate "parameters."

But even if one keeps using traditional notation, a real breakthrough might still be achieved. This happens repeatedly—at that moment when a "newly discovered" musical language suddenly begins to be understood, in that instant when the overcoming of technical difficulties is still causing problems—but at the same time appeases musicians who find themselves able to surmount obstacles that only yesterday seemed absurdly impossible. Likewise, it appeases the audience, which feels flattered by the fact that it is beginning to understand this unheard-of music as music. So it is that the waves of Wagner, Brahms, and Mahler at long last break on the shores of the sea of music. And perhaps tomorrow, who knows, we shall come to experience the breaking waves of Bartók, Stravinsky, and Schoenberg, and the day after tomorrow of Stockhausen, Kagel, and Ligeti.

And, in the end, there is yet another possibility that could overturn all preconceived plans and give new meaning to what has been worn out by long usage. A new generation of performers might arrive on the scene, or we might find new shoots of young growth in the older generation.

But for this to happen the orchestra must remain, and its outward homogeneity must be preserved, whatever delicate adjustments are made to improve its inner structure. And best of all will be to continue both approaches in equal measure—the centrifugal and the centripetal.

Written in German in the early 1970s. Russian translation in *Besedy s Al'fredom Shnitke*, compiled and edited by A. V. Ivashkin (Moscow: Kul'tura, 1994), pp. 228–230.

CHAPTER

19

THE PROBLEM OF GIVING OUTWARD EXPRESSION TO A NEW IDEA (1982)

"Every blank sheet of paper is a potential work of art, every finished work of art is an idea that has been spoilt." —L. Leonov

In speaking of the idea in a composer's head, we must be clearly aware that such an idea has a very complex structure and that it cannot be reduced either to what is purely technological (that goes without saying) or to a single rational concept of a political or philosophical order. It must be remembered that any creative idea contains something that cannot be measured and that part of it is beyond the control of the conscious mind. This part of it, in general, is the principal inner force that drives a composer to begin a work and to actualize the idea, to hold fast to it, to formulate it for himself, and, in broad outline, to find the technical means of putting it down on paper in musical notes, which is to say, to turn it into reality.

This initial subconscious idea provides the emotional wave, the driving force, which brings the composition to life—and without which it cannot make an appearance.

At the same time, whenever he works, a composer constantly persuades himself that it is utterly impossible to give final realization and expression to any idea. The future composition presents itself to his inner imagination in a completely different form; it is as if he can hear it ready for performance, although not in concrete form, and yet by comparison what is achieved later seems like a translation into a foreign language, a translation from an original text, which, in general, proves to be irretrievable. At any rate, that is how I see it. These views have always existed, applicable not merely to art but to any kind of cognition: "Thou shalt not make unto thyself any graven image," "A thought uttered is a lie," and so on—examples are endless. There is something analogous to this in art as a whole, but particularly in musical composition.

One of the most vivid expressions of this problem—a problem that is both tragic and yet one that inspires optimism—is Schoenberg's opera *Moses und Aron*. The two central characters—Moses, endowed with the gift of thought (he can hear and comprehend the truth, but is incapable of conveying it to people), and his brother Aaron, endowed with the gift of speech (he is Moses' translator and interpreter, the disseminator of his ideas), in essence embody two sides of Schoenberg. On the one hand, his striving for purity of musical thought, unpolluted by the telltale signs of conventional genres and semantic referents, and, on the other, his dogmatic sense of mission, which required "materialized" norms of construction translated into the language of logic. It was the tragic impossibility of giving form to "the pure idea," the need to compromise with reality, to translate inarticulate chaotic truth into a harmonious language convincingly organized, which prompted Schoenberg to seek liberation in atonality and so led him to the creation of commandments to confirm a new truth—the twelve-tone system. Schoenberg was fully conscious of the fact that this was only a compromise, "a truce." Practically speaking, he himself broke his own tablets by not acknowledging the "neo-twelve-tonalists" of the late 1940s and early 1950s, thereby emphasizing that the twelve-tone technique was personal to him, a temporary, conditional, and individual solution to a problem that had no ultimate Solution.

Probably the truth of the matter is that technology, the outward form of the expression of an idea, is merely a construction, a net that helps to capture the idea, but that is not itself the bearer of that idea. This makes it clear why no technical analysis can disclose the complete truth about any musical composition, and it tempts one to suggest that it is more intelligent to analyze a work using other criteria, for example, by trying to work out the philosophical concept behind it. But certainly this kind of analysis cannot encompass the work as a whole. If a work really contains a particular idea, the work is inexhaustible. This may well be why compositions that retain their vitality in our time are distinguishable from those that merely offer "museum" interest. This invisible "submerged" element is in fact the most important one. But should a composer feel depressed because he cannot grasp what is impalpable? Does all this mean that any rational technique is meaningless, that music theory serves no purpose, that in any case what is most important cannot be detected, and that one has to consider whether rational analyses and rational creative methods might be limited and pointless? Clearly that is not so. But if we turn to any basis of music in nature, if we attempt to find a rational foundation for music in nature and, using that as our starting point, find one in music as a whole, we are forced to conclude that there can be no such foundation.

At one time an electronic studio was set up in Moscow. It was the brainchild of E. A. Murzin, a professional engineer who had a very limited musical education. As a scientist, he attempted to discover a purely physical basis for music and any approach to it. He knew that there existed a natural tone—that is, an overtone series—and that these [tones] have a very complicated structure. He was also aware that three hundred years ago the idea of temperament appeared, that is, that there was a movement away from the natural overtone series into the approximate discreteness of a musical scale. In light of this he took the whole history of music from the time of Bach to be the result of a mistake, a miscalculation, and he called for a return to the natural overtone series—the source of music. This would enable one, by making use of natural fundamental tones and their pure overtones, to rebuild everything afresh. All the problems of music, the endless changes of direction, the split between the leading trends of music and their commercial exploitation, all of these Murzin interpreted as arising from what he saw as a historical mistake.

I have to admit that in the electronic studio I attempted to compose a work based on the natural overtone series, setting myself what I regarded as a purely experimental task. Without rejecting my own musical experience I tried to carry out an experiment on myself and on music. And I came to the conclusion that, as one's hearing moves deeper into the overtone series, as far as the thirty-second partial, it penetrates into a limitless but enclosed world—and that from the magnetic field of this world there is no escape. Not only does modulation into another tonality become impossible; it is even impossible, once one has become conscious of one fundamental tone, to take in a second, because, once one hears the first fundamental and listens to its overtones, one's hearing can no longer accept the idea of another one. It remains content with the first fundamental and the microcosm of its overtones, and the second fundamental is heard as a mistake in relation to the first.

It is thus probable that any piece of music is "a mistake" if we relate it to the original conception of nature and its fundamental tones. In the consciousness of every composer there is an analogous "mistake." The composer imagines an ideal concept and then is forced to translate it into musical notes. And it is only this "tempered" part of the concept that he can bring to the ears of his audience.

But at the same time the impossibility of avoiding this "mistake" enables music to continue its very existence. Every composer tries to achieve a breakthrough to the direct expression of some pre-existent music that he can hear but which has not yet been caught in actual musical sound. And this prompts him to seek new technical devices, because he wants to be able to hear what he has inside his head. So there are endless attempts to eliminate all earlier conventions and to create something new without them. And thus it happens that at some point in the latter part of his life, a composer who has been seeking to abandon a certain technical device creates a new rational way of regulating music. Looking at the twentieth century, we see that Schoenberg devised his twelve-tone system consciously; Stravinsky and Shostakovich did not devise their theories consciously, but we can see them for ourselves in their works.

All these many attempts to achieve a direct expression of music, the constant return to "overtones," the adoption of new rational devices, and the process of coming closer to the truth, all these reveal still more areas that cannot be grasped. This process continues without end.

Thus it might be said that the process of giving form to an idea is always to limit the idea. For some composers the best solution is *not* to give form to the idea. In this sense, by failing to finish his opera Schoenberg was in fact giving outward expression to his idea. The work remained unfinished, and this can be explained by a whole lot of biographical factors (in particular, Schoenberg's difficult living conditions made serious work impossible). But this is mere coincidence of external and internal explanations; the true internal explanation lay in the fact that the real way to give outward expression to his idea was to *fail* to do so.

In general it is wrong to judge a work on the basis of what the composer says about it. For example, we have grown used to judging Stravinsky from the polemical, sometimes arrogant, remarks he made about his works. We are sometimes inclined to deny, on the basis of their own comments, that the composers whose inner musical world is vast and complex—like Stravinsky's or Webern's—have this inner world at all; and, on the contrary, we have greater faith in the composers who do not talk about things that can be grasped externally, about technique, about the rational side of music, but who try to tell us what they wanted to express. In neither case is anything really said about the work itself. So it comes about that the composer's own judgments deserve our attention only to a very limited degree, since they sometimes give only an indication of the general problems that concerned him. For example, we might work out Webern's circle of interests from his lectures, *The Way to Twelve-Tone Music* and *The Way to Modern Music,* and from them deduce what his guiding principle and inspiration were, what appealed to him, and what rational conclusions he came to. But none of that makes clear what he was seeking with his inner hearing, and thus one should not be guided by his rational ideas in trying to evaluate his works. And in general the same applies to similar evaluations by other composers of the results they achieved in their music.

Published in the miscellany *Problemy traditsii i novatorstva v sovremennoi muzyke* [Problems of Tradition and Innovation in Modern Music], compiled by A. M. Gol'tsman under the general editorship of M. E. Tarakanov (Moscow: Sovetskii Kompozitor, 1982), pp. 104–107. Russian text reprinted in *Besedy s Al'fredom Shnitke,* compiled and edited by A. V. Ivashkin (Moscow: Kul'tura, 1994), pp. 64–66.

FROM SCHNITTKE'S ARCHIVE
(1970S AND 1980S)

The Last Judgment is not a theatrical performance involving a public prosecutor, an audience, and the police—it is an inner mystery of the individual conscience.

The phenomena of life exist on both a material and a spiritual plane. And if the spiritual side reaches its limit merely by the fact that it is the product of our thoughts and feelings, that in itself is enough to establish the existence of a spiritual world, a world which, even on this realistic level, is much more important than the material world. For example, Pushkin's thirty-seven-year life, strictly in the material sense, with all its real-life events, is incommensurable with the two-hundred year existence of Pushkin's spiritual world which, filled with associations, images, and multifarious interpretations, is endless, and the interpretations, though often mutually exclusive, continue inexhaustibly to replenish it. Moreover, since they are a fact of the spiritual world, that is simply the product of thought and feeling, the works of Pushkin, through all those people who have made contact with him and his works, continue to influence the course of real-life events, that is, the material world. Thus, we may boldly assert that the spiritual life of human beings (that is, their posthumous life) is a real fact and that this longer life is infinitely more important than their brief physical existence, potentially leading to immortality.

By taking an artist away from his contemporaries, death simultaneously raises him to the level of eternal spiritual existence where, although time and development are no more, there remains still the absolutely inexhaustible immortal life of works of art. What is individual about the works changes from what divides into what unites; differences become kinships, and a link is established between phenomena of different times and places.

DSCH and BACH are related, not in any exceptional way but by the fact that they both belong to this world of the infinite. DSCH and BACH—these two motifs are brought together and blended in the *Prelude in Memory of D. Shostakovich*:[1] the first in the clearly heard voice of the soloist, the second as an unseen voice coming from outside.

---

1. *Prelude in Memory of D. Shostakovich/Preludium in memoriam D. Shostakovich/Prel'udiia pamiati D. D. Shostakovicha:* Schnittke's piece for two violins (or one violin and tape), written in 1975. –ed.

Intuition is a manifestation of knowledge above and beyond the individual, a kind of link with an external, miraculous source. It is as though a work exists outside time and space; the composer does not create it, but seizes and decodes it. This is why every outstanding work of art is so indisputably familiar—we already "know" it.

Art is especially dependent on intuition (the history of music is "an antenna pointed at the future").

Written in the 1970s and 1980s. Published in Russian in *Besedy s Al'fredom Shnitke*, compiled and edited by A. V. Ivashkin (Moscow: Kul'tura, 1994), p. 231.

CHAPTER
21

ON JAZZ (1984)

We learn a lot from jazz. It liberates musicians from fixed patterns and clichés. Jazz reveals and "resolves" much, prompting us to all kinds of searches and changes from the usual. Previously I had the idea that the most important part of the art of composition was the way the work was made, how successfully the artistic plan was carried out. I had a poor understanding of the possibilities latent in the actual process of creating and interpreting music; I undervalued the significance of a mistake, a deviation from the norm. Now I realize that a "mistake" or the taking of a risk in the treatment of a rule is in fact the area in which the life-giving elements of art arise and develop.

An analysis of Bach's chorales reveals many infringements of the strictest rules of harmony at the time. But they are not infringements at all! It is precisely the devices of Bach's polyphony, so perplexing to the ear, which verge on infringements. They have their own justification in the context of the actual music, principally in its melodic basis. When mathematicians are trying to solve certain equations, they introduce so-called "false numbers," which, although eliminated as the equation is solved, assist in the process of reaching the right result. Something similar happens in the creative process of art. Mistakes (more precisely, what mental inertia makes us see as mistakes) are unavoidable in the creative process, and sometimes they are essential. For the formation of a pearl in an oyster lying on the ocean floor, a grain of sand is required—something "incorrect," a foreign body. This is just like art, where what is truly great is often born "not according to the rules." There are a multitude of examples.

From an interview conducted by A. Medved'ev in the summer of 1984 and published in "Nuzhen poisk, nuzhny izmeneniia privychnogo" [A Search Is Needed, Changes to What Is Usual Are Needed], *Sovetskii dzhaz* [Soviet Jazz] (Moscow, 1987), pp. 68–69. Russian text reprinted in *Besedy s Al'fredom Shnitke*, compiled and edited by A. V. Ivashkin (Moscow: Kul'tura, 1994), p. 193.

TIMBRAL RELATIONSHIPS AND THEIR FUNCTIONAL USE

The Timbral Scale

(1970s)

The development of the individual elements of music does not take place simultaneously. Although the system of functional harmony in European music is more than two hundred years old and the period of its obvious dominance has long since passed, the functional use of timbral relationships has become an autonomous technique only in the twentieth century.

In spite of Rimsky-Korsakov's assertion that instrumentation is a creative act, not mere embellishment, in spite of the revered Age of Orchestration as a subject of music theory, in spite of the examples of functional orchestral logic left to us by such geniuses as Mozart, Tchaikovsky, Wagner, and so on, timbre remained a subordinate element in the hierarchy of expressive resources. It helped to make themes more vivid, harmonies more colorful, form more precise, but it hardly ever became an autonomous element of musical thought. Timbre naturally had an extremely dynamic influence on the associative sphere of music, but this was always in conjunction with the more important elements of melody or rhythm. Even such a stereotyped timbral device as a fanfare is an embodiment of the timbre of brass instruments in specific rhythms and intonations.

The comparative properties of different timbres were used to achieve unity of form. For example, a thematic relationship was emphasized by a connection in timbre, a contrast was made more pronounced by using a new timbre. As long as instrumentation had only this secondary role, there was no need for any systematic and concrete treatise on the concepts of timbral relationships and contrasts.[1]

The stormy development of music in the twentieth century, however, has long been concerned with ideas about timbre. The emancipation of dissonance (in the works of Debussy, Schoenberg, Scriabin, and Ives) meant, in practical terms, the emancipation of timbre as well. Emancipated dissonance brought to light the direct expressivity of *coloristic* harmony, that is, of harmony as timbre. In 1908 Schoenberg

---

1. There are cases, however, in nineteenth-century composers' concrete decisions about instrumentation, in which one finds "modifications of timbral quality," "a gradual transition from one timbral nuance to another," "a timbral shift within a string group," "timbral bridges," "timbral continuity," "timbral dissonance within the musical texture," and "timbral disjunction." See A. M. Veprik, *Traktovka instrumentov orkestra* [Principles of Orchestration] (Moscow: Muzyka, 1961). —A.Sch.

crossed the boundary of tonality (in the finale of his second quartet), and by 1909 he had used the "harmony" of timbre as the sole way of defining the form of a whole composition (No. 3 from the Five Pieces for Orchestra, Opus 16). But it took a long time for this experiment to find direct continuation (unless one counts Varèse, who turned timbre into a full-fledged element of musical thought). Instead the newly discovered primary power of timbre was kept subordinate to the purposes of intonational intensification. Only in electronic music of the 1950s did timbre become a basic structural material, finally achieving pre-eminence in the sonoristic works of the early 1960s.

Since timbre is capable of being an autonomous and even a fundamental means of expression, a more concrete and systematic treatment of its characteristic features is required. And since relationships between timbres manifest themselves in both horizontal and vertical planes, it is appropriate to apply to them terms borrowed from harmony and polyphony: timbral consonance and timbral harmony, timbral dissonance and timbral polyphony, timbral modulation and timbral counterpoint.

Timbral consonance is a combination of related timbres that create a blended sonority difficult for the ear to analyze, in which the individual characteristics of instruments are fused into a single total color. A typical example of timbral consonance can be found, for example, in the harmonic timbres of the *Leitakkord* used by Schoenberg in Piece No. 3 from Opus 16.

The timbral consonance of individual lines leads to timbral harmony. One of the most vivid and bold examples of this may be found in the third movement of Stravinsky's *Symphony of Psalms*. A four-voice mixed chorus, together with five trumpets and cellos *divisi a 3*, which augment the choral harmony with independent heterophonic voices, create a combination so closely blended that even the trumpets are dissolved into the sonority of the chorus, giving it a kind of dissonant sheen, a shining aureole. [See example 22.1.]

Timbral dissonance is a combination of distantly related timbres that retain their own individual characteristics. If a multitimbred chord is very brief, the ear has no

Example 22.1. Stravinsky, *Symphony of Psalms,* 3rd Movement

Example 22.2. Shostakovich, Symphony No. 9, 4th Movement

time to identify the various timbres in it. Only when a timbral dissonance is prolonged can the ear gradually come to fix all its components. The two climactic chords in the fourth movement of Shostakovich's Ninth Symphony exemplify this. Combined here are a cymbal strike, a sharply accentuated then gradually fading perfect fourth sounded by a pair of trumpets, and a subdued echo from the strings. [See example 22.2.]

A consistent prolonged dissonance of timbres creates *timbral polyphony*. This usually serves to intensify the prolongation of melodic polyphony and explains why Webern made wide use of it in those of his works that were structurally most perfect (the Symphony, Opus 21, and the Cantata No. 2, Opus 31).

A gradual *timbral modulation* during the process of a formal development has always acted as a counterbalance to timbral contrast (the latter may be regarded as an abrupt timbral modulation). For example, in the second movement of Brahms's Symphony No. 1, the transfer of the theme from the oboe to the clarinet is camouflaged in a most subtle way: the clarinet enters four beats before the oboe stops playing, taking off from the oboe as if it were what was left of the oboe's sound. After the clarinet enters, the oboe loses its thematic independence, its part now merely figuration in the pulsing chords of the strings. [See example 22.3.]

Timbral modulation was widely used by Wagner, Mahler, Richard Strauss, and Rimsky-Korsakov, but for them it remained merely one means among many. Only in

Example 22.3. Brahms, Symphony No. 1, 2nd Movement

the twentieth century did compositions appear in which timbral modulation served as the basis for the logic of orchestration. Apart from Piece No. 3 from Schoenberg's Opus 16, one might also mention Bartók's *Music for Strings, Percussion, and Celesta* and Webern's transcription of Bach's *Fuga (Ricercata) a 6 voci*.

The use of timbral modulation and timbral relationships presupposes the existence of a timbral *scale*, that is, a succession of gradually changing timbres which, extended over a considerable distance, is capable of unifying *all* those transitional timbres into a coherent grouping. It goes without saying that—because of the vast number of different instruments, and also because of the individual colorations of instruments of the same type—there cannot be one simple and discrete timbral scale (like a pitch scale in equal temperament) for every situation. Furthermore, one composer's ideas about timbre may be more precise and thus may require a scale that is more subtly graduated than would be the case for another. Thus an infinitely differentiated scale of interpolating sonorities, which move one to the next and which include every imaginable richness from the world of sound, can be conceived only in theory—although it might be applied more readily to electronic than to traditional orchestral music. In the latter, by virtue of the three factors mentioned above (the individuality of the composer, the individuality of the instrumental ensemble selected, and the individual relationship of the performer and his instrument), only a more or less precisely graduated illusory scale is possible, as some sort of artificial construct that may provide rational control over the sound material in the process of composing.

Boulez, Stockhausen, Nono, Berio, Ligeti, and many others use a timbral scale in precisely this way: as a prearranged working plan. Certainly, in connection with this, the composer does not always have a conscious conception of this scale—he may follow it by instinct. But even so, the concept of a timbral scale can still be useful as a means of analyzing the score after the fact.

The analogy between timbral and pitch organization of music lies in the fact that in both cases there exists the possibility of a functional system with a scale of nuances and gradual modulations. But it is also revealed in the possibility of consciously avoiding traditional functional logic. It is no accident that the move away from the overt gravitational tendencies in functional tonality toward the concealed poly-semantic pitch associations of atonalism should have been accompanied by a similar move away from more conventional timbral affinities among orchestral groups, and toward daring combinations of instruments that at first appear unrelated. In the last three bars of Piece No. 1 from Webern's Opus 10 [example 22.4], we are presented with all the orchestral groupings in the following order: cellos/celesta → harp → flute → muted trumpet → celesta. But once one identifies precisely what these instruments are playing, one discovers an affinity among the contrasting timbres: they are all marked *pp–ppp*, the last three instruments are playing the same note, imitating each other, and there is an indubitable kinship of timbre between the harmonics of the cellos and those of the harp and the flute. In this same example is yet another highly significant linking motif—its context. In the context of the whole piece the last bars are a timbral "resolution" of the opening bar, in which the colors of the same instruments are presented in the following blend: muted trumpet/harp → celesta/harp harmonics/cello harmonics → flute trillato/harp.

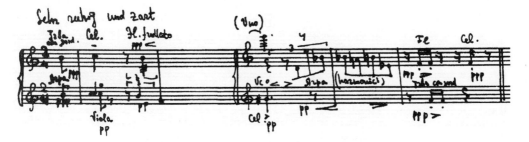

Example 22.4. Webern, Opus 10, No. 1

Thus the obvious ("tonal") timbral affinity of related instruments has been replaced by the less obvious ("atonal") affinity of related timbres from unrelated instruments. But the next step, too—the structural organization of atonal material by the use of twelve-tone technique—immediately entailed an analogous systematization of timbral logic. Starting with the Symphony, Opus 21, Webern assigned a distinctive timbre to each of the three fixed, four-tone melodic cells into which the twelve-tone series is divided. Here, once again, the contrast function of timbre is brought to the foreground, heightening the motivic and structural contrast (while the significance of the timbral affinities is relegated to the background). Although this modifies the individual melodic cell in a variety of ways, Webern does not change the instrumentation.

Those who followed in Webern's footsteps in the 1950s (Boulez, Stockhausen, Nono) were particularly interested in this tendency in Webern's musical thinking to disassociate and differentiate. In their efforts to achieve a total absence of repetition, expressed in the total serialization of all parameters, including timbre, they arrived at *timbral pointillism*—continuous jumps in timbre from note to note. At the same time, however, they failed to notice the timbral affinities, whose efficacy Webern had preserved. Only timbral contrast of the highest intensity remained both in the vertical and horizontal planes, continuous timbral dissonance. This is shown most clearly in Stockhausen's *Kontrapunkte* [example 22.5] and Nono's *Incontri* [see example 26.2, in this volume].

The total serialization of all the parameters, however, was not acceptable to the ear, and as the serial method became more thoroughly pervasive, the music sounded more chaotic.[2] To counteract the destructive forces of serialism, the most talented representatives of the "avant-garde" introduced factors designed to ensure the unity of a composition. The centrifugal trend toward the non-repetition of timbre began to interact with the centripetal tendencies toward unity of timbre.... The former dictated ensembles of assonant instruments (in Boulez's *Le Marteau sans maître* we have mezzo-soprano, alto flute, guitar, viola, marimbaphone, percussion), while the latter prompted a search for timbral affinities (all the performers in Boulez's score are the "alto" representatives of their differing groups, the voice being treated as first among equals, not as soloist). The former tendency pushed for an uninterrupted line

---

2. Xenakis was among the first to try to find a way out of this fatal circle. Instead of constructing a work on the basis of canonical law (that is, a series), he proposed the idea of constructing it on the basis of objective mathematical laws, namely, the Theory of Probability (stochastic music). —A.Sch.

Example 22.5. Stockhausen, *Kontrapunkte*

of continuously renewed timbres from note to note (even in his choral writing, expanding on the technique of hocketing, Nono settled on a pointillistic fragmentation of melody and words—even the individual voices do not always sing complete words, but syllables and sounds). The latter required timbral bridges, dynamic and phonetic links between the different points. [See example 22.6.]

In deciding on the performing group for a future work, composers immediately confronted the problem of trying to ensure unity of timbre, and this required them to pay attention to timbral affinities, forcing them to rely on a timbral scale.

The score of Nono's *Varianti* for violin, three flutes, three clarinets, and string orchestra provides an example of equilibrium between the pointillistic non-repetition of timbres and their uninterrupted affiliations. [See example 22.7.] In this work every note is independent with respect to its timbre (even in the solo part, no two adjacent tones can be produced by means of the same technical device), but every new coloration appears as a step in an unbroken modulation in timbre: string

Example 22.6. Nono, *Intoleranza*

harmonics herald the contrasting group of woodwinds, the solo violin appears as a consequence of the reduction in forces of the string orchestra.[3]

As we see, timbral modulation within a single timbre is a characteristic Nono device. Apart from the examples quoted (timbre modulation in a chorus and in a group of strings), we can recall, as an example of extremely subtle timbral gradation, the range of recolorations of timbre required of a single performer on the concertato violin in those same *Varianti*. Apart from the usual *arco* and *pizzicato*, we also have *sul ponticello, flautato, col legno, legno battuto,* and every possible combination of these techniques. And even for the solo soprano in the second movement, "Canti di vita e d'amore," we have *bocca chiusa, poco chiusa, poco a poco aprire, poco aperta, ordinario.* [See example 22.8.]

It is now possible to refer to the existence in practical terms of a functional system of timbral affinities as a highly important architectonic factor in contemporary music. The search for more and more new timbral affinities continues. There are modulations from music to speech (Gubaidulina's *Stupeni* [Steps]), from cymbal crash to chorus (Pousseur's *Elektra*). Electronic music opens up enormous possibilities in this direction, particularly in the interaction of "live" sounds with synthetic ones. Electronic music, however, is not the subject of these notes.

Written in the 1970s. The original Russian text has not been published.

---

3. This is a reversal of the device used in Berg's Violin Concerto, in which the soloist's playing is gradually absorbed into the collective sound of the orchestral violins, which enter a few at a time. —A.Sch.

(Figures for this chapter continue through page 112)

Example 22.7. Nono, *Varianti*

Example 22.7. (*continued*)

x) Kb.: Die Flageolette klingen immer wie mit kleiner Note in Parenthesi notiert!

Example 22.7. (*continued*)

Example 22.7. (*concluded*)

Canti di Vita e D'Amore
II.

Luigi Nono

Example 22.8. Nono, *Varianti*, 2nd Movement ("Canti di vita e d'amore")

23

KLANGFARBENMELODIE—
"MELODY OF TIMBRES" (1970s)

The first example of the consistent application of the principle of timbral modulation is probably Schoenberg's orchestral piece "Farben" ["Colors"], the third piece from Opus 16. If we take no account of those details of nuance that are of a decorative, quasi-thematic order, the whole fabric of this work is constructed on the constant timbral transformation of a single chord (C–G♯–B–E–A) that slowly and gradually, note by note, shifts from one transposition to another. The timbral and pitch recolorations of this chord constitute the sole impulse that shapes the work.

In the first, or exposition, section (the "principal theme" [see example 23.1]), the recolorations of the chord are regular both in length (each phase equals one half note) and in component timbres (a pair of timbral combinations with two stable linkages that recur periodically: two flutes, clarinet, bassoon, solo viola ↔ English horn, trumpet, bassoon, horn, solo double bass). The two timbres of each pair, linked together at the junctions, are very much alike, although the second timbre is always

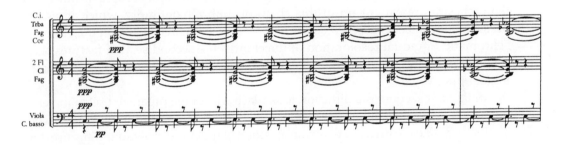

Example 23.1. Schoenberg, Op. 16, No. 3 ("Farben")

Table 23.1. Three Stages in the First Section of "Farben"

I	II	III
timbre stability	timbre stability	timbre stability
pitch stability	pitch shiftings	pitch stability
(initial transposition)	(element of diffusion)	(new transposition)
		introduction of new timbre and pitch element
		(quasi-thematic descending motifs)

somewhat more intensive than the first: flute < cor anglais, flute < trumpet, clarinet < bassoon, bassoon < horn, viola < double bass). While the timbral changes in the five voices of these chords are fully synchronic, their pitch changes are nonsynchronic. All the voices represent the same melodic cell (A–B♭–A♭, E–F–E♭, B–C–B♭, G♯–A–G, C–C♯–B), but the progressions from note to note take place at different times. Summing up, within the first section there are three stages [see Table 23.1].

After the fermata over the new transposition of the chord—which is reached at the end of the first section (bar 11) and sounds an octave lower in four cellos and a double bass, held motionless for the moment—the second section (the "second subject") begins with a reflection an octave lower, the new chord transposition played by the cellos and double bass. The timbral instability increases. Only the timing of the changes is preserved (i.e., the rhythm—except for the lower voice, where the phase length has been reduced to a quarter note), while the modulations in timbre and transposition lose their regularity. All the remaining instruments of the orchestra are caught up in this chain of timbral continuity, which loses any periodicity whatsoever. Whereas the first section was constructed on the basis of a "chromatic," gradual recoloration of the chords, the second section features acute timbral jumps. [See example 23.2.] Table 23.2, for example, shows the timbre changes in the upper voice.

In the first section, the diffusion took place within the organized pitch material, but now it grows more intense and embraces the timbral structure as well. The second section ends like the first, at a new transposition of the chord, now sounding an octave higher in harmonics on the violas, cellos, and the double bass [bar 25].

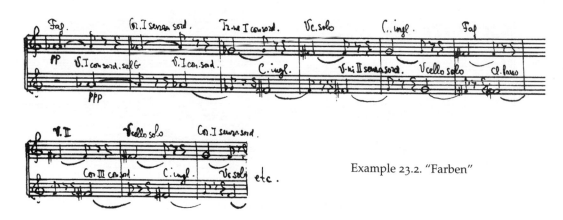

Example 23.2. "Farben"

Table 23.2. Timbral Changes in First and Second Sections of "Farben"

First section	Second section
flute ↔ English horn	bassoon → first violins
	con sordino sul G → horn → first violins → trombone
	con sordino → English horn → solo cello → etc.

In the third section (the "development") the diffusion embraces even the area of rhythm—the timbral changes in the voices of the chord are nonsynchronic, they increase in pace more and more toward the end of the statement, and instead of the previous pointillist arrangement of material in the score, brief three-note motifs emerge (still based on the same pitch cell from the first statement). The rapid change of tones, timbres, and rhythmic accent produces a structural instability that admits the intrusion of alien decorative elements (such as the descending chromatic scale in cellos and violas [in bars 28–29; see example 23.3]). These destructive, quasi-improvisational elements, which appear first at the end of the first section and continue their depredatory work in the second, now, at the end of the third, collide with the fragmented pieces of what was once a well-ordered structure, but is now, after prolonged internal spasms, disintegrating.

A modulatory cycle closes during the course of this measured structural disintegration, and the fourth section begins again [bar 32] with the original transposition of the chord. [See example 23.4.] Likewise the original regularity of timbral modulations (the phase equal to one half) is restored. But their measured rhythm, based on a pair of periodic combinations, is not restored, neither is the balance of timbre within the chords. Thus a spiral twist is inscribed, leading from timbral consonance to timbral dissonance, from a "tonal" monocentric timbral structure to one that is "atonal" and polycentric.

Probably it is not for anyone to succeed wholly in putting his ideas into actual practice. Schoenberg's leap of genius into a new world of sound, in which timbre is the main expressive element and is subjected to independent functional organization, long remained merely an incidental breakthrough. It is symptomatic that once the composer had announced the emancipation of dissonance, it fell to his lot to announce the emancipation of timbre, too—although it would have been more natural to expect this from Debussy and Ravel. Preoccupied in his investigation of the newly discovered world of atonalism, Schoenberg did not plunge any deeper into unfamiliar territory, although—fully conscious of its great significance, he gave it a name: *Klangfarbenmelodie* (melody of timbres).

For over sixty years this concept has remained a kind of ideal definition of music that does not yet exist, since no one has been able to put it into practice.

True, there have been approximations of it, as follows:

1. In Bartók's orchestral writing, where timbre (both simple and mixed) is given thematic and architectonic significance.

Jede Note genau so lang aushalten, wie vorgezeichnet; aber auch nicht länger!!!

Example 23.3. "Farben"

Example 23.3. (concluded)

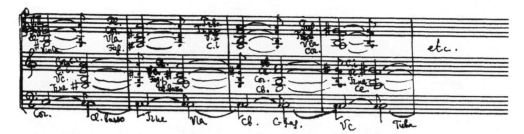

Example 23.4. "Farben"

2. In instrumentation with rapid timbral recoloration of lines, where the reciprocal timbral interchange assumes an independent function (Webern; early Shostakovich—Octet,[1] and his opera *Nos* [The Nose]; the post-Webern group—Boulez, Nono, and Stockhausen).

3. In the scores of Varèse, who treated timbres more radically than any other composer in the first half of the twentieth century (in his *Ionisation,* for example, timbre is the only musical material).

4. In musique concrète and electronic music from the early 1950s, when musical thought was expressed not linearly but entirely harmonically, and the composers fashioned a structure of timbre, creating new sonorities.

Schoenberg's presentiment of the future has been expressed still more definitively in two polarized tendencies in contemporary orchestral thinking:

1. In the sonoristic practices of the early 1960s, seen most clearly in the Polish school (Penderecki's *Polymorphia* and *Fluorescences,* Górecki's *Genesis,* Szalonek's *Sounds,* and others). Here timbre, in the immediacy of its effect, has become the only functionally organized element of the music. The experience of electronic music, revealed by way of a "reverse influence" on orchestral thinking, prompted composers to seek new timbres, either by using unconventional ways of producing sound or by way of an orchestral texture, which, by bringing together a collection of simple timbres, produced a new timbral quality.

2. In the micropolyphony used by Ligeti (or by the no less original, though less well-known Klaus Huber), in which the new timbral quality is also generated by the interweaving of many simple lines. However, the new quality is not so much an end in itself as a complementary result (although still subject to strict control).

To get at the essence of the technique, what matters is not so much how the composer's intentions are realized, but what they actually are, what is the starting

---

1. Schnittke wrote "Oktet" here, but the actual title of the work is (in translation) *Two Pieces,* Opus 11, for String Octet. —ed.

point for the idea—color or line, timbre or pitch. The outwardly similar sixty-line scores of Ligeti and Penderecki were created by completely opposite methods. For the former, the first intimation of the music to come is its polyphonic fabric, while its timbral realization is a derivative factor; for the latter, a work starts from the perspective of timbre, realized through the means of multivoiced scoring. The value of pitched intonation in Ligeti's *Lontano* or *Lux aeterna* is preserved (although also veiled by the extremely delicate web of micropolyphony), whereas the significance of motif and melodic cell in the choral and orchestral frescoes of Penderecki is limited (with the exception of *Stabat Mater*). Here we have heterophony, in which the overall timbral-harmonic mottling is more important. In this sense Ligeti is closer to Schoenberg, whose *Klangfarbenmelodie* did not completely destroy the melody of tones, either the horizontal melody of a three-note motif or the vertical "melody" of a five-note chord.

The more "cultural layers" there are in music, the more subtle it becomes. Enthralled by the conquest of new domains, humankind carries within itself all the experience of former conquests. When Schoenberg formulated the idea of *Klangfarbenmelodie*, it is unlikely that he had in mind the withering away of the realm of pitch. Rather he envisaged a shift of the center of gravity to timbre, while retaining the significance of melodic energy, albeit manifested in concealed form. The "melody of timbres" that Schoenberg imagined remains still a Utopian dream.

Written in the 1970s. The original Russian text has not been published.

CHAPTER

24

FUNCTIONAL VARIABILITY OF LINE
IN ORCHESTRAL TEXTURE (1970s)

Along with the clear and distinct functions of the instrumental parts in modern orchestral practice, one also encounters the principle of functional variability. Within the span of even a short formal segment (within a statement, a phrase, or a motif) the same voice fulfils different functions in succession. [See example 24.1.]

Example 24.1. a. From Shostakovich, Symphony No. 4, 1st Movement

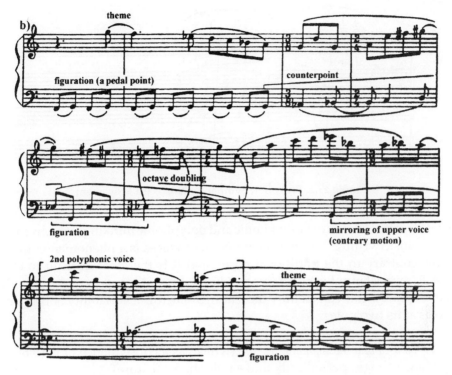

Example 24.1. b. Functional schema of the same passage

Within the span of two bars, the function of the cellos is continually changing—from an accompanimental figure on a pedal point, to counterpoint in contrary motion, back to an accompanimental figure, then to octave doubling of one of the implied voices in the violin part, then to mirroring the upper voice in contrary motion, and once again to accompanimental figuration.

As distinct from traditional practice in the treatment of lines, the change in function of the voices in this case is accomplished not coincident with clear-cut demarcations of the form (thematic statement, phrase, or motif) but independently of the syntactic division, and smoothly as well. This type of "free" treatment of the individual voice, unrestrained by the polyphonic web of the texture, was previously to be found in chamber music, but in the latter the change of function involved the *instrument* itself, not the *instrumental part.* At the basis of a score lay a precise plan for the distribution of parts, with a functional stability among the voices; only a shortage of instruments would make it necessary for a part to be switched from one instrumental voice to another.

In a polyphonic texture, changing functions among the voices has always been inevitable. At any particular moment, any voice could assume the role of the leading voice, thereby increasing its thematic function, while the other voices receded for the time being into a more neutral, background role. The assertion of the principle of functional variability in the modern orchestra, characteristic of Shostakovich, Prokofiev, Stravinsky, Britten (and other representatives of the neoclassical movement),

Example 24.2. Prokofiev, Symphony No. 7, 3rd Movement

is the result of a synthesis of homophonic and polyphonic thinking, of orchestral and chamber-music writing. Varying the function of voices is a phenomenon that is in principle contrary to the traditional norm, and it is therefore difficult to classify accurately the vast number of devices that lie on the continuum between polyphony and heterophony. One can identify the features of textural variability only by noting examples at its two poles:

1. *Variability of a monophonic texture* (which, as a consequence of variable doubling, changes periodically into a polyphonic texture).

   The oboe [in example 24.2], for literally a single instant, stops doubling the flute melody in order to create a full triad at the moment when two of the harmonic voices pause.

   [In example 24.3] the double basses play a rhythmically simplified variant of the cello part (as if they were incapable of dealing with shorter note values).

   The cello part [in example 24.4] gradually frees itself from active doubling of the first violins and finally becomes rhythmically independent.

2. *Variability of a polyphonic texture* (which, as a consequence of decreasing independence of the separate voices, changes periodically into a monophonic texture).

   Here [in example 24.5] we have two-part counterpoint in the strings, in which the intonational kinship between the contrapuntal voice and the principal theme is enhanced by their blending into an octave "unison," after which they again become independent.

Example 24.3. Shostakovich, Symphony No. 1, 2nd Movement

Example 24.4. Stravinsky, *Orpheus* (Pas de Deux)

Example 24.5. Prokofiev, Symphony No. 7, 1st Movement

Example 24.6. Shostakovich, Symphony No. 8, 1st Movement

[In example 24.6] a canon at the octave in the brass leads into doubling at the octave.

[In example 24.7] two flutes, freely imitating each other, create figural approximations of the thematic voice in the solo violin. But in a moment their independence is undermined by the appearance of three parallel octaves.

Example 24.7. Stravinsky, *Orpheus*

In the practice of functional variability, one real voice may carry out the functions of several voices in succession. The possibility arises of realizing a complex textural plan by using only two voices (as, for example, in the above example from Shostakovich's Fourth Symphony [see example 24.1]). Two real voices presented in short segments can substitute for a sizeable number of illusory voices. Traditional orchestral treatment of the parts (based on precise distinctions among the functions of instruments) would have dictated to Shostakovich the "materialization" of all his planned textural effects in a multilayered scoring. This would have entailed a rhythmically activated supporting accompaniment, a contrapuntal voice, a pedal in the middle register, an octave doubling of the theme, a bass on a pedal point, and so on. A "cleverly" orchestrated construction with an "elaborated" orchestral texture would have resulted, calling for a large and colorful collection of instruments.

Thus the principle of functional variability contributes to great flexibility in orchestral texture and promotes an economical use of orchestral colors.

Written in the 1970s. The original Russian text has not been published.

CHAPTER

25

A NEW APPROACH TO COMPOSITION

The Statistical Method

(1970s)

The post-Webern serialist composers of the 1950s (Stockhausen, Boulez, Nono) extended rational control to all parameters of composition, striving to subordinate them to a single structural idea (hence the term "structuralism"). This was initially expressed in the idea of a series: a tone row, most frequently consisting of twelve tones. When it was a question of constructing a rhythmical series—that is, of transferring the intervallic proportions of a series from the dimension of tone to that of rhythm—the need first arose to express a tone row not by using notes but by using numbers (*Structures* by Boulez; *Kreuzspiel* by Stockhausen). A certain duration was selected as the starting (for example, a thirty-second note or a sixteenth note) and was assigned to a particular note (either temporarily or for the entire composition), while the other notes in the row (depending on their intervallic distance from the starting note) were assigned various numerators, but with the common denominator of either a thirty-second or a sixteenth note.

Introduced in this way (or in some other way, as in *Gruppen* by Stockhausen), a row of numbers could become the index for changing textural density, dynamics, the number of sounding voices, the length of sections, and so forth. The series of numbers thus became the point of departure for the compositional technology, the first step in the realization of a creative conception (even of the most poetic one).

If it is possible to derive a numerical row from a tone row, it is equally possible to derive a tone row from a numerical row. As Stockhausen worked on his first electronic works, he encountered the untempered "infinite" pitch scale of the sinusoidal electric generator. In order to control the tones, he selected a certain limited number from the full spectrum of possible frequencies and arranged them in order of their gradually increasing number of vibrations, thus producing a scale, from which he derived the rows of numbers that defined in every dimension the structure of the whole. At the initial stage of composition, Stockhausen used *numerical* operations. Only in realizing the work on magnetic recording tape and in montage did he deal with the tones (although the numerical rows had been worked out with a definite sound in mind). The period of total serialism of this sort soon came to an end, but the idea of a *scale*, a *progression of numbers* that reflected successive qualitative changes, was transferred from the area of discrete, graduated phenomena (a tempered twelve-step scale, a pyramid of durations, relatively precisely fixed dynamics from *ppppp* to *fffff*, tempo, and bar structure) into the realm of phenomena previously not susceptible to quantitative measurement (timbre, form, thematic process, and, even beyond these, characteristics of expression, musical imagery, the play of styles, and the associative spectrum of music).

Previously the dominant principle in this area was that of dialectical antithesis, contrasts in theme, timbre, image, style, and affect, and the resolution of these contrasts provided the motivational force in the compositional process. The polar qualities were conceived as the stable elements, while between them lay a mobile realm of unstable, interconnected transitional qualities. The paramount form of tonal music—the sonata allegro—embodied the dialectical principle in its most obvious form: contrasts of theme, tonality, texture, rhythm, tempo, and timbre; and their resolution supplied the dynamics of sonata form for over two hundred years. The representatives of the New Viennese School experienced this dialectical principle in their own way. According to one of Webern's pupils, Filip Moiseevich Gershkovich, they regarded the basic constructive principle of a sonata as the contrast between its first and second subjects according to the way they were regulated structurally: *"fest— und locker"* ("firm—and loose"). This was not by chance: under the conditions of atonalism one ceases to be conscious of contrast of tonality. The principles of tonal logic were expressed more subtly and with less contrast in dodecaphony—as a manifestation of polycentrism, the interaction of many tonal gravitations. Under the conditions of dodecaphony, thematic contrast also ceased to manifest itself directly as intonational but rather indirectly, by way of texture, rhythm, and especially structure (see for example Webern's Symphony, Opus 21, or his *Piano Variations*, Opus 27).

Here the foundations have already been laid for the replacement of the bipolar principle by the multipolar—the contrast of polarities is weakened, and the individual qualities of the intermediate intervals between are strengthened. Statistical rationalization based on a scale of all the parameters of a composition in the end dulls the sharpness of polar contrasts, since the poles are bridged by ladders of intermediate steps. The polarities start to be felt as relative, susceptible to prolongation. This idea that all the qualities, and their quantification, are in fact relative had a profound influence on both the psychology and on the methodology of musical composition.

In the practice of thematic-tonal logic, a composition starts with a distinctive musical idea—a motif, theme, or harmonic progression (some part of this is true even for dodecaphonic logic)—and this idea then sets off on its journey through the space-time of a musical world, without any obligation at all to calculate every possible distance or to embody itself in every possible way. The resulting musical events are perceived as a manifestation of natural, elemental forces in dynamic confrontation both normative and fortuitous. In the process of composition the composer inwardly identifies with the sound images he generates, leading them through the sound world, and in specific cases—guided by the given situation and the overall plan—he makes decisions, but not at all on the basis of statistically possible variants. The determinism of the form as a whole allows for the frequent indeterminism of specific musical circumstances.

In the case of a structuralist approach, work begins with the calculation of a musical space within the boundaries and possibilities defined by its structural law (for example, a series or a mathematical progression). Only after that [occurs] is the space filled with musical images, the existence of which has an astrological relationship with the mathematically calculated structure of the whole. As he continues to work, the composer does not inwardly identify with the sound images; as he realizes them, he thereby gives precision and concreteness to variants predefined earlier, variants selected from the statistical combination of probabilities. The point of departure in the realization of the work is a statistical review of the musical material from which the artificial musical space—or, better, the musical building—is constructed.

Stockhausen's *Momente* (1961–1965) is one of the most expressive works of the last decade. As one listens to this "Song of Songs" of our time, with all its emotional force, it is difficult even to imagine that the form of the work is open, that is, variable (the sequence of episodes can change) and that the whole conglomerate of episodes, each of different character (or "moment"), of this open form are subject to rational organization, all the moments being classified by their principal textural features, with various interactions between different types of texture:

Principal types of "moment"
M *(Melodie-Momente)*—melodic "moments" (monody—heterophony)
K *(Klang-Momente)*—sonoristic "moments" (homophony)
D *(Dauer-Momente)*—durational, rhythmic "moments" (polyphony)

Examples of possible mixings
MK—mixed melodic-sonoristic "moment"
M (d)—melodic "moment" inflected by some sort of rhythmic "moment"
M (m)—melodic "moment" with a "feedback" (i.e., a supplemental melodic factor, derived from the given "moment")
D (d → m)—rhythmic "moment" with a "feedback" that is gradually supplanted by the influence of a melodic "moment"

Example of more complex interaction of two "moments"
Km KM (km), KM—the second "moment" (KM) is performed twice: the first time with a quoted reminiscence of the first "moment" (Km); the second time without this "reminiscence."

Ligeti, in working on his *Aventures*[1] for three voices and instrumental ensemble (1962–1965), subordinated to strict rational calculation not only the pitch material (that is, the notes and also an abstract text composed by him, consisting of 119 phonemes, grouped along scales of the smallest possible changes—there are fourteen different sounds for "a" alone!) but also the expressive features. In his sketches of this "small-scale opera with unreal, imaginary action," the following "layer types" of "the polyphony of affects"[2] are noted in Table 25.1, along with a systematization of dynamics and tempi.

---

1. Ove Nordwall, *György Ligeti: Eine Monographie* (Mainz: B. Schott's Söhne, 1971). —A.Sch.

2. All the terminology is taken from Ligeti and from Erkki Salmenhaara, who has researched Ligeti's work. —A.Sch.

Table 25.1. Layers of Affect and a Schema of Dynamics of Tempi

Layer Types in the Polyphony of Affects
Speech layer—11 characters
Expressive layer—7 characters
Softly whispering layer—8 characters
Absolute, motionless layer—7 characters
Humorous-erotic layer—9 characters

Schema of Dynamics and Tempi

Quickly—softly (8 gradations)		Slowly—softly (11 gradations, plus an undefined additional number)
Quickly—mixed (1 gradation)		Slowly—mixed (4 gradations)
Quickly—loudly (11 gradations)		Slowly—loudly (2 gradations)
	Variously—softly (6 gradations)	
	Variously—mixed (7 gradations)	
	Variously—loudly (2 gradations)	

Stockhausen, in his works of an "intuitive," "meditative" type (i.e., *Kurzwellen, Prozession, Aus den sieben Tagen, Spiral),* succeeded in making the statistical principle as absolute and algebraic as possible. In these works there is not a single musical note, merely a system of restrictive symbols or verbal indications, according to which the performers improvise. Only changes in the qualities of the music are precisely fixed by the use of the signs + −, or $^+_-$ $^+_+$ $^-_-$, and so forth, or by verbal indications. The actual quality to which these gradations apply is not shown at all: it is left to the performers or the guidance of chance. For example, + may mean the maintaining of the tempo, rhythm, register of the preceding performer or the one playing at the same time (or of the arbitrary sounds coming from the radio receiver); ± may mean a partial maintaining of one quality and a conflict with another, and so forth. Thus, the only factor organized by the composer is the direction of the movements along a graduated scale; the actual qualities to which the scale applies are not known in advance. What is composed is simply the dynamic structure of a musical composition, the actual musical material can be anything.

But this is an extreme case. More frequently composers follow the principle of a scale for specified, concrete musical material:

Timbre: The Yugoslavian composer Vinko Globokar, having discovered a whole series of new sounds for brass instruments, is guided in his work by the principle of a timbral scale, modulating from timbres that are familiar to ones that are aggressively strange.

Style: In the "Galop fantastique" from the opera *Votre Faust,* Henri Pousseur retraces the whole course of European harmony from the functional system to dodecaphony, modulating from style to style (the episode starts with quotations and false quotations "from Gounod," moves through Liszt, Wagner, and Schoenberg, and ends with Pousseur himself).

Forms: In the "super-collage" third movement of his Symphony, Luciano Berio follows a scale of increasing deconstruction of collage: (a) literal quotation of a Mahler scherzo; (b) quotation, but with added, stylistically unrelated, counterpoints; (c) "punctuated" [i.e., segmented] quotation that preserves the thread of the *cantus firmus* in a hidden "counting out" of its temporal relationships; (d) fragmentary quotation, but without preserving the thread; and, finally, (e) prolonged absence of quotation.

It is true that a work composed by statistical methods is by no means always accompanied by a collection of graphic diagrams and computations. Like the principles of non-repetition, atonality, ametricality, and other rational devices used by the West European avant-garde, the idea has entered into the subconscious, and from there it directs the composer's work.

In recent years the significance of the principle of using contrast has emerged once again. It continued to exist in concealed form even in classic examples of serialism (the formal conception of Boulez's *Le Marteau sans maître* subtly reproduces the Webern principle of "firm" and "loose" structure).

Furthermore the consistent use of the statistical method in itself inevitably led to the discovery of new areas of contrast: a scale to indicate this quality, going down to zero, logically should have gone even further into *minus-space*. Ideas developed concerning positive ["plus"] and negative ["minus"] musical spheres, and attempts were made to realize them in some conventional form—such as, in Stockhausen's *Plus/Minus*, in which the performing group is variable; one can, for example, use sound-recording or radio as the minus sphere. (Even more subtle representations of musical minus-space are possible. For instance, the end of V. Silvestrov's Violin Sonata, where the real sound is over but the performer continues silently to pretend to play, or Cage's piano piece *4'33"*, consisting entirely of silent gesticulations by the performer.)

The principle of using contrast finally returned to the forefront thanks to the wide-ranging extent to which collage techniques have been applied in the last decade [the 1970s]. The stylistic contrast between the basic material of a work (most often atonal, unconventionally tonal, or "modal") and quotations (which stand out as a consequence of their emphatically tonal language) is immeasurably more effective than modulations along a statistical scale. As we listen to Berio's Symphony, it is not so much that we distinguish his own music in the third movement from the music he quotes from other composers, but that we draw a distinction between the music of the atonal school and tonal music. We hear principally the contrast between the music of Berio, Schoenberg, Berg, Webern, Stockhausen, and Globokar, and the music of Mahler, Ravel, Strauss, and Beethoven.

Does this mean a return to the dynamics of simple contrasts? Time will tell, but nothing can be repeated precisely. If the principle of contrast comes back into music, it will happen not only with the "statistical" stage of development taken into account but also with some inevitable new element, the nature of which is impossible to foresee.

Written in the 1970s. The original Russian text has not been published.

STEREOPHONIC TENDENCIES IN MODERN ORCHESTRAL THINKING (1970s)

The functional use of space in music intended for concert performance is partly a consequence of the experience of electronic music. The first electronic work that went beyond the limits of pure experimentation, Stockhausen's *Gesang der Jünglinge* (1955–1956), owes the power of its artistic impact, in many respects, to the author's happy idea of presenting the sound material to the audience through five loud-speakers. This immediately infused life into the dead synthesized material.[1] Carrying out parallel work on his *Gruppen* for three orchestras (1955–1957), Stockhausen transferred to the orchestra the idea of using space functionally. As often happens, yet another reason also motivated this: the actual metrical-rhythmical structure of the work, which was based on frequent changes of tempi and tempo polyphony (the simultaneous coexistence of several tempi), required that it be divided among three orchestral groups with three conductors.

This marked the beginning of a broad penetration of stereophony into orchestral as well as chamber music. We can now speak of a whole arsenal of devices for making functional use of space. In part, these further develop the achievements of

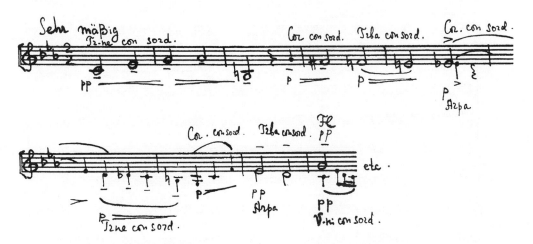

Example 26.1. Webern's orchestration of Bach's *Fuga (Ricercata) a 6 voci*

---

1. Since electronic music is not the subject of this essay, there will be no further discussion of it. —A.Sch.

Incontri

Luigi Nono

Example 26.2. Nono, *Incontri*

Example 26.2. (*concluded*)

antiphonal choral singing with its tradition of imitative or contrasting polyphony. In *Gruppen* (in which the three orchestras are similarly constituted) one repeatedly encounters (at moments of tempo "unison") interchanges between related instrumental groups:

> 70–77: "Drums" and "bells" in the three orchestras (chimes, harp, celesta, electric guitar, pizzicato strings, marimbaphone, tom-tom, bongo, tumba, etc.)
> 114–120: Pseudo-fugato for the brasses in the three orchestras.
> 121–122: Interchanges and repartee between the "drums," "bells," and brasses of the three orchestras.

An unusual expression of an antiphonal idea reduced to a formula can be found in Górecki's *Elementi per tre archi* (1962). Here a string trio directed by a conductor sits in triangular formation, one in the center and the other two at the edge of each side of the concert platform. The antiphonal arrangement of the performers is accompanied by two stereophonic effects:

The first, the real effect, is *static*. The sounds are separated in space, and this is especially perceptible when the musical material is contrasted in various combinations.

The second creates the illusion of being *dynamic*. The sounds move either one way or both ways from one player or group to another as they are imitated. This effect is the result of the ability of the ear to perceive the space between separated sound sources as if it were actually the movement of the selfsame sound to the new location.

Modern stereophony derives not only from an antiphonal approach but also from the principle of timbral modulation within the musical material, as shown in Webern's concept of instrumentation. His continuous timbral recoloration of a melodic line, at the very boundaries of the motifs themselves, inevitably produces a dynamic stereophonic effect. His melodies change coloration as they unfold, being passed along from one player to another. The illusion of their connectedness, the filling-in of the space between the sounds, derives from the timbral kinship of the different instruments. [See example 26.1; see also examples 31.1 and 31.2, in this volume.]

In the pointillist technique used in the early 1960s, timbral recoloration became even more frequent, and the stereo effect that resulted from it even more noticeable.

Such bold sudden shifts from timbre to timbre, confined within the closed space of the orchestral platform, imparted a heightened tension to the sound of the orchestra [see example 26.2]. Forces were generated, like those created by yeast, which erupted within the orchestra from the inside and eventually set the whole mass in motion, making it spill out over the edges of the confined space of the concert platform. At this point the capricious character of serial music in terms of timbres and dynamics was most naturally matched by continuous non-imitative interchanging of material between the groups.

In this instance [by Stockhausen, example 26.3], the effect is a true stereophony, but one that is *static*: the sudden movements through space take place only in the perception of the audience, while the performers themselves remain fixed in their places. The desire for a real, dynamic stereophony prompted composers to new experimentation. To achieve this, either performers or listeners had to be put in motion.

Example 26.3. Stockhausen, *Gruppen*

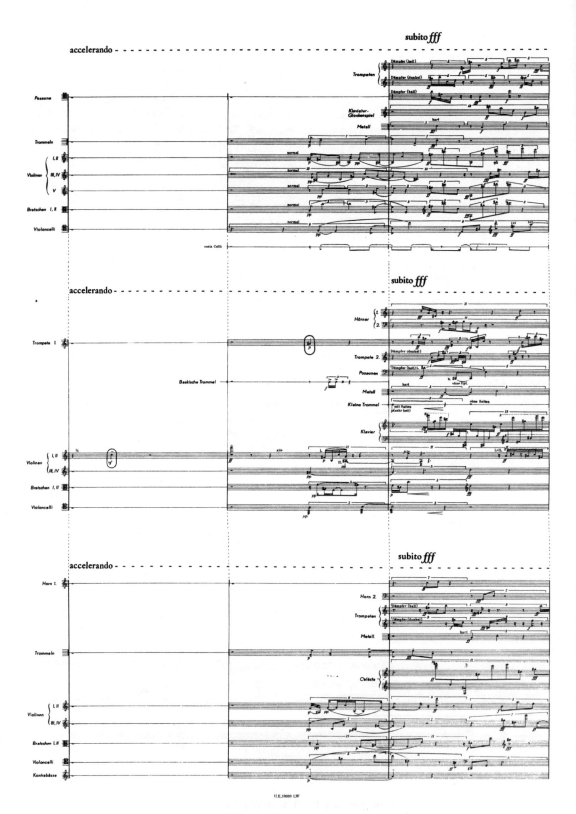

Example 26.3. (continued)

Example 26.3. (*continued*)

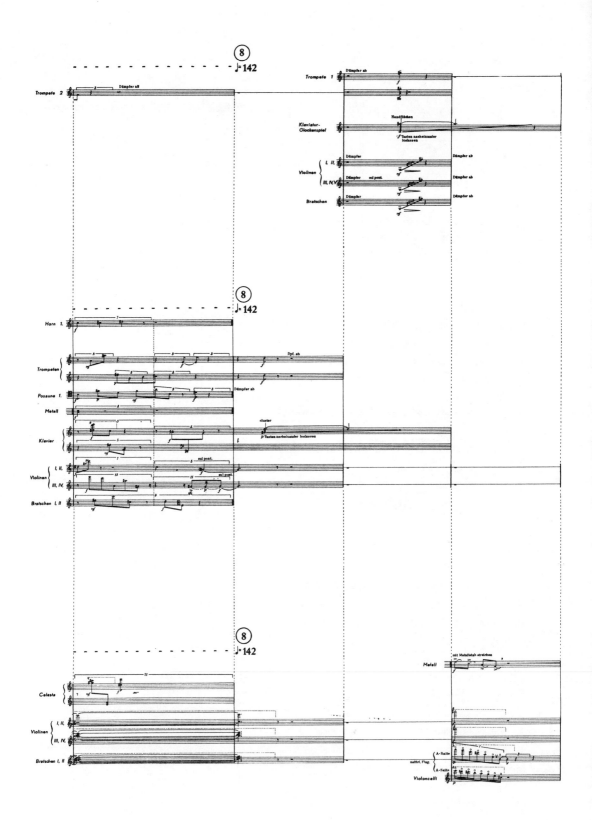

Example 26.3. (*concluded*)

Both the one and the other were accomplished. In Xenakis's *Eonta* for piano, two trumpets, and three trombones, the brass do not have fixed positions on the platform. At the outset, they are hidden behind the piano (which is playing stormy music), then they move to a more visible position, from whence they start walking about the stage. Music performed like this is inevitably permeated as well by the rhythm of the players' movements.

Sergei Slonimsky's (born 1932) *Antiphones* for string quartet (1968) begin with the players completely disassociated in space. Only the cellist sits in the usual position; the others play offstage. By proceeding through a whole series of intermediate combinations, all the players eventually arrive at spatial "consonance" in the usual configuration of a string quartet.

In contrast, such time-space performative music-theater[2] as Stockhausen's *Ensemble* (1967), *Musik für ein Haus* (1968), *Musik für die Beethoven-Halle*,[3] and *Sternklang* (1971) had in mind an audience wandering freely among the performers, who remain in fixed positions, an audience who would perceive a continuously changing balance of sound.

Both of these tendencies—the one aiming at the utmost variability in its achievement of a non-repetitive stereophonic balance, and the other aiming at a requirement that the sounds themselves move continuously—are vividly demonstrated in Xenakis's *Terretektorh* (1966). Here the orchestra is arranged in the form of a star, with the audience situated between its points. In such a situation, the sound balance is literally an individual experience for each member of the audience, depending on where he or she is located. If one adds to this the effect of a revolving circle of sound, originating in the shifting of the music from point to point of the star, it is possible to speak of a truly *dynamic* stereophony.

In conclusion we should add that the stereophony of the 1950s and 1960s, like most of the other technical devices used by contemporary composers, was anticipated at the beginning of the century by Charles Ives. In the second movement of his Fourth Symphony (1910–1916), two[4] conductors coordinate the separate orchestral groups, which are nonsynchronic in tempo, each one playing a kaleidoscopic collage of popular music. The *Unanswered Question* (1906) also offers three streams of music that are independent in space and time: a rhythmically measured chorale in the strings, questioning phrases from a distant trumpet, and ominous replies from four flutes.

Written in the 1970s. The original Russian text has not been published.

---

2. Similar to those works of a "conceptionalistic" tendency in modern painting and sculpture intended for a single showing in a particular place at a particular time ("drawings in the sand," "self-destructive sculpture"). —A.Sch.

3. No corroborating reference to this work has been found. Perhaps Schnittke was thinking of Stockhausen's *Kurzwellen mit Beethoven* (1969). —ed.

4. Schnittke's manuscript erroneously says "three." —ed.

27

USING RHYTHM TO
OVERCOME METER (1970s)

Conflict between rhythm and meter, to a greater or lesser degree, has always characterized music. Rhythmic and dynamic syncopations whose accentuation does not coincide with the meter of a motif (giving rise at times to two simultaneous meters—one notated, the other actual) are quite typical of Mozart, Beethoven, and Brahms, who at times created additional tension by making us wait for a metrical "resolution," that moment when phrasing and meter finally coincide [see example 27.1].

The representatives of the New Viennese School took this device a step further. Not content, however, with a conflict between just two meters (one real, one notated), they strove for a musical "prose" devoid of rhythmic periodicity. Webern achieved this seeming "ametricity," or absence of meter, by a subtle interplay of intrinsically simple periodic rhythms. Let us remember that the most characteristic note value for his dodecaphonic period was the quarter-note; he generally avoided such complex groupings as the quintuplet, septuplet, and the like.

In the works of the serialists of the 1950s (Boulez, Stockhausen, Nono, Pousseur)[1] there developed a more stringent requirement that rhythm be completely independent of meter, the latter being indicated in the score as a mere convenience for synchronizing the parts (like the network of lines on a globe indicating latitude and longitude), but lacking any real rhythmic power. The principle of non-repetition, which had precluded the possibility of the appearance of a claimant to the role of "tonic," was extended by the representatives of serialism, following the example of Messiaen, to include rhythm as well, and led to the appearance of the rhythmic series. The "atonicism" of a rhythmic series is determined by two factors:

1. non-repetition of rhythmic values;
2. rhythmic and metric accents that do not coincide.

The rhythm of the percussion instruments in Stockhausen's *Kreuzspiel* (1951) can serve as the simplest example of a rhythmic series [example 27.2]. The series here consists of various groupings of sixteenths, ranging from 1 to 12.

---

1. Beyond the scope of the present essay lies an entire, vast arsenal of rhythmic devices discussed in detail by Valentina Nikolaevna Kholopova in her book *Voprosy ritma v tvorchestve kompozitorov pervoi poloviny XX veka* [Problems of Rhythm in the Creative Work of Composers of the First Half of the Twentieth Century] (Moscow: Muzyka, 1971). —A.Sch.

Example 27.1. a. Mozart, Symphony No. 40, 3rd Movement;
b. Beethoven, Piano Sonata No. 31, 2nd Movement;
c. Brahms, Quartet No. 2, 4th Movement

rhythmic modification

Example 27.2. Stockhausen, "Kreuzspiel"

When they follow each other in an unbroken succession, however, rhythmic series are inevitably transformed into rhythmic periods, notwithstanding their internal variations, because the sum of the rhythmic units always amounts to 78. These rhythmic periods of 78 ♪ or 78 ♪♪♪ dictate both the nominal meter, that is, the notated meter—which is most often 6/8 or 3/8, since 78 is divisible only by 1, 2, 3, and 6, or by 13, 26, and 39; obviously 3 and 6 are the most convenient metrical units—and also the form. Precisely as a consequence of the latter, Boulez's *Structures I* (1952) amounts to a variational chain of periods, all proportional in duration.

Nono struggled against this fatal periodicity by using rhythmic structures not derived from a tone row but based on independent successions. In his *Canciones a Guiomar* (1962–1963) [see example 27.3], he attempted to achieve continuous rhythmic renewal of the fairly neutral tonal material (a rising whole-tone scale for six sopranos and a falling one for six contraltos) by setting it out in six rhythmic rows.[2]

But the most effective method of overcoming meter proved to be dividing the bars (or the "phases," in the case of Stockhausen) or the beats within a bar into a varied number of rhythmic units (the *Formant* in Stockhausen's case, where the number of *Formanten,* or rhythmic units, may total as many as twenty-six).[3]

Not all such rhythmic units are necessarily used in the process, of course. On the basis of a rhythmic series it is possible to form groupings of values, or values with pauses between them.

---

2. [See table 27.1.] The rhythmic unit is the triple quaver. —ed.

3. For Schnittke, the term *Formant* is equal to "rhythmic unit" in "additive" values. For Stockhausen, however, a *Formant* is normally a stable basic "timbre" or "timbre unit." —ed.

Table 27.1. Six Rhythmic Rows in Nono, *Canciones a Guiomar*

1 – 5 – 13 – 25 – 13 – 5 – 1	1 – 2 – 4 – 7
1 – 2 – 4 – 7 – 4 – 2 – 1	1 – 3 – 7 – 13
1 – 4 – 10 – 19 – 10 – 4 – 1	1 – 3 – 8 – 14
1 – 3 – 8 – 14 – 8 – 3 – 1	1 – 4 – 10 – 19
1 – 3 – 7 – 13 – 7 – 3 – 1	1 – 5 – 12 – 24
1 – 5 – 12 – 24 – 12 – 5 – 1	1 – 5 – 13 – 25

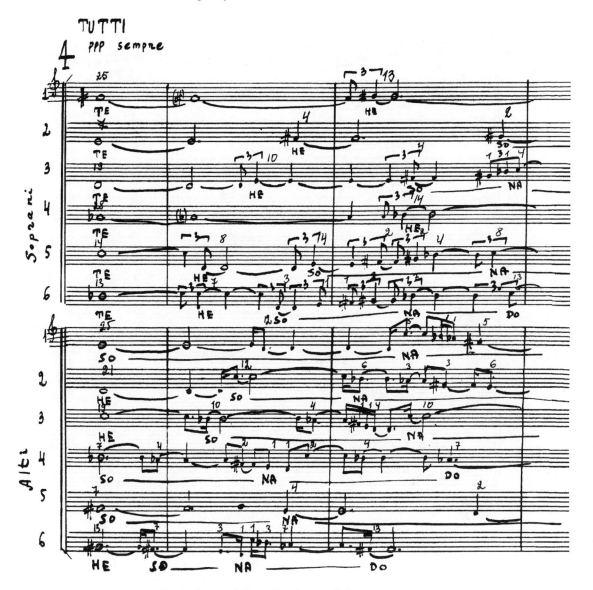

Example 27.3. Nono, *Canciones a Guiomar*

Nono and Ligeti make less "total" use of rhythms based on *Formanten* than does Stockhausen. They are content not only with fewer *Formanten* but also with the beat's being subdivided into fewer units, that is, one to six. By varying the additive values, they achieve, in the context of an "additive" polyphonic texture, the effect of "hovering" or indeterminate rhythm [see example 27.4].

Written in the 1970s. The original Russian text has not been published.

(Figures for this chapter continue through page 146)

Example 27.3. (*concluded*)

Example 27.4. Ligeti, *Lontano*

Example 27.4. (*concluded*)

CHAPTER
28

STATIC FORM

A New Conception of Time

(1970s)

The concept of "static composition" is usually linked with the works of Ligeti, such as *Atmosphères* (1961), *Volumina* (1961–1966), and *Lontano* (1967). Ligeti was the first to risk formulating a theoretical interpretation of the concept (which previously had only a negative connotation), as well as to create in his micropolyphonic scores an actual artistic representation, a musical symbol, as it were, of stasis. But stasis as a real factor had already existed in music before Ligeti and was manifested in two ways, material and conceptual:

1. By abandoning the sensation of time in music as actively "pulsating," as connected first of all with the vivid "foregrounding" of meter and metrical rhythms. By moving toward *ametricality* (the repudiation of meter, or else its subjugation), and, in general terms, by eliminating the feeling of time through deactivating the metrical rhythm or somehow neutralizing its power to activate.
2. By denying that the dynamic forward movement of form is the sole, irreversible possibility—by creating open variable forms (which permit a multiplicity of realizations) or by creating forms that in principle are static (a form of "moments").

The possibility of taking music out of time by interrupting its inherent pulse has always existed. Fermatas, accelerandos, and ritardandos, tempo rubatos, cadential ritards, all these devices of temporal instability have mitigated the periodic, thus purposeful and dynamic, motion of music.

Yet even more subtle examples of stasis than these have long been a part of music. For example, metrical accents are weakened in the adagios of Beethoven and Schubert, and there arises a melodious, flowing, seamless music whose meditative profundity captivates listeners and carries them away from any real sense of time (one has the feeling of making contact with eternity). In these same Beethoven adagios one encounters unexpected intrusions of contrasting material that interrupt the periodic flow of the form, sudden changes in tempo and prolonged pauses, which seem like stoppages of time (remember Joshua [Iisus Navin], who stopped the sun!).[1]

---

1. This is a biblical reference, to Joshua 10:13. —ed.

Thus, at opposite poles stand two factors that lead to the disruption of a sense of time:

1. the absence of formal changes and long sustained periodic rhythms;
2. unexpected formal changes and abrupt nonperiodic rhythms.

Both a highly structured approach carried to the extreme and an unstructured approach followed to the utmost will lead to the same result: the loss of a sense of time, a feeling of stasis. This stasis is not always an advantage. It may even have been unintentional, an unplanned consequence that works against the composer's conception. Such was the case in early "academic" examples of serialism (for instance, in Stockhausen's *Kreuzspiel* [1951] or Boulez's *Structures I* [1952]), where total control over all parameters and the attempt to activate them to the limit led to the loss of any organic, rational feeling for the whole—to a chaotic jumble of conflicting and mutually destructive energies, and as a consequence, to stasis from hypertension.

It was no accident that devices to counteract this overvaluation of the element of surprise rapidly began to work their way into the practice of strict serialism. Periodicity, which had run contrary to the a priori postulate of non-repetition, had been tossed out the door, only to return through the window. It reappeared in little islands here and there (although in a somewhat more complex form). Remember the vocalized syllabic articulation of the form in the instrumental movements of Boulez's *Le Marteau sans maître* (1942–1954, rev. 1957). And Stockhausen, in a new version of his early work *Punkte* (1952, rev. 1962), introduced numerous repetitions of certain bars, using these interludes to interrupt the continuous transformation of the material. In a commentary on *Punkte* written in 1964, the composer considers these repetitions precisely as "a cessation of movement, the fixing of a moment, a snapshot." Such devices as these compensate for the lost dynamics of periodicity and provide a refreshing exception to the "rule of non-repetition," thus giving direction and organizing power to the unbridled energies released by the "shattering" of metrical rhythms.

It is paradoxical that the exceedingly dynamic principle of non-repetition taken to the absolute leads to chaos, that is, to stasis, while a limited use of the principle of repetition, in itself static, relieves this stasis, creating an unforeseen sensation of organization, that is, of dynamic form.

Obviously, the creation of a closed, dynamically directed form requires a certain balance between static and dynamic elements, with preference given to the latter.

* * *

In the present essay, however, we shall not deal with that stasis which is subordinate to and highlights a sense of dynamic motion (something inherent in music), but instead with the deliberate adoption in a number of works of recent years of a form that is in itself static in principle.

The conception of an "open form" that is antidynamic in principle is expressed most consistently by Stockhausen. "Moment-form involves new relationships between the duration of a performance, the duration of a work, and the moment": this quotation serves as the heading to Stockhausen's text[2] for the musical broadcast "Endless Form" ["Die unendliche Form"], transmitted by Cologne Radio in 1960.

In his article "Erfindung und Entdeckung" [Invention and Discovery] (1961),[3] Stockhausen formulates not only a new way of treating "the moment" but also, obliquely, his conception of open form:

> As the moment-forms were being generated I tried to create states and processes in which each moment is something individual, central, that can exist independently in its own right and at the same time always in correlation with what surrounds it and with the whole; in which all the events from a definite beginning to an inevitable ending are arranged not in fixed order (the "moment" not merely being the consequence of what precedes or the cause of what follows, i.e., one element within an organic span of time), but are concentrated on the "now"—on each and every "now"—and are simultaneously manifested in vertical slices that cut across the horizontal presentation of time into a timelessness that I call eternity; an eternity that begins not at the end of time but that is attainable at any given moment.[4]

The whole is not created by a total conglomeration of events, rather each moment is the reflection of the whole, and the succession of events loses its dominant significance for the expression of an idea. Herein lies the poetic motivation for those numerous open-ended and variable forms with all their inescapable and willfully organized stasis (Stockhausen's *Momente* [1961–1972], *Zyklus* [1959], *Stimmung* [1968], and *Mixtur* [1964–1967]; Boulez's Third Piano Sonata [1955–1957] and *Improvisation sur Mallarmé I, II, III* [1957–1959]; Pousseur's *Votre Faust* [1969], *Ode* for string quartet [1960–1961], and *Caractères* [1961], etc.). There is a deepened meditative contemplation of the whole by way of its myriad reflections, rather than a particular individuality acting during a brief slice of time along one of millions of possible pathways. Thanks to the unregulated progression of events and a free application of the principle of repetition, the irreversibility of time seems to be overcome, and the possibility arises of traveling into the future and into the past, and even of existing in all time simultaneously. Beneath the outward stasis of an open-ended nonprogressive form are concealed magnetic fields of polar attractions, intersecting at every point of the form and filling it with the explosive force of compressed dynamics.

Fundamentally different premises engender static form in the case of Ligeti. His music is constructed on the total rejection of external dynamics and is presented as "music of the microworld." The most typical texture in Ligeti's orchestral works (*Apparitions* [1956–1957; orch. 1958–1959], *Atmosphères* [1961], *Lontano* [1967], and *Ramifications* [1968–1969]) is an outwardly motionless cloud of sound, a multilayered "mass" woven out of a multiplicity of noncontrasting, most often imitative polyphonic lines. The stasis arises as a consequence of the leveling influence of an abundance of homogeneous elements that could in themselves be dynamic but are

2. See "Momentform" in Karlheinz Stockhausen, *Texte zur elektronischen und instrumentalen Musik*, Vol. 1 (originally published in 1963; reprinted Cologne: M. DuMont Schauberg, 1998). —ed.

3. Stockhausen, *Texte zur elektronischen und instrumentalen Musik*, Vol. 1, pp. 222–258. —ed.

4. Stockhausen, op. cit., p. 230. —ed.

neutralized by a dogmatic, total adherence to the technique. When a canon comprises five imitating voices, they are still audible. But when there are thirty or forty of them, all that can be perceived is the global result, a dense, slowly swaying web of interweaving lines. Here the kinetic dynamics of active interplay between rhythm, timbre, and intonational gesture are replaced by the potential dynamics of the most subtle of micropolyphonic processes.

The contrasting elements that make occasional appearances among the static episodes serve not to restore formal dynamics but to discredit them in a tragically ironic way. Typically, these are abrupt rendings of the texture (Ligeti calls them *caverni*) that seem to express a ludicrously pointless hysteria, or else they are perfectly constructed bridges to nowhere. This intensifies the overall feeling of stasis (already pervaded by a furtive sense of tragedy), which is thrown even more clearly into relief by the vain attempts at generating dynamics and contrast. Only the mysterious fermentation of micropolyphonic processes or the weightless floating in time-space not subject to measurement on a metro-rhythmic scale comprehend the secret dynamics of static music.

No absolute goal can ever be achieved, including the goal of absolute musical stasis. Even Cage's piece for piano 4′33″ [1952], in which the performer merely simulates by gesticulation an imaginary music without producing a sound, even that does not achieve absolute stasis. The hearing of the audience is sharpened by their expectations, and they perceive the inevitable inadvertent noises in the concert hall (even the quietest ones) as a kind of pre-music. Even the useless, ineffectual motions of the pianist create the illusion of a kind of "non-music" not materialized in sounds.

Just as "dynamic" form is not absolute, so, too, "static" form is relative. The new concept of *musical stasis* does not mean that dynamic elements are completely eliminated and that immobility triumphs. It merely points to a changed relationship between what is static and what is dynamic—the uncovering of hidden dynamic resources when outwardly the forms and materials tend toward stasis. Neither Stockhausen, Boulez, Ligeti, nor Cage achieves absolute stasis. In the process of approaching outwardly static forms as closely as possible, they have only uncovered new inherent dynamics.

Written in the 1970s. The original Russian text has not been published.

PARADOX AS A FEATURE OF
STRAVINSKY'S MUSICAL LOGIC (1973)

I. Works from the 1920s and 1930s

A study of Stravinsky's creative output reveals two seeming contradictions: the first is immediately obvious, the second more obscure but closely linked with the first. The first hits one in the eyes: it is the inexplicable absence of stylistic consistency in his music. Closer analysis reveals the second: the paradoxical character of his musical ideas, the way he turns the unexpected into the normal.

The first contradiction has been dismissed quite convincingly by the French writer Michel Butor. In his essay "La musique, art réaliste,"[1] in which he refers to a classification of musical materials (*couleurs* [colors]) based on the way they affect the listener, he writes of the "geographical" and "historical" coloration of Stravinsky's works. Stravinsky, according to Butor, uses elements of musical styles from the past along with folk-music intonations, modulating "from one exotic coloration to another, from one historical coloration to another, just as in a classical sonata one can modulate from one key to another."

This idea of Butor's renders the first contradiction illusory. The entire tortuous path followed by a mind that seems so inconsistent is revealed (if one takes an eagle's-eye view) to be the consequence of a single creative method, the quickest and most logical way to encompass the musical space of past and present from various directions. Particularly valuable here is the idea that Stravinsky's method extended the use of folklore even into the musical language of European classicism. It follows from this perspective alone that the word "stylization" is not applicable to the music of Stravinsky.

In light of Butor's argument, therefore, Stravinsky's development is shown to be consistent and *fully integrated*. No rupture occurred between the "Russian" and the "neoclassical" stages, no surrender to the fashionable trend of serialism, simply an assimilation and reworking of different musical dialects.

But all the same, a qualitative leap was made, and it occurred in the middle of the "Russian period," sometime between *The Rite of Spring* [*Vesna sviashchennaia/Le Sacre du printemps*] (1912–1913) and *The Wedding* [*Svadebka/Les Noces*] (1914–1917, 1923). Arguments against this based on chronology carry no weight: true, the opera *The*

---

1. The essay "La musique, art réaliste" appeared in Michel Butor, *Répertoire II* (Paris: Editions de Minuit, 1964). —ed.

Nightingale [*Solovei/Le Rossignol*] was completed in 1914, but it was started in 1908. The starting point in a Stravinsky work, generally speaking, is far more significant than the ending point. If we place the works near the "turning point" in the order in which the composer started them, we are able to investigate how the changes occurred, where that turning point took place. In this perspective, the turning point turns out to be less a change of direction than a logical continuation along the same path:

> *The Nightingale* [*Solovei/Le Rossignol*]—1908
> *The Firebird* [*Zhar-ptitsa / L'Oiseau de feu*]—1909
> *Petrushka/Pétrouchka*—1910
> *The Rite of Spring* [*Vesna sviashchennaia/Le Sacre du printemps*]—1911
> *The Wedding* [*Svadebka/Les Noces*]—1914
> *Renard/Baika*—1915
> *L'Histoire du soldat*—1918

Superficially, the turning point may be described as an abrupt change in technical resources, accompanied by a clear rejection of the intoxicating clamor of a large orchestra with its multilayered timbre and harmony, and a turn toward the restrained and efficient linearity of a small instrumental ensemble. But the roots of this change go much deeper: they may be found, in Stravinsky's own words, in a change in his "poetics of music."

(*N.B. Clearly one should regard "poetics" not as aesthetics or technique, but as the point at which these two intersect, the manner in which technique is conditioned by aesthetics, something like "the aesthetics of technique" or the "technique of aesthetics." —A.Sch.*)

Since all of Stravinsky's most important works of the period of the turning point are connected with the theater, the change in his poetics of music is seen most clearly in the change in his attitude toward the theater.

Stravinsky's theater in the period before the turning point is the theater of realism (albeit with elements of symbolism). It is realistic in the way it gives expression to the action and the characters, even if these also involve concealed symbolic meanings. *Firebird*, the *Rite*, and *Petrushka* all continue and develop the tradition of Russian fantastic fairy-tale opera (here, transformed into ballet). The principles of realism are operative: the musical characterizations are portraits of the dramatis personae, and the musical atmosphere is descriptive of landscape—in a word, musical *imagery*. After the turning point, the situation changes: now the musical characterizations are masks, and the atmosphere is created by decorative means—in a word, musical *symbols*. The latter is the theater of *convention*. Some of its features had already appeared earlier in the symbolic quality of characters, the way their psychology was portrayed in a non-individualized manner (such are the characters of the "Firebird," "Petrushka," and the "Moor," as well as numerous others).

Remember the *Golden Cockerel* [*Zolotoi petushok*]:

Pered vami v staroi skazke	Before your eyes in this old fable
Ozhivut smeshnye maski.	Comic masks shall spring to life.

Tol'ko ia lish' da Tsaritsa	Yea, I alone, and the Tsaritsa,
Byli zdes' zhivye litsa.	Were living people here.
Ostal'noe—tlen, mechta.	All the others, debris and daydream,
Prizrak blednyi, pustota . . .	Pallid specter, barrenness . . .

One can fairly say that the whole of Stravinsky "took off" from Rimsky-Korsakov's *The Golden Cockerel* (1907) and his *Kashchei the Immortal* [*Kashchei bessmertnyi*] (1902), however much Stravinsky himself might deny it. The parallels between *Petrushka* and the *Golden Cockerel* are obvious: both Petrushka and the Astrologer come to life threateningly "as the curtain falls," as if to prophesy some kind of retribution. The "Chizhik" ["Birdie"] song in the *Golden Cockerel* anticipates the "street" music in *Petrushka*, and so on. But much more important is the fact that, as we can see, the future Stravinsky is to be found here—the composer of *Renard*, *Histoire du soldat*, *Mavra* (1921–1922), as well as other later works.

In Stravinsky's music for the theater in the "pre-turning-point" period, music was a component of a *tautological* spectacle; it doubled everything—action, atmosphere, events, and characters. In the "post-turning-point" works, the music becomes a component of a *contrapuntal* spectacle—it makes no attempt to provide a complete picture of the characters and the action. In the stylized theater, the theater of convention, just a few musical signs suffice: the contour of the "object," a symbol, its *hieroglyph*.[2] We no longer encounter that sonorous spaciousness found in the *Rite*, that boldly authentic characterization of actors and puppets found in *Petrushka*. We return to the theater of Shakespeare. Instead of a musical picture of the "Underworld" in *Orpheus/Orphée* (1947), we are given a musical *illumination*, a *diagram*.

Not only are the objects and characters now described in symbolic terms, so too are the events and actions. The conventional symbol, the hieroglyph, merely expresses the idea, the *meaning* of what is happening, but does not pretend to create the illusion of a real event. Such a method is psychologically more subtle, and more economical from a directorial point of view. The listener, having been given a musical cue, senses in advance what is going to happen. The composer, the performer, and the director merely present the audience with a problem involving character and/or situation, while the actual resolution of the problem depends on the individual viewpoint of each audience member. The audience member is thus presented not with just one solution of the problem on stage, but instead with a challenge, a summons to solve the problem in his or her own emotional imagination. The level of audience participation is raised. The audience member experiences not just the emotion experienced and enacted by the composer and the performers (which remains *secondhand*, no matter how powerful) but also an emotional stimulus to experience it *firsthand*. Thus, the emotional cogency of the work is not reduced but, on the contrary, enhanced. The actual *situation* on stage becomes tragic in its own right, not merely the emotional *gesture* of something experienced by the com-

---

2. In this instance we are not using Plekhanov's theory of the hieroglyph as the starting point. In the Soviet period this was harshly criticized. —A.Sch.

poser. The subjective tragic nature of the *experience* is supplanted by the objective tragic nature of the *presentation*.

A poetics such as this also, quite naturally, required a different treatment of the musical material. What was needed here was not a musical language of *experience* (independent of the time period of the subject matter) but a musical language of *depiction* (of necessity connected with the musical topics of the era being depicted). Today, one cannot compose something *living* in the musical language of the eighteenth century (without setting oneself some sort of specialized task); to try this would inevitably lead to dead stylization, a corpse galvanized into life. But one can compose in a contemporary language, imparting archaic attributes to contemporary intonations; or, conversely, one can compose in an "antiquated" language, but follow a contemporary developmental logic. The resulting musical logic will inevitably involve a sense of *paradox* because it no longer falls within the framework of a single style or a single era.

Since this paradoxical musical logic is an organic quality of mind, not merely the expression of a conscious artistic purpose, it becomes for Stravinsky not the exterior trappings of a work but its *driving principle* and permeates every dimension of its compositional technique, even the technique of orchestral voice-leading. We should note at once that in Stravinsky's works the degree of this "paradoxicality" develops *in depth*, from composition to composition. At the beginning of the "neoclassical period" we can still differentiate between the contradictory elements. Listening to *Pulcinella* (1919–1920), we are able to decide mentally, "This is a genuine melody by Pergolesi, whereas this is Stravinsky's contradictory harmonization" [see example 29.1].

But in *Orpheus*, for example, the blend of what is paradoxical, its *organic constitution*, has reached such a high level that we can no longer detect the bonding between the elements. Now we have a new style, which opens the music to a new

Example 29.1. Stravinsky, *Pulcinella*, Part I (Sinfonia)

formal logic, the logic of a consistent, artistically controlled a-logicality. An organic synthesis of opposing stylistic resources is achieved. Now the paradoxical quality is imperceptible: no point of logical contradiction can be detected. Stravinsky loves to balance precisely on this knife-edge between the logical and the absurd, between the "old" and the "new," between "truth" and "deception."

Let us investigate this in a number of works, beginning with the concert suite from *Pulcinella*. Outwardly everything is "as it was in the eighteenth century"—the instrumentation (pairs of woodwinds without clarinet, string quintet *concertino* and string quintet *ripieno* "alla concerto grosso"); the genre designations and forms (a suite comprising a Sinfonia, Serenata, Scherzino, Tarantella, Toccata, Gavotta, Duetto, Minuetto, and Finale); and the harmonic/melodic language (diatonic, the absence of "fully realized" chords, instrumental independence, periods dutifully marked by cadential punctuation, trills, an emphasis on the "conventional types" of melodic motion—scales, arpeggios, etc). But a close study of detail reveals the full duplicity of this *baròcco*. (Here it is relevant to recall the Spanish portraits of Picasso in his late period, in which everything seems to be as it was in the sixteenth century— camisole, lace, beard, and the like, but you suddenly discover that the nose "works" both in profile and frontally, the eyes are asymmetrical, the lace of the jabot is barbed wire disguised....) In Stravinsky's score, what is revealed above all is the mystifying nature of the polyphony, or what appears to be its polyphony. It turns out that a basic precept of eighteenth-century harmonization is broken, a precept not only of the eighteenth century: the rule of independent voice-leading that forbids parallel octaves and unisons. In this score we meet them at every turn:

1. At cadences, a coming together at the octave or the unison of parts that were previously independent [see example 29.2]. Something similar can be found in classical voice-leading when "parallel octaves" occur at the moment of resolution to a fundamental tonic. But in the example cited, the practice extends back to an earlier moment in the form.

2. Stravinsky also uses this "loophole" in traditional harmonization the other way round: if parallels are permissible at the cadence, then why not at the beginning of a phrase? [See example 29.3.]

Example 29.2. *Pulcinella*, Part I (Sinfonia)

Example 29.3. *Pulcinella*, Part VI (Gavotta)

3. Finally, if parallels are permissible at the beginning and the end, why not use
them to emphasize all the important turns of melody? And so a parallel
variant of the melody appears [example 29.4].

Example 29.4. *Pulcinella*, Part III (Scherzino)

By elaborating on particular exceptions to what was not allowed by the "rules"
of classical voice-leading, Stravinsky arms himself with an immense arsenal of
pseudo-classical devices. He even adapts for his needs the superposition of dissonant figuration above a harmonic foundation [example 29.5]. Or else he makes
paradoxical use of a pedal point: for example, the tonic-third dyad becomes a pedal
point (which, of course, was anticipated by Beethoven in the Finale of the Ninth
Symphony, and even earlier by D. Scarlatti).

Still more daring, the tonic and its ninth appear as a pedal point, only to reveal
themselves a bar and a half later [example 29.6] as suspensions to the dominant third
and fifth.

Example 29.5. *Pulcinella,* Part III (Scherzino)

The "taste" for the second in eighteenth-century music (as a suspension or a passing note, and such) is subtly capitalized on by Stravinsky in the *Duetto.* Here, the deliberately dissonant seconds in the brass create the illusion of certain unprepared suspensions that materialize and then resolve. But there *are* no suspensions. What we have are freely appearing seconds that then *seem* to be resolved. In reality, they are nothing more than bait for the listener, who bites with alacrity, imagining himself to be in the world of the musical *Baròcco* [example 29.7].

Sometimes, for the sake of complete authenticity, he imitates the playing of natural horns either (1) by means of intentionally awkward voice-leading, (2) by

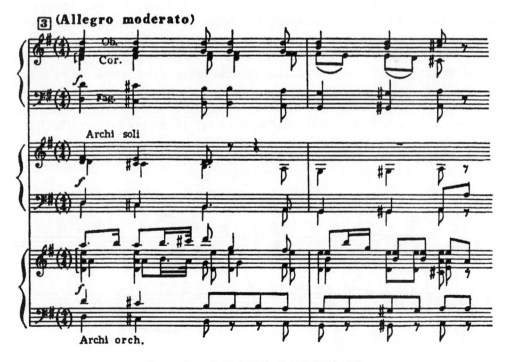

Example 29.6. *Pulcinella,* Part I (Sinfonia)

Example 29.7. *Pulcinella*, Part VII (Duet)

taking away a segment of the theme from the French horns (which are being treated as if they were natural horns that "cannot play" a passage) and transferring the segment temporarily to the bassoons [see example 29.8], the instruments most closely related in timbre to natural horns, or (3) by means of a deliberate orchestrational imbalance in chordal voicing: two French horns along with two non-doubling oboes "with equal rights" play four-note chords *forte* ("in the eighteenth century, the coordination of dynamics between instrumental groups was unknown"; moreover "in the eighteenth century natural horns sounded less resonant...").

A favorite device of Stravinsky's requires special attention—his cryptic voice-leading, his abstruse textural strategy. Often the polyphonic basis of the texture is so unstable that it is impossible to distinguish between the main contrapuntal voices and their variants (the opening bars of *Pulcinella*, already cited, exemplify this).

Speaking generally, the technical approach in *Pulcinella* is that of *pseudo-stylization*. It is not yet the illusive paradoxical neoclassicism of the *Symphony of Psalms* or the *Symphony in C*. In *Pulcinella*, we can still draw the line between those elements involving classic stylization and those characteristic of mature neoclassicism. The synthesis of what is "alien" and what is "his own" is still not organic. But to find where one ends and the other begins in *Apollo* is much more difficult. Here the stylized "substance" is far more complex. It is not simply "in the old style," but "in

Example 29.8. *Pulcinella*, Part I (Sinfonia)

the old style through the eyes of Tchaikovsky" (the seventeenth century viewed through the prism of Tchaikovsky's *Serenade for Strings*, Opus 48)—in other words, a three-fold mystification. The first impression is of the ballet theater of the time of Lully, with its classical subject and typical instrumental ensemble ("[les] vingt-quatre violons du roi"). But on closer inspection we discover a swan ballet in the style of an elegant *pastorale* at the Maryinsky Theater. Finally, we perceive the shadow of the all-controlling Puppet-Master looming over the stage; then we realize that it is nothing more than a puppet ballet being staged for today.

This "temporal three-dimensionality" of the music is achieved by a similarly paradoxical musical logic: the traditional musical components interact here in a completely unexpected way. In the very first bar of the prologue [see example 29.9], an intonational "deception" lies in wait for us: a cadential trill on the leading tone—rounded off with a *Nachschlag*—never resolves but is left hanging in the air.

It is instructive to note that straightaway in the first five bars, Stravinsky sets up for himself the widest range of possibilities. Bar by bar and note by note, he "allows himself more and more": an unresolved cadence gives him the right in the second bar to make free use of diatonic dissonances (non-tertian harmonies). The next move in the fourth bar involves the appearance of a chromatic dissonance (an augmented octave treated as a suspension to the root of a V_3^4 chord).

Only one thing remains, to undermine the tonality, and this happens in the fifth bar. Such is the merciless and dogged power of Stravinsky's paradoxical logic. Having bared his teeth, he can do what he wants. He may pretend to be diatonically meek and mild, decently four-square, but we won't forget with whom we are dealing, and all the while we'll accept any sort of tonal shock as right and proper. Then in the finale, when he forswears the shocks, we take it as somehow uplifting and noble.

Example 29.9. Stravinsky, *Apollo Musagetes*, Prologue

Example 29.10. *Apollo Musagetes,* Prologue

Many more logical "sallies" lie ahead! In the very middle of the prologue an unrealized sonata allegro suddenly appears (vaguely recalling the "sonatina" in Tchaikovsky's *Serenade for Strings,* not because the material is similar, but because it functions similarly: a burst of activity after a slow introduction). But the two traditional contrasting subjects ("an energetic main theme and a *cantabile* subordinate one") crumble away in our grasp, because of their structural infirmity—pseudo-themes, a pseudo-sonata. The voice-leading, too, is pseudo: the faithful bass line, solidly underpinning the key and supporting the melodic voices as it strides along broken triads, arrives at the cadence, where it should fully reveal its functionality, only to limp feebly off course in the most confusing manner [see example 29.10].

It is only natural that after such a display of weakness, a second claimant should appear, making short sharp attacks [see example 29.11]. Two bass lines are often

Example 29.11. *Apollo Musagetes,* Prologue

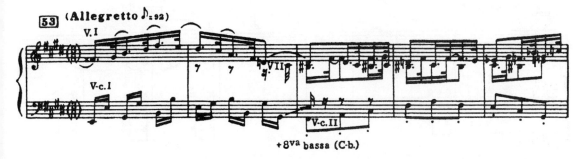

Example 29.12. *Apollo Musagetes,* Terpsichore Variation

encountered in Stravinsky's scores, most frequently an ostinato bass and a real one. The appearance of a usurper, as above, is a common tactic. One of the composer's favorite tricks is to introduce a quasi two-voice texture that is inevitably discredited, either psychologically (when a *single* character sings in *two* voices, as do the Cockerel and the Fox in *Renard,* or as does God in *The Flood,* so perfect that He has two voices) or simply as a consequence of the unstable, illusory quality of the two-part passage itself [see example 29.12].

The discrediting of what was apparently planned as a logical process, the leading of a developmental process into confusion and absurdity, these are cultivated by Stravinsky quite consciously. Take the cozy second theme (owing something to Vienna and Strauss) of Apollo's Variation: without lasting for even five bars it skids off track and gets tangled up in "almost tonal" and "almost metrical" manipulations. Its attempt at rehabilitation in the second statement—a feeble repetition of the opening two bars a semitone higher, then a final stop—fails miserably. The development reaches a dead end, calculated ahead of time, of course. The situation can be salvaged only by an ostentatious gesture: the elaborate violin cadenza ("Never fear, all this was planned in advance"). [See example 29.13.]

Example 29.13. *Apollo Musagetes,* Apollo's Variation

Example 29.14. *Apollo Musagetes,* Pas d'action

Then yet another pseudo-classical pose is taken, *un pas d'action.* A very promising theme à la Tchaikovsky goes sour without having been developed properly. Its accompaniment, in a most delicate rhythm, is harmonized most indelicately, far "past" the theme. Meanwhile, a decorous ostinato based on the certitude of a tonic triad, automatically allows the violas to preserve an unruffled air of propriety, despite what is happening all around them [see example 29.14].

The device of making the tonic triad into a pedal point is also encountered later on in the ballet score [see example 29.15]. It would be absurd in every similar case to create a new norm of musical language, as if to say, "Just see what an iron rule the composer has followed intuitively in this apparently illogical music." Stravinsky consciously veers away from the possibility ever of turning these technical devices (in the examples cited) into a formula. All this has a psychological motivation, but it is deliberately not fitted into a technological system.

He also discredits polyphonic devices. In the section "Apollo and the Muses" we unexpectedly encounter a "total" canon: two voices in turn state the theme, then a third presents the theme in augmentation, and a fourth in diminution. The latter treatment (i.e., the theme in diminution) is completely symptomatic: the theme now becomes figuration, thus effectively discrediting it. A closer look also reveals the

Example 29.15. *Apollo Musagetes,* Pas de deux

Example 29.16. *Apollo Musagetes*, Pas d'action

theme as antipolyphonic: it comprises pitches arranged along a tonic triad with an added sixth. The sonorities that result from combining the various versions of the theme are inert and uninteresting: quasi-polyphony, a quasi-canon, and a quasi-theme [see example 29.16].

Stravinsky makes wide use of this technique of pseudo-polyphony in all kinds of linking "gambits" based on the conventional routines of transition between structural units that have more clearly individualized thematic content. Generally they focus attention on an approaching recapitulation, structural climax, or coda. Very often they appear as scalar motion at different speeds in the same direction [see examples 29.17, 29.18, 29.19].

Example 29.17. *Apollo Musagetes*, Polymnia Variation

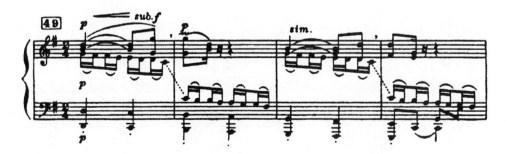

Example 29.18. *Apollo Musagetes*, Polymnia Variation

Example 29.19. *Apollo Musagetes*, Apollo's Variation

In such cases, momentary inadvertent "parallelism" between voices moving in the same direction at different speeds is inevitable. This cannot be heard; moreover, it is also evident in music of the classical era.

The "negotiable space" between a one- and a two-voice texture opens up great possibilities for tricks of harmonization. Along with the unstable two-voice texture already examined (which strives to move "back" into one voice; see example 29.12), we also encounter an unstable one-voice line "pregnant" with two voices. Rarely are these "glimmers" a genuine two-voice texture, but merely the illusion of such. Just one voice, not two, but with its shadow running on ahead [example 29.20]; or perhaps a single voice with a "shadow" cast over its "purity" [example 29.21].

Example 29.20. *Apollo Musagetes*, Coda

Example 29.21. *Apollo Musagetes,* Coda

You can never take Stravinsky's word for anything, even when he calls a work *Symphony in C.* In this work everything possible is done to discredit C and C major. Even in the introduction, the oft-repeated leading tone B, stated powerfully in unison octaves, challenges C. C, in fact, rarely appears in the symphony (either in the themes or in the harmony); it is envisaged, but not actually there. The introductory B for good reason acquires the significance of dominant precursor to E. In fact, the E embedded in C begins to control the tonal structure of the symphony. The E appears continuously in the bass, not only in the exposition of the principal theme, for example, but even in the final chords of the first and last movements. Here, Stravinsky reminds us of Tchaikovsky's characteristic use of the tonic with an added sixth before a final unison, but turned around the other way (the sixth, C, above the bass note E is in fact the root of the basic tonality) [examples 29.22, 29.23, and 29.24].

Example 29.22. Tchaikovsky, *Francesca da Rimini* (ending)

Example 29.23. *Symphony in C,* 1st Movement (final chords)

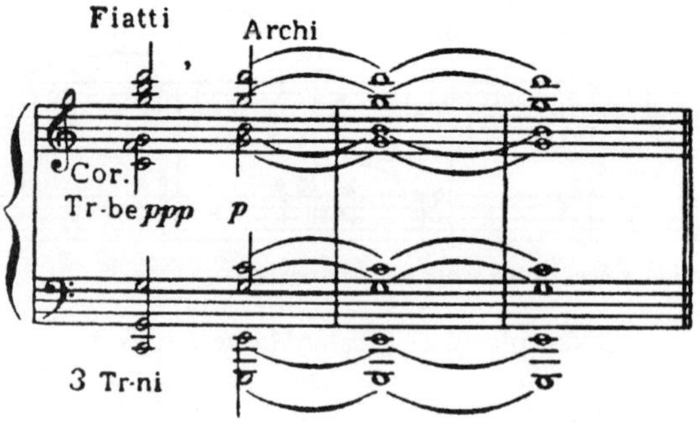
Fiatti
Archi
Cor.
Tr-be ppp
p
3 Tr-ni

Example 29.24. *Symphony in C*, 4th Movement

In this C "stricken by flux," everything becomes duplicitous: the classical dominant–tonic relationship of B and E is treated as an internal event in C major. C major itself is presented not head-on but somehow sideways, or more precisely from the inside out (through E minor). We have what appears, therefore, to be a classical intention fundamentally undermined by an inner paradox. Having expressed a literal preference "in words" for a tonality, Stravinsky accentuates not its tonic quality, but rather its powerful anti-tonic qualities: a quasi-tonic, a quasi-tonality.

Still and all, everything is "like the Viennese classics"—the development, the external ornamentation, the instrumental complement. Before the second section, for instance, one even encounters the hint of a dominant of the dominant, following all the rules: a stern Beethoven-style orchestral *all'unisono* sounds a trumpet-like octave D that heralds G major. But this octave bombast is a fake. Instead of G major, its antipode—F major—appears. But not for long, of course. Toward the end of the exposition, F major slips down into E major (the clandestine tonic of the symphony). The development begins from this obviously unstable and problematical starting point ("a tonality far removed from C major!"). A genuine, meticulous thematic development follows, but with its whole meaning undermined by the deliberate absence of tonal tension. Pseudo-instability. Pseudo-development. The very formal process of a sonata allegro is thus discredited, and doubt cast not merely on the "C" but also on the "Symphony."

The second movement also conceals traps for unwary listeners. Sometimes they are teased by a two-voiced thematic chameleon that keeps changing in timbre (sometimes from note to note!). [See example 29.25.] Sometimes they are tormented

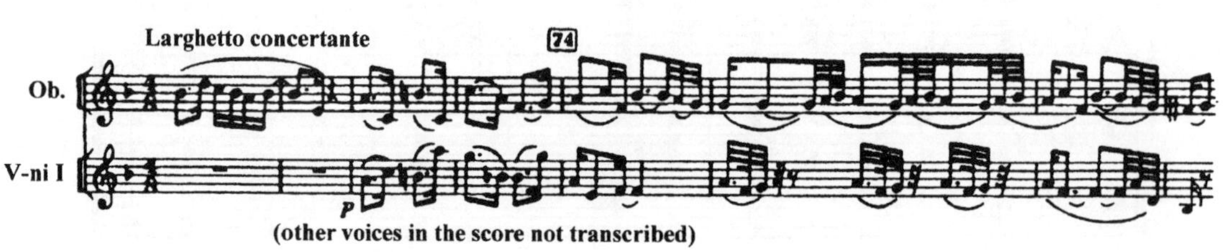
Larghetto concertante
74
Ob.
V-ni I
p
(other voices in the score not transcribed)

Example 29.25. *Symphony in C*, 2nd Movement

(other voices in the score not transcribed)

Example 29.26. *Symphony in C*, 2nd Movement

by the effort to remember where these brilliant, quasi-pianoforte passages for flute and clarinet originated: "Surely there has been something like this earlier." But there hasn't! This is an invention of Stravinsky: he has transferred to the orchestra an actual bit of brilliant pianistic passagework à la Weber [see example 29.26].

Typical practices in contemporary composition also acquire an ironic sense in Stravinsky, polytonality for instance, which is frequently cast into doubt. If one compares the trumpet and French horn parts in the second thematic element of the third movement, it becomes clear that there would be no polytonality if French horns and trumpets played in the same key. "Maybe the polytonality is the result of a mistake in transposition?" This is the logical, if erroneous, conclusion one is inclined to draw from looking at the score. The idea is even supported by the fact that as soon as the feeling of polytonality is overcome (that is, "the mistake is corrected"), this particular thematic element actually disappears (not counting two brief reminders at the start of the reprise and in the coda) [see example 29.27].

But this "game with transposing instruments" is not over. A four-note ostinato bass supports an imitative neoclassical coda, the entries oddly skewed by their polytonal setting [example 29.28]. Yet even this polytonality raises doubts ("Is it not true that in olden times they used horns and trumpets of different pitches in the same composition? Probably these ought to sound in the same key...").

One finds the same sort of playfulness with the conventions of modern and old-fashioned score-writing in other Stravinsky works as well. For instance, in the Polka

Example 29.27. *Symphony in C*, 3rd Movement

Example 29.28. *Symphony in C*, 3rd Movement

from the Suite No. 2 for small orchestra, "polytonality results from a mistake in transposition: the trumpet should be in B-flat, not in C, the clarinet in A, not B-flat—then everything would sound just fine" [see example 29.29].

Returning to the *Symphony in C*, the listener on hearing the first three notes of the finale (fourth movement) may have the wild idea "Isn't this the beginning of Tchaikovsky's Sixth Symphony?" [See example 29.30.]

The composer's psychological calculation is cunningly precise: the final bars of the first movement have already prompted the listener into subconscious memories of *Francesca da Rimini* and "Zimnie gryozy" ("Winter Daydreams," the subtitle of Tchaikovsky's First Symphony), but these were immediately swamped by an abun-

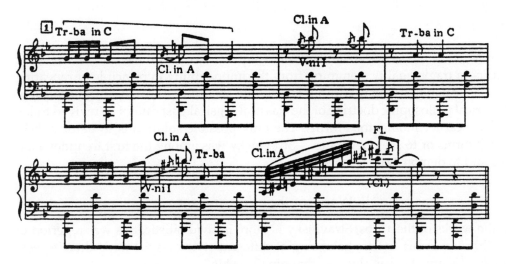

Example 29.29. Stravinsky, Suite No. 2, Polka

dance of new impressions. Now suddenly we seem to hear the bassoon introduction to the first movement of the *Pathétique* (Tchaikovsky's Sixth Symphony), but for some reason, here it is at the beginning of the last movement of the Stravinsky. True, but then a bassoon also plays a little further on in the Tchaikovsky (a different one!). We are shocked. We lose track of time, unsure of the hour, the day, the date. We even have doubts about the month and year. But Stravinsky is subtle and inscrutable: having momentarily stunned us with a crazy analogy, he has now moved far away from his mischievous hint: "The two bassoons are playing their duet so seriously and calmly, we were surely mistaken!"

The finale proper begins: "an active, energetic, purposeful theme...." But where is it going? When, after all the peripatetics, it returns at the reprise (at long last we hear a theme in C major!), the appearance of the introductory *all'unisono* B from the first movement effectively devitalizes this "active" theme and, after a brief one-bar struggle, it gives way without the slightest hint of tragedy to the main theme of the first movement. And so the last movement ends. C is simply not reached, thanks to the opposition of the fatal B. The irony of both the formal conception ("Symphony") and the tonal conception ("in C") is obvious: this is only the shell of a symphony, filled with surrogate thematic and tonal development. A quasi-symphony. A quasi-tonality.

Example 29.30. *Symphony in C*, 4th Movement (beginning)

So now we begin to understand all the oblique tragedy, as it were, of Stravinsky's music—a tragic quality stemming from the impossibility in principle of repeating the classical models today without falling into absurdity. The naive profundity and rhetorical philosophic doctrine of the classical musical past cannot be revived today in their earlier momentous forms. The only possible solution is to parody these grand forms or to seek new ones.... Stravinsky was among the first to understand this and to demonstrate it to us.

II. Works of the 1940s and 1950s[3]

In the works of the 1940s, Stravinsky is more individualistic: this was a period of equilibrium in his tireless balancing of different styles. As we have already seen, before this time he was always "changing his skin":

1. the Russian "painterly" period (*Firebird, Petrushka, The Rite of Spring*);
2. the Russian "graphic" period (*Renard, Les Noces, Histoire du soldat*);
3. the period of neoclassicism (starting with *Pulcinella*).[4]

The neoclassicist "coefficient" of works in the "third manner" also varies. Some are out-and-out personifications (*Pulcinella* and *The Fairy's Kiss/Le Baiser de la fée* are constructed wholly on quoted material). Others have general stylistic features of one or another period of music history (*The Symphony of Psalms* and *Oedipus Rex* have no direct sources but are still obviously archaic in style). A third category represents a complex and indivisible synthesis of characteristics from various "times" and styles (e.g., *Apollo/Apollon*, the *Symphony in C*, the *Concerto for Piano and Wind Instruments*, and the like).

The works from the third category are especially original, thanks to the almost surrealistic mixture of times incidentally remembered from music history or more precisely the simultaneity of these times: on the "Mount Olympus of Music," Haydn can meet Tchaikovsky, Vivaldi can meet Weber, and Handel can meet Rimsky-Korsakov.

Certainly the organic nature of this stylistic interpenetration in the works of Stravinsky continuously developed, reaching a crest in the 1940s. If in *Pulcinella* we saw Pergolesi through the eyes of Stravinsky, then in *Oedipus* we saw the ancient

---

3. In the published Russian version of this essay, the numbering of musical examples for Part II begins with example 1. In the present edition, the numbering sequence from Part I continues through Part II; thus the original example 1 for Part II corresponds to example 29.31, below. —ed.

4. We remind the reader that this periodization of Stravinsky's work is a convention: it involves only his outward *re*-incarnation, not his inner immutable essence, not a re-*incarnation*. Moreover, the features of preceding periods were sometimes preserved and revived in later works (e.g., the obvious reminiscences of the Russian period in *Mavra* and even in still later works, all the way to *Orpheus*). And vice versa, devices used in the later styles are anticipated earlier (e.g., certain features of neoclassicism in *Renard* and *L'Histoire du soldat*). —A.Sch.

world as imagined by Monteverdi through the eyes of Stravinsky, and in *Apollo*, antiquity as imagined by Lully expressed in the manner of Tchaikovsky—who surely anticipated neoclassicism in his *Serenade for Strings, Variations on a Rococo Theme,* and *Queen of Spades* [*Pikovaia dama*]—all through the eyes of Stravinsky, and so on. In the end, the number of mutually interpenetrating and "interweaving" shades of great composers increased so much that one can only rarely recognize them in an instant. The only one who remains recognizable is "Woland," who leads the "Ball."[5] Try, if you will, to define the stylistic pedigree of *Orpheus* or the *Symphony in Three Movements*: in every bar we find Stravinsky, in every bar neoclassicism. But the source model cannot be identified!

Once having pondered the problem, you may be surprised to realize that, in essence, you have raised the question of the existence of an independent Stravinsky who possesses a distinctive "script" of his own, unrelated to anyone else's. Does this imply that the whole of the composer's previous forty-year career (indisputably great) turns out to be nothing more than a prolonged search for an individual style? But then you recall the undeniable individuality of all his earlier work, literally of every bar in it.[6] Clearly this is a phenomenal instance of development in reverse: a movement from the general to the individual (contrary to Thomas Mann's notion in *Joseph and His Brothers* [*Joseph und seine Brüder*] about the development of an individual identity, from what is a subjectively individual and particularized position toward one that is objectively individual, a movement away from opposing oneself to the world to one of blending with it).

Stravinsky's presence in universal time, this shimmering subtlety of style, could not have been more suited to the eternal subject of the ballet *Orpheus* (1947). This music breathes a profusion of stylistic associations: the archaic diatonicism of the few ancient chants known to us (e.g., the Introduction and the Finale); the somewhat cool and monumental decorative conventions of the operas of Monteverdi and Gluck, likewise of Berlioz's vocal-symphonic pictures (the scenes depicting Orpheus in Hades, e.g., the "Dance of the Angel of Death" and the Interlude from Scene 1 and the Interlude from Scene 2); the agitato *dansant* of the ballets, operas, and even the symphonies of Tchaikovsky and Prokofiev (e.g., the "Air de Danse" from Scene 1 and the "Pas des Furies" from Scene 2); the "endless" *lamento* of the mournful Bach-like arias (e.g., the "Air de Danse" from Scene 2); the Ravel-like choirs of strings (e.g., the Introduction, the "Pas des Furies," the Interlude, and Orpheus's second "Air de Danse" from Scene 2). These associations are inevitably subjective for the listener (one person will remember one thing, someone else another), but also inevitably they are extremely varied and irreducible to any single stylistic tendency.

The compositional methods used by Stravinsky are just as varied. We hear nonfunctional "white-note" diatonicism (e.g., the Prologue and the Epilogue; the "Pas d'Action" when Eurydice is returned, from Scene 2), functional triads and seventh chords (predominating in all the ballet numbers), parallel diatonic and

---

5. Woland, identified as the Devil, from Mikhail Bulgakov's novel *The Master and Margarita* [*Master i Margarita*], an enormously popular work in Russia since the late 1960s. —ed.

6. With all its stylistic heterogeneity, the *Rite* represents the peak of the composer's creative output and his most characteristic work. —A.Sch.

chromatic chord successions (e.g., the Prologue and the Epilogue; the middle section of the "Air de Danse" from Scene 1; the "Pas des Furies," the Interlude, and Orpheus's second "Air de Danse" from Scene 2), free linear polyphony (e.g., the "Pas de Deux" from Scene 2), and we even encounter clearly realized serialism (e.g., the "Pas d'Action" with the Bacchantes from Scene 2 is almost entirely constructed on the basis of a microseries of three pitches).[7] But all these devices, most of them quite traditional (even academic at the time the ballet was composed in 1947), are individualized by Stravinsky, revivified by the "living water" of his genius. How does he do it?

Polyfunctionality, Polytonality

Triads and seventh chords give the music of *Orpheus* a classical "cleanliness" and "regularity" of expression, but they acquire a new power as a consequence of their polyfunctional superpositioning, in connection with which the chord changes in the various layers of the musical texture are not synchronized. A variety of typical polyfunctional techniques may be found:

1. A lack of functional correspondence between the bass and the upper voices of the harmony, which is often expressed in the use of two "polar" functions simultaneously, for example dominant harmony above a bass line in the tonic (this undoubtedly stemmed from the traditional pedal point and ostinato, which often created bifunctionality). [See examples 29.31 and 29.32.]

Example 29.31. Stravinsky, *Orpheus*, Scene 1

Example 29.32. *Orpheus*, Pas de Deux

---

7. For an analysis of this episode, see Yurii Kholopov, "Nabliudeniia nad sovremennoi garmoniei" [Observations on Contemporary Harmony], *Sovetskaia muzyka* 25, No. 11 (November 1961), pp. 50–55. —A.Sch.

2. A lack of functional correspondence between the melodic voices and the harmony, which is also associated with the simultaneous use of opposing functions. [See examples 29.33 and 29.34.]

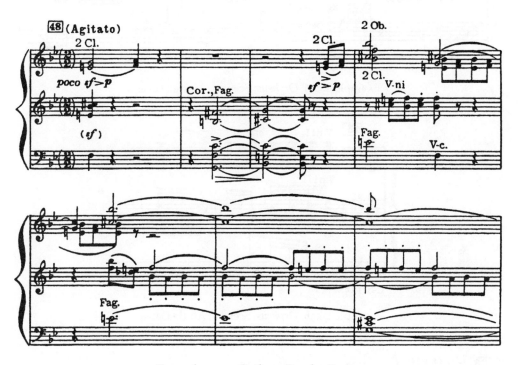

Example 29.33. *Orpheus,* Pas des Furies

Example 29.34. *Orpheus,* Scene 2, Air de Danse

3. A lack of functional correspondence between two or more layers of harmony, which also arises on the basis of a broader understanding of pedal point (e.g., the complete tonic triad used as a pedal point, which is encountered even in classical music; cf. the first sonority heard in the finale of Beethoven's Ninth Symphony). [See examples 29.35, 29.36, and 29.37.]

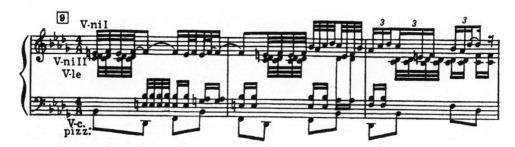

Example 29.35. *Orpheus,* Scene 1, Air de Danse

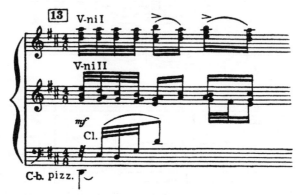

Example 29.36. *Orpheus,* Scene 1, Air de Danse

Example 29.37. *Orpheus,* Scene 2, Dance of the Angel of Death

4. A lack of functional correspondence between the harmonic framework of two or more polyphonic voices. [See examples 29.38, 29.39, and 29.40.]
5. A lack of functional correspondence between the harmonic framework of voices in a texture that mixes harmonic/homophonic and polyphonic elements. [See examples 29.41, 29.42, and 29.43.]

Sometimes the lack of functional correspondence between elements results from a dogmatic stylization of devices taken over literally from traditional polyphonic techniques (a commitment to linearity that entails a polyfunctional "freshening" of the device). [See examples 29.44, 29.45, and 29.46.]

Example 29.38. *Orpheus,* Scene 1, Air de Danse

Example 29.39. *Orpheus,* Interlude

Example 29.40. *Orpheus,* Interlude

Example 29.41. *Orpheus,* Dance of the Angel of Death

Example 29.42. *Orpheus,* Pas de Deux

Example 29.43. *Orpheus,* Pas de Deux

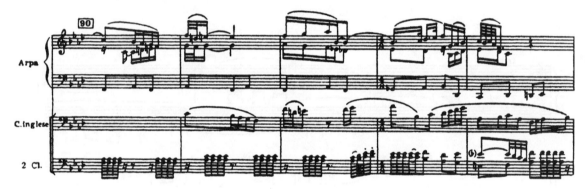

Example 29.44. *Orpheus,* Air de Danse

Example 29.45. *Orpheus,* Scene 3, Orpheus' Apotheosis

Example 29.46. *Orpheus,* Orpheus' Apotheosis

On the subject of linearity, the differences between the linear thinking of Stravinsky and Hindemith should be emphasized at once. Hindemith's linearity is based on the union of nontraditional, intonationally abstract, semantically neutral melodic *lines*, relatively uncontrolled in the vertical dimension (or at least controlled by norms artificially created by Hindemith). Stravinsky's approach to linearity is founded in a blending of traditionally defined, intonationally concrete, semantically characteristic *melodic* lines.

A more consistently applied linear approach sometimes leads in *Orpheus* to polytonality:

1. A lack of correspondence in tonality between the bass and the other voices in the harmony. [See examples 29.47 and 29.48.]
2. A lack of correspondence in tonality between three layers—the bass, the melody harmonized in parallel triads, and the pedal harmony. [See example 29.49.]

Example 29.47. *Orpheus,* Scene 2, Pas des Furies

Example 29.48. *Orpheus,* Scene 2, Pas des Furies

Example 29.49. *Orpheus,* Scene 2, Pas des Furies

In both items 1 and 2, the layers in different keys are also differentiated in timbre. Following is a rare example of polytonality in a unified timbre: a melodic figure in first violins casts the "shadow" of a "variant doubling" in a foreign key over the central material, a melody and accompaniment in the strings, all fully in harmony with the main key. [See example 29.50.]

Example 29.50. *Orpheus,* Scene 2, Pas des Furies

Other characteristic features of Stravinsky's part-writing were also more thoroughly developed in *Orpheus:*

1. Functional variability as a consequence of an inconstant number of independent voices with momentary divergence and convergence of the melodic lines. [See examples 29.51, 29.52, and 29.53.]

Example 29.51. *Orpheus,* Air de Danse

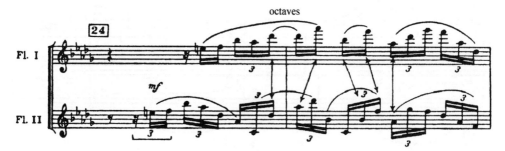

Example 29.52. *Orpheus,* Air de Danse

Example 29.53. *Orpheus*, Air de Danse

2. Varied doublings, ranging from variations in register (e.g., zigzag doubling, sometimes at the unison, sometimes at the octave) to brief, independent offshoots from the main voice. [See example 29.54.]

Example 29.54. *Orpheus*, Scene 2, Pas des Furies

3. The "cycling" of separate voices in the texture within the span of a provisional, quasi-enclosed micro-mode (in such a context, movement beyond the confines of the micro-mode tends to be perceived as a cadential gesture). [See example 29.55.]

Example 29.55. *Orpheus*, Scene 1

4. Multivariable treatment of the part-writing associated with a masking of the basic "independent" voice parts in the musical fabric by the addition of instruments playing quasi-voices that sometimes double the primary lines in the texture, sometimes not. In the example given below, the timbre of the "quasi" voices—trumpet, trombone (and later oboe and English horn)—prevails over the timbre of the strings playing the basic lines in the texture. [See example 29.39, p. 175.]

The score of *Orpheus* as a whole, however, is characterized by greater specificity of instrumental function than is found in Stravinsky's later works (which prepared the way for his subsequent turn to *serial* techniques).[8]

Stravinsky's "serial" period is highly distinctive. There is, of course, no hint of a capitulation to his more farsighted rival, who divined one of the characteristic tendencies of the age earlier than Stravinsky did.[9] On the contrary, this is just another of Stravinsky's faces. He is capable of "admitting" anyone at all into himself, while retaining his own identify. This is not the first time, after all, that he stakes his own individuality on the turn of the cards, subjecting it to a new test. But even this time round, his individuality emerges unscathed, even strengthened. Neither was his adoption of dodecaphony accidental. One can find many devices in his arsenal that prepared the way for his move to a new technique:

1. the ostinato—any ostinato can serve as the most primitive form of a series, an unchanging succession of sounds repeated over and over;
2. provisional micro-modes whose boundaries define for a certain time the intonations in an episode;
3. the varied display of one and the same intonation, melodic motifs presented in a variety of metric and rhythmic contexts, reminiscent of the endless rhythmic variations of a series;
4. the functional variability of the texture and, so characteristic of serial technique, the rapid reconfiguring of the texture, as well as the timbral recoloration of the thematic voices;
5. a "universal" mobile musical language that allows for any stylistic inclination, analogous to the way in which the various intervals in a twelve-tone row may even at times crystallize into "traditional" combinations (triads, seventh chords, scale-like diatonic and chromatic passages, and the like) and through them momentarily reproduce one musical style or another.

One could probably find in Stravinsky other links with serial technique. But it is much more important to discover what distinguishes his serial works from those of

---

8. By "later works" Schnittke means *The Rake's Progress* (1947–1951), the Mass (1948), the Cantata (1952), the Suite from *Pulcinella* (1947). Below, Schnittke also identifies *Agon, Canticum Sacrum,* and *Three Songs from William Shakespeare* as transitional works. —ed.

9. We recall Schoenberg's caricature of Stravinsky as "little Modernsky," wearing a wig—just like Bach! (Suite, Opus 25). —A.Sch.

the New Viennese School. Quite obviously, Stravinsky could not submit to the norms of a style hitherto alien to him, just as he could never submit to the norms of any school or trend. As he imitated each new manner, so he immediately reinterpreted it. Having regulated the way he adopted the norms of others, he created his own. The elusive essence of Stravinsky's technique lies in the fact that, rejecting generally accepted rules, he created his own for each separate occasion—only to break them immediately himself. And this is also the way he proceeded with the twelve-tone system.

Despite all these indisputable links with serial technique, Stravinsky could not immediately cross the stylistic barrier in the way that other venerable composers, such as Krenek, could easily do. The transitional works—*Agon, Canticum Sacrum, Three Songs from William Shakespeare*—are dualistic; in these works the familiar neoclassical polystylistic method of the mature Stravinsky coexists with separate serial and dodecaphonic episodes.

In the ballet *Agon* (1953/1957) the material is organized into two contrasting intonational spheres, the serial and the tonal, in opposition to one another (similar to the way in which Rimsky-Korsakov contrasted the major/minor scales and the "artificial" scales in *Sadko, Kashchei,* and *Kitezh*). Furthermore, the intonations of several of the tone rows in *Agon* are gradually drawn out of the tonal episodes.

Let us look more closely at these tone rows [figure 29.1]. Everywhere here we encounter characteristic groupings of four chromatic pitches within the span of a minor third; the pitches are not arranged as a straightforward scale but are grouped in pairs constituting either a minor or a major second [figure 29.2].

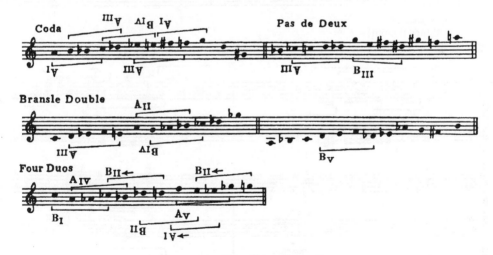

Figure 29.1. Tone Rows from *Agon*

Figure 29.2. Pairings of Major and Minor Seconds in Micro-Series from *Agon*

Permutations of the above micro-series serve as the intonational basis of the Double Pas de Quatre. [See example 29.56.]

One also encounters a second four-note micro-series comprising two melodic cells, these too based on seconds but within the span of a major third; this pattern is constructed on the principle of semitone-tone-semitone [see table 29.1]. The row used in the Four Trios that end the ballet is based on this [see figure 29.3 and example 29.57].

Example 29.56. Stravinsky, *Agon,* Double Pas de Quatre (T = pedal point)

Table 29.1. Patterns from Four Trios

Figure 29.3. Micro-Series from *Agon*, Four Trios

Example 29.57. *Agon*, Four Trios

In one way or another, all the twelve-tone rows of *Agon* are constructed from intonations of these two micro-series, either reproduced literally or in transformations. The first of the two micro-series has a particularly important role; one encounters it everywhere. Most interesting, it is also present in the tonal themes. [See examples 29.58, 29.59, and 29.60.]

Example 29.58. *Agon*, Pas de Quatre

Example 29.59. *Agon*, Gailliarde

Example 29.60. *Agon*, Second Pas de Trois, Bransle Simple

This particular micro-series originates in the very first number of the ballet (the Pas de Quatre) under the influence of the prevailing modal-melodic context. The melodic material in this introductory number (as well as many of the other tonal episodes in the ballet) has a Lydian flavor,[10] with its tendency to strive upward in the circle of fifths. [See example 29.61.]

Example 29.61. *Agon,* Pas de Quatre

The two neighboring Lydian tetrachords in the circle of fifths (e.g., on F and on C) already give rise to a polytonal struggle between two tonics. The resulting polytonality, two simultaneous tonics with roots a fifth apart, colors the harmonic plan of all tonal episodes in *Agon.*

In the middle (Double Pas de Quatre) of the opening number, however, appears a natural countertendency toward the Phrygian[11] or flat side of the tonal spectrum, that is, downward along the circle of fifths. And the four-note group we have indicated [figure 29.2] expresses schematically *both* modal tendencies—upward toward the "sharp" side, as well as downward toward the "flat" side. This four-note intonation figures also in later numbers of the ballet, fulfilling the same ambivalent modal function [see examples 29.58 and 29.59].

After having originated in the context of tonal thinking, this four-note intonation becomes the only thematic material in the outer sections of No. 2, in other words, it becomes a tone-row, a series (but still in a tonal context, since the separate phases of its development are marked by the "columns" of tonic and dominant octaves in D minor) [see example 29.56, p. 182].

The micro-series is now prepared; it has been realized, but still within the salutary and familiar context of tonality. The first burst into purely serial logic occurs in the middle of the number. Here, five small series of 3, 4, 5, 6, and 7 sounds operate simultaneously [see example 29.62].

One curious detail: a *triad* as a *series.* Situated in a more favorable context with respect to register and timbre, the triad lays claim to the role of tonal center, but its tonal authority is fictitious, like the authority of the English sovereign. Toward the end of this episode there is even a transfer of authority to a "successor": into the midst of completely atonal play among three series, an E minor triad is introduced

---

10. A complete Lydian scale need not be present in a situation such as this, only its tendency, as a consequence of its raised fourth degree, toward the "sharp" side of the tonal spectrum. —A.Sch.

11. Here again we mean not the complete Phrygian scale, only its characteristic tendency toward the "flat" side of the tonal spectrum. —A.Sch.

Example 29.62. *Agon*

from outside, once again by the trumpets, creating something like a cadence (cf. *Agon*, mm. 91–95).

The reprise/coda that follows the cadence momentarily restores D minor, but then serial organization is finally established. Everything is constructed on the intonations of two series—one of four pitches, the other of five (cf. *Agon*, mm. 96–99, 104–118).

Only at the end is a quasi-tonic harmony on fifths introduced, again from outside, as the formal cadential gesture (cf. *Agon*, mm. 118–121).

But the weakening of the authority of the tonic does not yet mean its complete banishment. True, toward the end of the ballet the serial organization asserts itself quite decisively. Nonetheless, the coda, a full repeat of the ballet's first number, restores the tonality. The return itself is achieved quite subtly: the seventh chord in the horns that serves as the transition between the dodecaphonic and the tonal episodes is built on the last notes of the four different versions of the series. [See figure 29.4.]

Figure 29.4. *Agon*, Transitional Chord

This chord closes off the preceding dodecaphonic cycle of development and opens the door to the return of tonality (the further we depart from tonality in *Agon*, the closer we come back to it). [See example 29.63.]

Example 29.63. *Agon*

Example 29.64. *Agon*

Similarly, the effect of cadence, of tonic stability, is achieved at the end of the Bransle-Double [which begins at bar 336]. Here, the final pitches of the two twelve-note rows are transferred from several "unreliable" and melancholy clarinets to the assertively distinctive timbre of trumpets. [See example 29.64.]

In defiance of the automatic nonperiodicity of the prevailing serial fabric, a striving to organize the broad divisions of the form by reference to the periodicity and structural precision of tonal thinking runs through many of the ballet's numbers. This is achieved in a variety of ways.

First, *varying principles for organizing the material in various divisions of the form* allow Stravinsky to articulate the form even in the absence of full perfect cadences. Thus, in the Double Pas de Quatre, the first section is wholly constructed of the four-note series analyzed above, while the middle section, as we have seen, sets forth five series of varying intervals. In the reprise/coda the four-note row returns again, but there is also a polyphonic summation of the various sections of the form along with the five-note row from the middle section. [See example 29.65.]

Example 29.65. *Agon,* Double Pas de Quatre

A similar ternary plan is encountered in the Bransle-Double. Its middle section, which presents various intervals derived from a stable, complete twelve-note chord, contrasts in texture with the two framing outer sections, the latter involving a two-voice, then a three-voice combination of lines sharply differentiated in timbre and register. [See examples 29.66 and 29.67a,b,c.]

Example 29.66. *Agon,* Bransle-Double

Example 29.67. *Agon:* a–b. Bransle Double; c. Complete twelve-tone chord

Second, *an exact couplet-like repetition of sections of the form,* which results in formal *periodicity* in the literal sense of the word (not a feature of serial music on the whole, with rare exceptions, the finale of Webern's Cantata No. 2 being one). Form in both the Bransle-Double and the coda of the Gailliarde is conspicuously marked by varied repetitions of a *period* (but without traditional cadences). The coda of the Gailliarde is an example of a passacaglia, rare in Stravinsky (its nucleus is a twelve-tone row whose sharply accented notes are played in turn by two trombones and a piano). [See example 29.68.]

Example 29.68. *Agon,* Gailliarde

Finally, almost all the excerpts just described may be regarded as serial, but *cannot be considered atonal.*

In many cases Stravinsky creates something like a tonal center, but one that is in fact melodic, not harmonic. He achieves this not by transposing the series, but by constantly moving away from one and the same pitch and always ending on the same pitch. What the tonic is in this case, the first or the last tone, is difficult to decide. Most likely, the whole row is the tonic since it is not re-ordered (the passacaglia just mentioned is an example). A melodic tonal center also appears when the prime and the retrograde versions of the row are linked, given that the first and last pitches are inevitably identical, hence they are perceived as the tonic (e.g., the Bransle-Double).

In certain cases, the effect of a quasi-harmonic tonal center arises from the introduction "from outside" of cadential triads or other fixed sonorities with tonic

implications (such as were pointed out in the Triple Pas de Quatre). Similar ca-
dential-like pedal chords introduced "from outside" articulate the form in the
passacaglia. [See examples 29.69 and 29.70.]

Example 29.69. *Agon*, Gailliarde

Example 29.70. *Agon*, Gailliarde

Finally, the tonic center of gravity can be supported continually by means of a
pedal point, which overcomes the centrifugal force of serial organization. [See
example 29.56, p. 182.]

The aforementioned middle section of the Bransle-Double provides a paradoxical example of total stability in a twelve-tone row; it is in essence entirely constructed
on a static twelve-tone chord that is never heard as a whole but always in various
"segments." Typically for Stravinsky, his excursion through the various levels of this
twelve-tone chord is completed by its transposition, which serves a cadential,
"braking" function [example 29.71; see also example 29.67].

Example 29.71. *Agon*, Bransle Double

Example 29.72. *Agon*

Example 29.72. (*continued*)

Example 29.72. (*continued*)

Example 29.72. (*concluded*)

Given such subtlety of harmonic logic, the voice-leading too has polysemous functional implications; the ways in which it changes multiply by comparison with the earlier "non-serial" works of Stravinsky. The composer adopts the practice characteristic of the New Viennese School of dividing the melody into short motifs entrusted to disparate timbres. This practice had arisen from necessity—a single instrument was not always capable of playing an atonal theme broken up into widely spaced intervals, but later on, as is well known, Webern made use of the practice consciously (e.g., in his orchestration of Bach's *Fuga/Ricercata a 6 voci*), as did the post-Webernites, who took it as far as *pointillism*. The new property of this practice extends from the fact that a melody modulating in timbre gains a certain additional stereophonic quality, a spatial fullness that is particularly marked at those points where two timbres "link." The abundance and frequency with which new timbres are introduced create the illusion of a vast number of independent voices, which we hear somehow incompletely, in fragments. In *Agon*, this approach appears most vividly in the coda of the Triple Pas de Quatre. [See example 29.72.]

A detailed analysis of the voice-leading in the serial episodes of *Agon* is not really worthwhile, because in serial technique constant changes in orchestral voicing become the norm. But there are occasions in serial technique when the orchestration, in particular the orchestral voicing, decisively influences the form, such as in the example cited above of the simultaneous sounding (as a transition between atonality and tonality) in the chord played by the horns, of the four final pitches of four parallel rows, previously assigned to quite different instruments. Here, the introduction of the chord in the horns marks a boundary between the preceding and following formal divisions at a critical moment, the advent of the reprise. [See example 29.63, p. 185.]

But it is no less instructive to analyze the organization of the tonal episodes in *Agon*. Here, as in *Orpheus*, the tonal development is subject to the principle of polyfunctionality, the simultaneity of cause and consequence, of tonic and dominant, expressed however not in the triads and seventh chords of functional root relationships at the fourth or fifth, but in tetrachords, pentachords, and the like, that exhibit ascending ("Lydian") or descending ("Phrygian") modal tendencies. [See examples 29.61 and 29.58, pp. 184, 183.]

The final notes of these micro-modes are combined in quasi-tonic chords of the fourth or fifth, all of them polyfunctional and representing an unresolved collision of several tonal centers. [See examples 29.61, p. 184, and 29.73.]

Example 29.73. *Agon,* Pas de Quatre

Example 29.74. a. *Agon*, Interlude

Example 29.74. b. *Agon,* Interlude

If the final "stable" chords are themselves polyfunctional, this makes the contrasted elements in the musical texture all the more autonomous tonally and functionally (right up to the clear-cut polytonal differentiation of the various layers,
which is generally underscored as well by timbre). [See examples 29.74a,b.]

Stravinsky makes broad use in *Agon* of the traditional devices of imitative
polyphony, but they are always given a new meaning by the composer, such as the
polytonal canons at the fifth and fourth in the Gailliarde (which once again reflect
the "sharp" side and "flat" side of the theme's modal tendencies). [See examples
29.75 and 29.59, p. 183.]

Example 29.75. *Agon,* Gailliarde

An analogous polytonal canon at the lower fourth, in two horns and piano, is
encountered in the refrain of the Pas de Deux. Since the horns are transposing
instruments, the canon as notated appears to be at the octave; perhaps Stravinsky
was once again playing his favorite game of ambushing the listener, "quasi in C" (cf.
Suite No. 2, the *Symphony in C* [example 29.76]).

Example 29.76. *Agon,* Pas de Deux

Even the usual canon at the unison for two trumpets in the Bransle-Simple sounds unusual because of the continuous collisions between the "Lydian" F-sharp and the "Phrygian" F-natural in the two voices (still the same concurrent tendency toward both the "sharp" and the "flat" sides; see example 29.60 [p. 183]).

As may be seen from the examples above, while making use of the traditional polyphonic devices, Stravinsky ironically exaggerates them or reproduces them too literally. For a moment he submits hypocritically to the rules of "decent" polyphony, which leads him to an even more indecent counterpoint (e.g., the simultaneous statement, in the cadences of the Gailliarde, of two variants of the same line, one in diminution, the other in augmentation [see example 29.77a,b]).

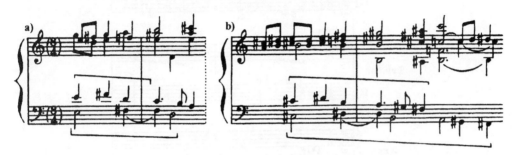

Example 29.77. a–b. *Agon*, Gailliarde

A device long familiar from Stravinsky's previous work also recurs in *Agon*—the interplay of short micro-modal ostinatos whose rhythmic relationships continuously change. In final analysis, this approach amounts to a technique of invertible counterpoint made automatic. [See example 29.78.]

The Saraband-Step remains unique in the deceptiveness of its outwardly unpretentious structure and voice-leading—a binary form with two clear cadences, on the dominant F and the tonic B-flat, and a two-bar codetta that amounts to an "embryo" of the reprise. Despite all the self-evidence of this form, the listener stumbles at every step into logical "traps." Start with the fact that the second section is a retrograde version of the first, but only from the third bar in intervallic structure, whereas by visual impression it appears to be from the first bar (in fact, the direction of the melodic contour of the solo violin and, in the second bar, of the trombones is here inverted; but only the direction of the passage is inverted, not its actual intervals). The following bars (3 through 8) of the second section are actually an inversion of the corresponding bars from the first section, but now rearranged vertically and with a multitude of deviations from literalness, not only in the vertical distribution of the voices but also in the intervals themselves. Thus, some elements from the first section are retained in the second, in uninverted and untransposed form, while others are changed, so as to return to the main key (as happens in the tonal answer in a fugue). [See example 29.79.]

To sum up, then, we see that both in his tonal and in his serial logic, Stravinsky strives equally to overcome the dogmatism of a device, either by deforming it or by using exaggerated literalism (the latter is doubly lethal). This testifies to the organi-

Example 29.78. *Agon,* Pas de Quatre (micro-modal ostinato)

cally paradoxical inner nature of his logic, the logic of a great mind bold enough to be conscious of the impossibility of following literally the norms of classicism (which in many respects had already grown passé), but at the same time cautious enough not to have faith in new doctrines that even today have not sanctioned the building of a new musical edifice.

Originally published as "Paradoksal'nost' kak cherta muzykal'noi logiki Stravinskogo" in *I. F. Stravinskii: Stat'i i materialy* [I. F. Stravinsky: Articles and Materials], compiled by L. S. D'iachkova and edited by B. M. Iarustovskii (Moscow: Sovetskii Kompozitor, 1973), pp. 383–418.

(Figures for this chapter continue through page 200)

Example 29.79. *Agon*, First Pas de Trois (Saraband Step)

× = deviations from literal inversion

Example 29.79. (*concluded*)

TIMBRAL MODULATION IN BARTÓK'S *MUSIC FOR STRINGS, PERCUSSION, AND CELESTA* (1970s)

Bartók, in his *Music for Strings, Percussion, and Celesta*, was among the first composers to risk making timbral modulation the basic approach to orchestrating a complete work. His very choice of instruments (strings and percussion!) at once forced him to look for affinities in timbre, without which there would be no unity of sonority. The solution he found was unusually simple. Not one instrument from the percussion group (including the harp, piano, or celesta) appears in the score without its particular timbre being somehow prepared in the strings. But to achieve this, Bartók had to determine the timbral connections between strings and percussion. What were those qualities peculiar to the strings that would help Bartók relate these two seemingly antithetical orchestral families?

1. The characteristic nonuniformity and lack of periodicity in the fluctuating resonance of mass strings in general, whether performing as a multivoiced string choir or in vibrant *tremolo* (the latter comes close to the *tremolando*-like sound of beating on cymbals, tympani, and snare drum).
2. The vast spectrum of string overtones, unique to each individual instrument in the string group. (The natural voicing of the overtone series of a string instrument lacks the comparative stability of the series heard in a wind instrument; instead, it keeps mutating, creating a sound spectrum whose complex format is a kind of sketch in shifting, fading overtones.)
3. The whole array of string performance techniques similar in timbre to that of percussion instruments—*pizzicato, col legno, sforzando, sul ponticello, suoni flautati* (harmonics), *tremolo, glissando*, and the like.

Bartók made masterful use of all these timbral affinities. Let us now investigate how and in what order the percussion enters.

Movement I

First, the tympani enter imperceptibly at bar 34, doubling the double basses on a tremolo pedal point [see example 30.1].

Example 30.1. Bartók, *Music for Strings, Percussion, and Celesta*

At their next appearance, in bar 53, the tympani play a modest, but now independent role. Again there is a drumroll pedal point in the bass, but without the doubling string basses; it starts *pianissimo* and crescendos to a full, percussive *forte* in bar 56.

The cymbals enter in bar 51 [example 30.2] with a brief crescendo roll that ends in a mezzoforte crash simultaneously with the climactic general accent in the strings (a wonderful concord of timbre between cymbals and the intensive polyphonic branching in the strings).

Example 30.2. *Music for Strings, Percussion, and Celesta*

The ringing of the triangle, struck at the height of the climax in bar 56 [see example 30.3], is heard as a prolongation of the overtone spectrum created by the extraordinarily vivid E-flat in three octaves played by violins and violas (up to now octaves have been shunned, except in the basses).

Example 30.3. *Music for Strings, Percussion, and Celesta*

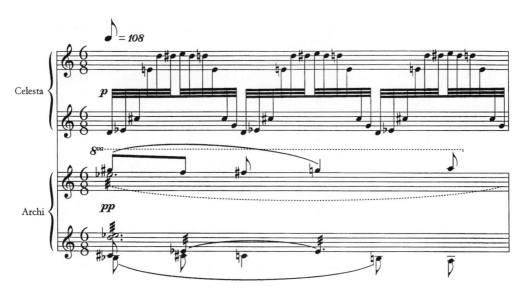

Example 30.4. *Music for Strings, Percussion, and Celesta*

The celesta's entry in bar 72 [see example 30.4] is also veiled, its delicate arpeggios shrouded by the high tremolo strings.

In all these examples, the percussion timbres are obviously quite deliberately obscured, their timbres emanating from the timbres of the string section as a consequence of doubling the strings literally or else providing sonorous supplementation—a "sharpening" of the latent timbral qualities of the strings by the percussion. The percussion instruments are treated here as a means of prolonging the timbre of the strings.

Movement II

Whereas in Movement I the modulation "from strings to percussion" is generally accomplished through tremolos of various sorts (in both percussion and strings), in Movement II the modulation is accomplished through the "percussive" techniques of string performance, every sort of *pizzicato, col legno,* and the like. This is how the piano makes its entry [see example 30.5], doubling the focal pitch of the string

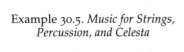
Example 30.5. *Music for Strings, Percussion, and Celesta*

pizzicato (there is no need to expatiate upon the timbral relationship between *staccato* on the piano and *pizzicato* in the strings).

The tympani enter similarly, doubling the motif in fourths of the second string orchestra [see example 30.6]; the sharp, abrupt bow strokes in the low register of the strings produces a rumbling related in sonority to the sound of tympani.

Example 30.6. *Music for Strings, Percussion, and Celesta*

Having been introduced through a transitional string timbre, henceforth the piano and the tympani become independent and present their own independent thematic material.

The short rolls on the snare drum in bar 115 are heard as a natural sharpening of the trills in the strings [see example 30.7].

Example 30.7. *Music for Strings, Percussion, and Celesta*

Particularly varied are the techniques for widening the range of shadings in string *pizzicato*—from harsh, spiky blows in the piano [example 30.8a], snare drum [example 30.8b], and xylophone [example 30.8c], to subdued tinkles in harp and celesta.

The doubling is not always strict. In bar 199 [example 30.9a], the harp plays the string figuration in reverse, and in bar 267 [example 30.9b] the harp doubles the octaves in the strings with parallel [first-inversion] $\frac{6}{3}$ chords. But here, too, the timbre of the harp is eclipsed by that of the strings, so that in both instances the harp merely contributes variant "shadings" to the *pizzicato* strings.

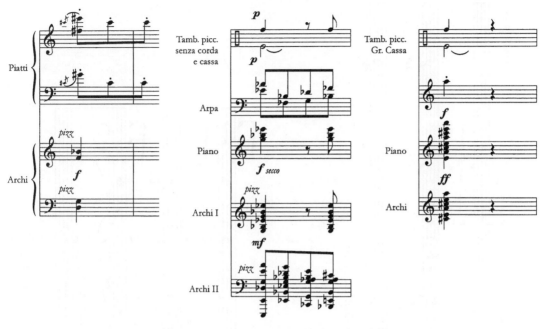

Example 30.8. *Music for Strings, Percussion, and Celesta*

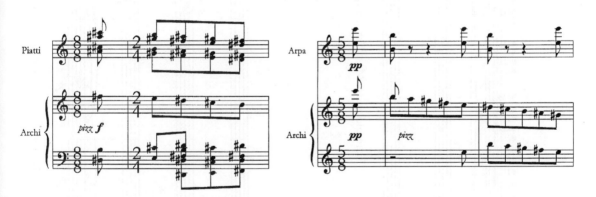

Example 30.9. *Music for Strings, Percussion, and Celesta*

Movement III

Only in this third movement are the percussion instruments finally treated as an independent group, having been carefully groomed by the timbral modulations in the preceding two movements. The duet between the xylophone and the tympani [example 30.10], with its barely audible sounds emanating from an unknown source, engenders a tense and mysterious atmosphere.

Such moments of timbral "purity," of percussion alone, are extremely rare. They occur only at the beginning and ending of the third movement. Otherwise, timbral "hybrids" of the sort noted above continue to predominate:

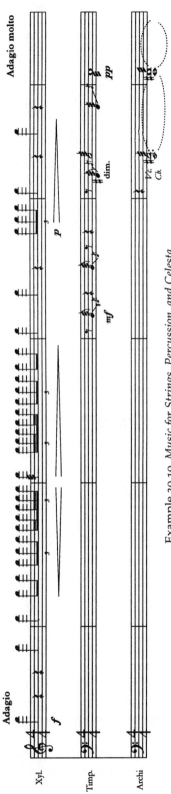

Example 30.10. *Music for Strings, Percussion, and Celesta*

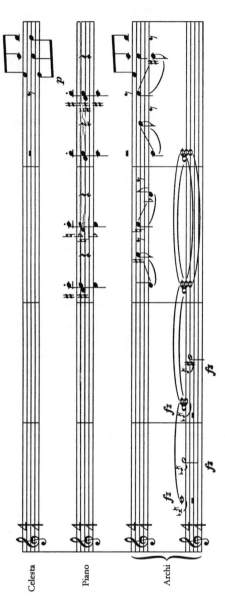

Example 30.11. *Music for Strings, Percussion, and Celesta*

1. Hushed tremolos by the bass strings and tympani [see, again, example 30.10].
2. Delicately dissonant timbral sonorities constituted of trills, *tremolos*, and *glissandi* in the strings [example 30.11], along with variant presentations of the same figuration by harp, celesta, and piano [example 30.12].
3. Climactic chord in mixed timbres [example 30.13].
4. Thirteen timbral variations on every possible variety of *staccato* and *pizzicato*, along with analogous timbres in the percussion. [See example 30.14, items 1–13.]

Example 30.12. *Music for Strings, Percussion, and Celesta*

Example 30.13. *Music for Strings, Percussion, and Celesta*

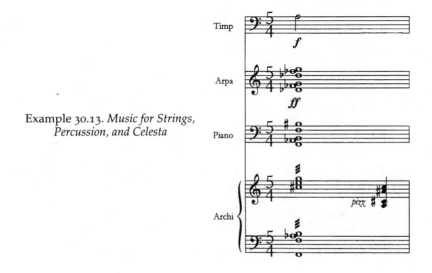

Example 30.14. (Items 1–13) *Music for Strings, Percussion, and Celesta*

Examples 30.15–30.17. *Music for Strings, Percussion, and Celesta*

Movement IV

No new timbral combinations are found in the fourth movement, but here too the principle of timbral affinities between the different families is strictly observed. The practice already familiar from earlier movements predominates: varied combinations of different instruments, correlated in timbre, playing the same figuration. But there are also some unexpected timbral combinations:

1. The reiteration of seconds in the piano and, in the strings, a dissonant harmonic texture that seems related in sonority [see example 30.15].
2. An even more subtle timbral affinity is achieved when the same "dinning" seconds in the piano are imitated by violins spaced over three octaves [example 30.15]. Here, the small intonational discrepancies among the individual instruments, made inevitable by the high register and the forceful bowing, create around each sound something of an imprecise aura of seconds closely related in timbre to the seconds sounded in the piano. [See example 30.16.]

The evidence for Bartók's having consciously calculated this effect of a "zone of seconds" in the sonority of strings playing in unison is confirmed by his having doubled the piano seconds by cellos playing in unison in a register so high as to ensure a wide band of intonational discrepancy [example 30.17].

All the above examples from Bartók's score have one thing in common. In every case, the percussion instruments are introduced not suddenly but through preparatory timbral modulation. As the work proceeds, the representatives of the different instrumental families almost always carry out the same formal function, supporting and supplementing one another to create a consonant timbral harmony.

Written in the 1970s. The original Russian text has not been published.

CHAPTER

31

THE PRINCIPLE OF
UNINTERRUPTED TIMBRAL AFFINITIES
IN WEBERN'S ORCHESTRATION OF BACH'S
FUGA (RICERCATA) A 6 VOCI
(1970s)

In his orchestration of the six-part ricercare from Bach's *Das musikalische Opfer*, Webern perhaps came closer than anyone to achieving a scale of timbres. One cannot say that timbral contrasts are absent from the score. They occur both in the horizontal plane (a muted trombone states the theme, and the flute answers) and in the vertical (see bar 36: flute, solo first violin, second violins, and tympani). A glance at the score instantly reveals its obvious *pointillism*—the six voices of a strict fugue are fragmented into motifs scattered throughout the orchestra (just as in Webern's original compositions). Yet, when listening to the music, we notice not the slightest scatteration. The orchestra sounds to us like a unique super-instrument that blends all the orchestral colors, balanced to perfection as in an organ. The timbral contrasts are fused into a unified totality by means of subtle calculation: not one timbre appears without timbral preparation, and not one new timbre is left without consequences for the whole.

The entire future score is already implicit in the orchestration of the subject on its first appearance. Obeying the rule of non-repetition, Webern makes use of eight timbres in the opening nine bars (counting the first bar of the countersubject) [example 31.1]: (1) muted trombone, *non legato e portamento*; (2) muted horn, *non*

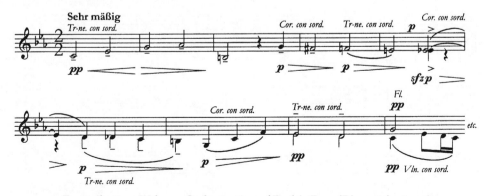

Example 31.1. Webern, Orchestration of Bach's *Fuga (Ricercata) a 6 voci*

legato e portamento; (3) muted trumpet, *legato*; (4) muted horn, *legato*, and harp; (5) muted trombone, *legato e portamento*; (6) muted horn, *legato*; (7) muted trumpet, *portamento*, and harp; (8) muted second violins, *legato*.

Everything here seems outwardly to serve the goal of variety: frequent change in instrumentation and type of articulation, constant variation in accentuation and duration of the constituent motifs. Along with this, however, unifying forces are also at work, and these have a crucial influence on what is heard. All the successive changes, except for the final transfer to muted violins, follow along three basic gradations of a timbral scale based on muted brass: muted trombone—muted horn—muted trumpet. Even the pluckings of the harp in bars 4 and 7 (which later seem to precipitate the string *pizzicato*) are heard as "pointings" of the brass accentuation.

A more definite division marks the entry of the countersubject [example 31.2]. Here the muted trumpet theme bifurcates along two related timbral lines: flute in a low register and violins *con sordino* (the mutes multiply the number of partials, bringing the timbre closer to that of muted brass). The changes of timbre that follow continue along these two new timbral scales, both starting with a muted trumpet. In the first: muted trumpet → flute → clarinet → oboe → clarinet or harp. In the second timbral scale: muted trumpet → second violins, muted → solo viola, muted → second violins → viola, *pizzicato* → solo second violin → second violins, *tutti pizzicati*.

Example 31.2. Webern, Orchestration of Bach's *Fuga (Ricercata) a 6 voci*

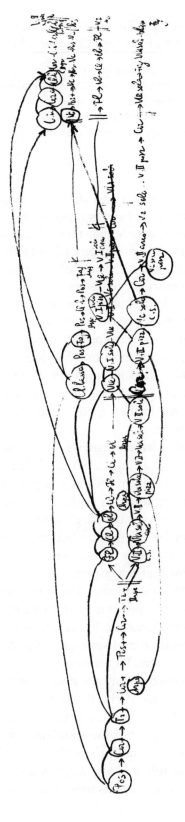

Example 31.3. Timbral Affinities in Webern, Orchestration of Bach's *Fuga (Ricercata) a 6 voci*

**Table 31.1. Timbral Modulations
in the Subject and Countersubject**

trombone→(to horn or harp)
horn→trumpet→(to flute or second violins)
flute→clarinet→oboe
second violins→solo viola
harp→solo viola, *pizzicato*

The new branchings (woodwinds and strings) from the original muted brass timbral scale will continue and remain integrated during subsequent statements of the subject. In addition to these, yet another timbral scale branches off, comprising harp and *pizzicato* strings (the latter prepared earlier by the pluckings of the harp in the first statement). Later on, after *pizzicato* violas, violins, and cellos, this scale is rounded out by the tympani entrance in bar 35.

Thus, within the span of only the subject and the countersubject, virtually all the orchestral timbres have been introduced in successive, interlocking timbral modulations [table 31.1]. True, the sensation remains of a somewhat abrupt "jump" in timbre from muted trumpet to flute, despite the affinity between the low registers of the two instruments. The jump is later filled in, however. The timbre of the bass clarinet, which begins the third statement of the subject, resembles that of each of the two instruments with which it shares the theme, both the bassoon (representing the wood-winds) and the muted trombone.

Without continuing with further analysis of the score, let us examine the principle of interlocking timbral affinities within the abbreviated context already provided in the first four statements of the subject. [See example 31.3.]

As we have seen, timbral gradations stretch between the contrasted timbres, connecting the extremes not only within a single timbral scale but also within all the possible timbral scales available in this particular group of instruments. What results is an uninterrupted, completely unified web of timbres within a single closed multipolar system—a system that corresponds to the requirements of Webern's "atonal" thinking, which did not dismiss the powerful gravitational forces of tonicality and pitch-scale tendencies, but gave them new values. Thanks to the polysemy of the timbral affinities, each individual timbre becomes multifunctional, simultaneously a link in several timbral scales, a point of intersection, and thus the potential center of the whole system. The uninterrupted timbral modulations do not create a kaleidoscope of timbres but combine into a dynamically stable system that preserves its integrity as the center of gravity shifts from one timbre to another. As we recognize the actual sound of any particular instrument, we become conscious of its infinite timbral affinities with all the others and have the illusion of hearing them too. Each component, even the smallest (recall the modest harp plucking as it doubled the muted brass), acquires along with its own concrete significance the capacity to influence the whole, even in its most distant reaches. A dialectic interaction arises between the general and the particular, between contrast and uniformity, with which Webern was consciously concerned and for which in his course of lectures, *Wege zur neuen Musik,*[1] he formulated the theoretical concepts of *Faßlichkeit* (clarity) and *Zusammenhang* (connectedness).

Written in the 1970s. The original Russian text has not been published.

---

1. Anton Webern, *Wege zur neuen Musik,* edited by Willi Reich (Vienna: Universal, 1960); *The Path to the New Music,* translated by Leo Black (Bryn Mawr, Penn.: Theodore Presser, 1963).

THE THIRD MOVEMENT OF
BERIO'S *SINFONIA*

*Stylistic Counterpoint, Thematic and
Formal Unity in Context of Polystylistics,
Broadening the Concept of Thematicism*
(1970s)

The third movement of Luciano Berio's *Sinfonia* for eight soloists and orchestra (1968–1969) is constructed entirely on quotations from the music of the nineteenth and twentieth centuries. Each quotation serves a thematic function. This approach represents a new, more generalized type of thematicism, in which the semantic unit is not confined to an intonation as such, with its conventional expressive responsibility, but rather to an entire intonational bloc (the quotation), an intonational coalition with an enormous range of emotional, stylistic, and historical associations.

Two factors ensure the overall unity of this movement:

1. an orderly formal conception (polystylistic contrapuntal variations over a *cantus firmus*, the latter being the scherzo movement of Mahler's Second Symphony) [example 32.1];
2. a variety of intonational, timbral, and expressively associative *linkages* that connect the passages involving direct quotation. These linkages facilitate smooth transition from quotation to quotation, from style to style, all the while preserving unaltered the literal musical text of the Mahler original (everything, including even the orchestration).

The most traditional of these linkages are types based on melodic intonations. All the latter, and the stylistic counterpoint associated with them, exhibit intonational affinities with the thematic material of the *cantus firmus,* Mahler's scherzo:

1. The "tambourines" (with the flute grace notes) from the beginning of the first movement of Mahler's Fourth Symphony [example 32.2] are akin to the *appoggiature* in the low register of the clarinets from the scherzo of the Second Symphony.
2. The major-minor "iridescence" of Mahler's scherzo switches over into the major-minor intonation that starts the quotation from Alban Berg's Violin Concerto [example 32.3].

Example 32.1. Quotation from Mahler, Symphony No. 2, 5th Movement (Scherzo)

Example 32.2. Quotation from Mahler, Symphony No. 4, 1st Movement

Example 32.3. Quotation from Berg, Violin Concerto

3. The simultaneous sounding of a major and a minor third also characterizes the quoted material from Debussy's *La Mer* [example 32.4a,b,c].
4. The chromatic splashes of Ravel's *La Valse* are easily montaged in Mahler's scherzo [example 32.5].
5. The descending chromatic passages in the Mahler scherzo are answered by quoting the ascending chromatic figures from Berg's *Wozzeck* [example 32.6].
6. The "clashing" chromatic figures "at a distance" in Mahler's theme call up the quotation from Stravinsky's *Agon* (the micro-series based on the non-stepwise filling-in of a minor third) [example 32.7]. Any atonal chromatic material can be easily integrated into the domain of Mahler's intonations and harmonies, given their potential for atonality. In every case, however, more concrete intonational affinities are also present.

Example 32.4. Quotations (a, b, c) from Debussy, *La Mer*

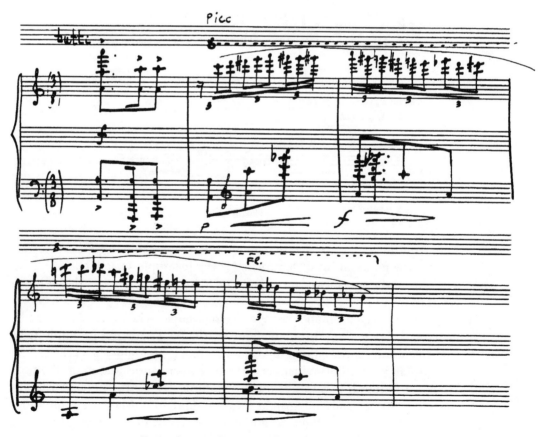

Example 32.5. Quotation from Ravel, *La Valse*

Example 32.6. Quotation from Berg, *Wozzeck*

7. The initial diatonic fourth in the Mahler scherzo along with its continuation, either diatonic or chromatic, have correspondences with both the violin solo in Webern's Cantata No. 2, Opus 31 [example 32.8], and (in its vertical projection) the well-known chord from the third of Schoenberg's Five Pieces for Orchestra, Opus 16 [32.9a,b].

8. A major-minor "splintered" third, utterly lacking in modal effect, is nominally present in the quotations from Stockhausen's *Gruppen* [example 32.10] and Webern's Cantata No. 2.

Example 32.7. Quotation from Stravinsky, *Agon*

Example 32.8. Quotation from Webern, Cantata No. 2

a)

b)

Example 32.9. a. Quotation from Schoenberg, Op. 16, No. 3;
b. Quotation from Mahler, Symphony No. 2

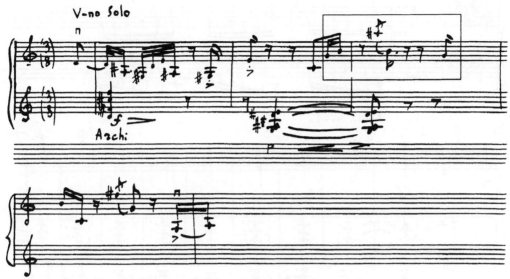

Example 32.10. Quotation from Stockhausen, *Gruppen*

Following are still more examples of intonational affinities between the Mahler *cantus firmus* and the polystylistic counterpoint found in the linkages and elsewhere:

9. The falling diatonic tetrachord heard in the trio of Mahler's scherzo [example 32.11a] and, at its climactic "rebound" [example 32.11b], is encountered as well in the quotation of the "Beloved's" *idée-fixe* from Berlioz's *Symphonie fantastique* [example 32.11c].
10. The three-beat wave-like pulse, the similarity in tessitura, tonal plan, and timbre (that same clarinet, which dominates the Mahler scherzo, brightened and freshened here by re-coloration in the relative E-flat major)—all these make the quotation of the folk-like pastoral piping tune from the finale of Beethoven's Sixth Symphony seem entirely organic [example 32.12].

Not content just with affinities in intonation, Berio also integrates the many styles of his musical material by means of less perceptible affinities. The comments and rejoinders by the vocal ensemble at the very beginning of the scherzo herald a subtle network of hints, allusions, and oblique associations that unify all the seemingly disconnected images into a poetic musical picture of the modern world being shaken and torn apart. The quasi-ironic interrogatory retorts—"deuxième symphonie," "quatrième symphonie," "deuxième partie," "première partie," "quatrième partie," "troisième partie"—immediately say to the listener, "Pay attention to the text, no matter how absurd it may be; it also has formal connections with the music. But that's not all, you will surely feel the expressive and associative connections between the stylistically alien layers of the music."

When the issue of formal unity is approached as it is here, the intonational affinities are seen as an external factor. Apart from them, deeper affinities among the elements also function, affinities that deserve as much attention as the thematic,

intonational ones. In fact, in this work the thematic function is accomplished not only by the demonstrative, easily heard, "above-water" layer of the musical material, but also by the non-demonstrative, implied, "underwater" complement of associations, analogies, and oblique correspondences. Thus, between Mahler's scherzo and the quotation from *Wozzeck*, apart from the coincidence of the chromatic intonations already noted, there is also a plainly ironic literary association. "Hören Sie? Ja dort!"; then, "Jesus! Das war ein Ton!"—these exclamations are heard from the Captain and the Doctor as Wozzeck drowns. Then one remembers that Mahler's scherzo itself makes use of the melody of a song about St. Anthony of Padua preaching to the fishes from Mahler's song cycle *Des Knaben Wunderhorn*. But beneath even this manifest literary link hides yet another one. In both situations, in Mahler's scherzo and in the scene from *Wozzeck* (as well as in Berio's *Sinfonia*, which unites them all), an overall sense is evoked of precarious, shaky ground slipping away beneath one's feet.

An even more subtle correspondence exists between the willfully eclectic quotations flashing by in Berio's *Sinfonia* and their timbral embodiment. In fact, the very performance ensemble itself embodies the eclectic universalism of modern musical practice: the usual instrumental complement of a large symphony orchestra is augmented by two saxophones, an electric guitar, an electric organ, and an electric harpsichord. But the decisive factor is the participation of the vocal octet, the Swingle Singers, which one cannot hear without subconscious recollections of virtuoso performances of modernized, commercialized versions of the classics.

Finally, the most subtle unifying factor, which imbues the work with a tragic quality, is the precise correspondence between the ephemerality of Mahler's scherzo, as it flows rapidly through the work, and the deliberately imperfect form of the whole.

A nostalgic sense of the impossibility of achieving conceptual and formal perfection, which had distinguished West European music of the nineteenth century, permeates Berio's *Sinfonia*. As though identifying himself with the dying individualistic humanism of the art of the past, the composer revives in a "death-bed review" images of nineteenth- and twentieth-century music from Beethoven to Stockhausen, and even himself (thereby relegating himself to the past as well). The composer seems to be saying, "Just as it is impossible to bring these wonderful memories back to real life, so too is it impossible to restore the living musical form— assuming that precisely 'form' is meant, and not 'construction'—a form that has been destroyed by the shocks of ideological demystification and eroded by the intellectual skepticism of technological preoccupations." And he proves his point with an experiment designed to generate and bring about the premature destruction of the new polystylistic form.

At critical moments in the historical development of the language of music, salvation always came from outside. The attempt to strengthen a rotting tree by

(Facing page, top) Example 32.11. a–b. Quotations from Mahler, Symphony No. 2, 3rd Movement; c. Quotation from Berlioz, *Symphonie Fantastique*
(Facing page, bottom) Example 32.12. Quotation from Beethoven, Symphony No. 6, Finale (pastoral piping tune)

grafting on shoots from its wild relatives is nothing new. Examples of such hybrid-ization fill the history of music, the crossbreeding of what has grown old with what has been long forgotten, to make the tree of music fruitful again. One of the most recent examples is Webern, who "crossbred" the homophonic-harmonic forms of nineteenth- and twentieth-century music with the polyphonic formal processes of sixteenth- and seventeenth-century music.

Berio seems at first sight to have taken another step in the same direction: his polystylistic variations on a *cantus firmus* are the fruit of crossing Webern's homo-phonic-polyphonic hybrid with new, "wild" material, with the jumble of sounds that reaches us daily from radio and television through open windows and pursues us on public transportation. But unlike his predecessors, Berio himself refuses to confirm a new form in his *Sinfonia*; it dies just as it is being born. Swamped by the polystylistic quotations, the guiding thread (the *cantus firmus*) first "sinks underwa-ter" but remains unbroken, floating up to the surface from time to time in precisely the necessary bars, as if the Mahler scherzo has not been interrupted but merely ceased at times to be audible. But then, under the pressure of the accessory quota-tions, the thread breaks; afterward, those fragments of the scherzo that float to the surface seem no longer to be linked by an "underwater" connection. Now, the alien polystylistic musical material intrudes itself without being syntactically subordi-nate to the broken *cantus firmus*. The tempo changes and, right up to the transgres-sive appearance of the climax of the Mahler scherzo, a tangled mass of quotations rolls on freely, without any formal framework. The musical form suffers catastrophe.

Written in the 1970s. The original Russian text has not been published.

LIGETI'S ORCHESTRAL MICROPOLYPHONY
(1970s)

Lontano [At a Distance]—the very title of this work expresses Ligeti's idea and his technical approach. The listener is enveloped in the most delicate web of sound through which, like distant phantoms, appear familiar shadows of romantic music. Sometimes they become clearer and come into focus in dazzling beams of light, heralding a miracle, but at the last moment the golden nimbus fades and everything mists over. Now the mist thickens, then we see sharply defined dark shapes, but the gloom proves as unstable as the light. Everything is unsteady, full of meaning, elusive. As in Plato's cave we glimpse only reflections of a higher reality, but we are powerless to grasp it. As in a dream, we hear only echoes of some vast sonorous world, but on awakening, we cannot remember it.

At the basis of this work, however, lies precise calculation. The most delicate network is woven from a single thread. The micropolyphony of the piece, which the ear cannot separate into its component parts, proves to be a strict multivoiced canon (at times, a double canon).

Example 33.1 gives a schema of the work.

The intonational thread itself lacks implication—no gradual sharpenings of intonation, no expressive leaps. The most characteristic motif, a falling minor second, is deprived of conventional expressive effect (the traditional motif of a "sigh") by a return to the initial note, which neutralizes it (a "sigh" is expressive; "inhaling" and "exhaling" are not). Only the profile of the tessitura suggests a dynamic factor, with its perpendicular widening from an initial middle register and its eventual slippage downward into the lower register toward the end (obvious in the diagram).

This is the "horoscope" of the work, its secret formula, nowhere expressed openly. In its actual realization, filtered through the multicolored world of the orchestra, it generates a stream of individual lines that imitate each other and slip away from each other. Some last a long time, following along a substantial part of the fatally predestined course, while others perish immediately, only their shadows remaining briefly visible.

Already on the very first page of the score a micropolyphonic canon takes shape as follows. The instrumental parts, new ones being added continually, are all linked to an initiating note (A-flat above middle C) and are introduced in order of timbral modulation from the less to the more vivid and distinctive timbres: 4 flutes—4 clarinets—3 bassoons—4 horns—trumpet—oboe. Not all of them are destined to

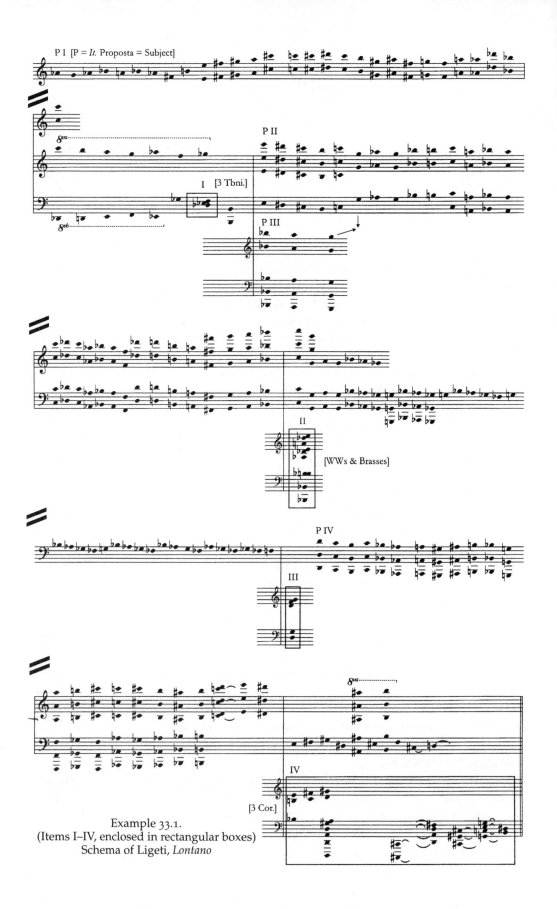

Example 33.1.
(Items I–IV, enclosed in rectangular boxes)
Schema of Ligeti, *Lontano*

survive the first melodic phrase intact, only the flutes and clarinets. The bassoons, horns, and trumpet fade away on the very first tone, and the oboe on the second (in order several bars later to present a new melodic offshoot). But, apart from the real timbres of the wind instruments, there are also incorporeal harmonics in the strings, functioning as internal pedal points, which are introduced by turns simultaneously with the winds and continue sounding for a very long time, like traces left behind by the wind instruments. The order of their entries constitutes yet another voice in the canon, as if in free augmentation. Thematic imitation also entails dynamic imitation, a chain of wavelike greater and lesser crescendos-diminuendos that offers the opportunity for each timbre to emerge momentarily from the overall sonority and then dissolve into it once again [example 27.4, p. 145].

Before the first "phase" of the canon finishes, the voices of the following "phase" make their entry, to begin with as incorporeal shadows, as harbingers in double-bass harmonics, then in actuality in the oboes (here the abandoned motif of the "sigh" is extended through further development). Thus continues the weaving of a delicate web of micropolyphony in which the different colored threads turn for a moment toward the sunlight only to fade immediately into shadow.

The textural elements in this sound picture are easily differentiated in the vertical plane. The voices of the canon, their contrapuntal offshoots, and the internal pedal tones (which sometimes blend into chords) are clearly distinguishable. All these elements originate in a single source, since they represent different stages of a theme observed simultaneously. The functions of the voices in the texture change at every moment as a consequence of the fact that the performers of segments of the theme do not play them at the same time. A voice in a more animated zone is perceived as thematic, while another in a less vigorous segment is heard as an internal pedal tone. Thus, the entire musical fabric with all its contrasting elements reflects the theme as seen simultaneously from different perspectives. This in conjunction with the "hovering" rhythm, skillfully avoiding metrical accents (thereby leveling out any sense of time), creates the illusion of free flight devoid of ordinary time and specific gravity. In this way the work acquires maximum structural unity, all its textural components not merely springing from the theme, but themselves *being* the theme.

Four times, however, foreign textural elements of non-thematic, "irrational" origin intrude into this ideally perfect fabric. Although they always make their entry unnoticed, their appearance inevitably interrupts the projected flow of the form:

1. A chord in three trombones cuts short the coming together of two lines in opposing registers and gives rise to the entry of a new double canon (although its two streams soon flow into each other) [example 33.1(I)].
2. A softly articulated chord in woodwinds and brasses, barely audible in itself, interrupts an expected buildup in the strings, which one by one fall away, seemingly dragged down by the static invisible mass of the chord and dislodged from the action [example 33.1(II)].
3. [A note in Schnittke's hand refers to item 3 as being on the back of a leaf of his typescript, but this fragment of his text has never been found. Example 33.1(III) does, however, give Schnittke's illustration for this point. —ed.]

4. The third cycle of dynamic buildup is also cut short by the unnoticed entry of a soft chord in three horns. Later on, the chord secures continuation in the "shadow" of a chorale that ends the entire composition [example 33.1(IV)].

Thus, the non-thematic elements in this work serve a cadential function. They close off one of the ways in which the theme might move forward, and they open up another.

* * *

Having mastered in a theoretical sense the "strict style" of serialism of the 1950s, Ligeti the composer rejected it as a dogmatic technique. Nonetheless, the entirety of his personal style is obliquely linked with serialism:

1. *The "aesthetics of avoidance":* Ligeti uses avoidance not only in the technological sense (e.g., avoiding simultaneous octave entries in different voices or perfect fifths) but also in a more general expressive sense. He avoids dynamic expectation of climaxes, for the first time in the history of music turning stasis from a negative element into a positive one. He avoids direct topical associations. Like a cloud constantly changing its form—actually visible only from a distance, but at close range intangible and diaphanous—his mysteriously meaningful music eludes any straightforward verbal interpretations.
2. *The strictest possible control of the texture:* He devises polyphony of a vast number of imitative voices, precisely calculating the resultant texture in all its dimensions. Rhythm, timbre, and dynamics are structurally controlled, just as in the works of the serialists, not however on the basis of a series (treated cabbalistically as a "formula for life") but on the basis of a rational methodology that serves to make the expression of the fundamental poetic idea as clear as possible.

For Ligeti the process of composition begins not with a calculation of form but with close attention to the sonorous image of the future work—a sonorous image somehow independent of the composer's will, one that exists in his imagination and demands outward expression. Technology, in such a case, with all its rationality, serves as a means for actualizing a mirage in sound, rather than as a tool for building a musical edifice. Two essences at opposite poles interact in an incomprehensibly paradoxical way: a poetic style that is refined to a point beyond the real and a constructive logic that is precise to the point of being schematic. The interaction of these two essences comprises the intensity and dynamics of Ligeti's music, the work of a composer who revealed the world of musical stasis with all its secret energies.

Written in the 1970s. The original Russian text has not been published.

VI

SCHNITTKE AS SEEN BY OTHERS

34

GIDON KREMER ON SCHNITTKE (1989)

IVASHKIN: When did you first get to know Schnittke's music, and how has your perception of it changed since that time? Do you think there has been some evolution in it, or do you see it as a kind of single unified composition?

KREMER: Those are complex questions. But my general feeling, in any case, is that our perceptions change considerably. I recall something, not directly connected with Alfred, but still relevant to him: how in my student days (1967, 1968, or thereabouts) I reacted to Shostakovich. I was so indifferent toward someone generally acknowledged to be a genius that I find it hard to explain whether this was because of the familiarity of his music or because I myself was young and foolish—but, in any case, I seemed to find it all too familiar. And, to give you a specific example, when I heard the first performance of his Second Violin Concerto, personally I found nothing particularly new in it. It seemed to be drawn out, completely academic, marking no step forward from his first Violin Concerto.

Twenty years went by. (For the moment I skip over everything else.) And last year for the first time I made real contact with the work, played it myself, and noticed that my approach to it was completely different, and that I was hearing it in a completely different way. Whether this was because by then I had played his last quartets, whether it was because I was twenty years older, whether it was because Shostakovich was no longer with us—whatever it was, my attitude to the work had changed completely.

My view is that in a certain sense we ourselves evolve and that evolution takes place on account of time. Time brings correctives, reappraisals, and it also defines something. So if we speak of Alfred now (what I have been saying can serve as a kind of epigraph to this), I can say that I remember now the day when I asked Eri Klas the name of the lady who first brought Schnittke's name and work to my notice, or at any rate prompted me to start looking for his music and to ring him up. She lived in Estonia. To tell the truth, I scarcely knew her, but clearly we had some kind of conversation or interview. I don't remember, and she is no longer alive. Eri Klas thinks it was Ophelia Tuisk, and I think it must have been, although I cannot say for sure. I didn't even have the feeling that that was when I had first heard Schnittke's name. But probably it was, because people were talking about him then, and when I was in Estonia in 1967–1969, I did hear his name, although it meant nothing to me. I often take an interest in works without knowing the composer. I sometimes think that this is an advantage, because if you do know the composer and, God forbid, he dedicates a work to you (and in addition you are a close friend of his), then you are obliged to perform the work or, if you refuse, to think up excuses, and that creates tension. What happened in this case was that I made my own choice (although obviously someone had recommended Schnittke's music to me), and in order to clear up certain things about the performance, I rang up Alfred and we met. That day he gave me the music to his Second Violin Concerto, on which he had written: "To Gidon Kremer, in the hope of one day hearing something of my work." That's how our friendship began. I think it was in 1970.

The Second Violin Sonata *(Quasi una Sonata)* I have played a great deal, every-where I could. Sometimes I couldn't, like that time in Riga, when they didn't want to hear it and suggested I play Beethoven instead. But where I could, I played it, and audiences were completely shocked by it. But that was part of my plan—I wanted to disturb audiences, not let them doze off.

Then other works by Alfred began to come into my life—and not only the Second Violin Concerto, which I played again in 1973 in my series, The History of the Violin Concerto, in Vilnius, Kaunas, Sverdlovsk, and Lvov. I also played it in many cities in the Soviet Union, but I don't remember the exact order. In 1976, I played the Quintet—perhaps there was something else before that—then the *Preludia*.

Moz-Art was composed later, in 1976, for a New Year's concert. If you recall that New Year's concert, that was my first "Lockenhaus," my first experiment in that way, and Alfred also took some part in it. Our paths crossed frequently throughout those years—either because he had an idea and he shared it with me, or I had an idea, and I felt the need to consult him about it. Then, of course, the Concerto Grosso No. 1 became so important in our relationship—not only did we give the first perfor-mance together, but we also had the idea of going abroad together. And at that time, since I enjoyed relative independence in intolerable circumstances, I managed some-how to put the idea into practice and to involve a pianist no one had heard of, Alfred Schnittke, so that he could see the world. I thought that this was not just wonderful for us (the composer was actually performing) but simply essential as far as he was concerned.

IVASHKIN: Incidentally, out of this came his Second Symphony.

KREMER: Yes, I remember the situation in St. Florian.[1] For many reasons that tour was very stressful. I think that my decision at that time—to adopt a different position and to cross the border in such an unusual way—undoubtedly had intrigued him. It was a fairly intensive trip, and he was able to meet ordinary people and fellow musicians. I remember his enthusiastic response to a meeting with Stockhausen. And I discovered later that Stockhausen was equally enthusiastic. I could talk about this for hours, but I want to bring things into focus and talk about music.

If you take Schnittke's music from the time of his Second Sonata to the present day, for me its essence has not changed. As far as I am concerned, Alfred has always been unashamed of what he is, unafraid of trying to do something different. If

---

1. St. Florian: Austrian monastery near Linz, Anton Bruckner's burial place. —ed.

anything, he was afraid of success. Even when success came, he once said to me: "Success disturbs me. It's time to write something that will not be successful." I think there is a good deal of Alfred in this comment, because the reference points to his searchings for values lying outside time. That is very important. So many composers have tried to make successful careers for themselves by using time as their point of reference, using something that has been said to them or foisted on them. Alfred is a great mirror of time because he never flirted or played with it, but lived in it. And he was directed by the desire (and still is!) to reflect time not as if he were making diary entries, but by using the standpoints and categories of what is eternal. His reference points are not transient values. But, even though his values are eternal, he has no qualms about being in conflict with himself, with time, even with what he writes. And in my opinion anyone looking merely for completeness, for something smooth and comfortable in his music, will be making a mistake. There may be something smooth and comfortable in it, but there is always the opposite. His music is always built on contrasts.

You asked me if his music changes.... In the East they have an opposition—the Korean airline even adopted it as its logo—yin and yang, white and black, yes and no. Putting it simply, these are two forces, one centrifugal, the other centripetal. Yin and yang are a higher philosophical generalization of what I am trying to say. This tension is created by contrast—you can sense it in the Second Violin Sonata—in the contrast of the pauses, of chords or sounds, of material that seems to be trying to develop, but cannot.

In the Fourth Violin Concerto, written sixteen or eighteen years later, there is also this conflict or contrast. The whole work is built on the elusive quality of genuine despair and observation of this, on a striving for the beautiful and its simultaneous transformation into vulgar banality. These are eternal categories precisely because they are not merely "black and white"; they combine with one another and themselves create a new category. And only Alfred has the power to grasp this category and, subordinating it to his imagination, turn it into a musical score. I believe that in his case this process is so charged with drama and emotion that it cannot leave people indifferent. I have seen this tremendous power working on an audience that is unaware of the subtleties, unaware of the perfection. As Gennadi Rozhdestvensky remarked today, "In formal terms it is all done geometrically and mathematically."

This music has a direct influence on you. And this is Alfred's great strength. Reliving his experiences or investing them with definite musical form, he finds a way of getting out to the audience. I think he acquired this ability by having to work in the cinema to earn his living. In Moscow at the Stroganovsky [College of Fine Arts] there is a department of "monumental pictorial arts." In Russia there is a whole age connected with monumental pictorial arts, and the cinema is the "main art," the most "important" for all of us, even though it has a number of negative "consumer" faults, since it is meant for a mass audience. Alfred, while opposed to this, was still able to retain his musical identity and preserve his integrity in writing for film. Even here he was incapable of betraying himself. So when he says that his real music is a continuation of his film music, or vice versa, I see in this the kind of acknowledgment that is essential to any really great man: strength of character finding its continuation in weakness of character and weakness in strength.

This makes for unity in his work as a whole, like Mahler, whose music was shocking merely insofar as it combined what seemed to be incompatible. Hearing Alfred's Third Symphony today, I am struck once again—as I have been so many times—by the parallel with Mahler. It occurs to me that they are related to each other in their own ways. The essence of the music has not changed, although of course there is a change of style, a change of features, if you like, because there was a precise moment (perhaps about the time of the Piano Quintet) when Alfred conceived the desire to use more harmony or more so-called polystylistic music.

The tango in the Concerto Grosso is also certainly a reminder of how to combine incompatible elements. But in one sense this tango is a continuation of the *Serenade* written thirty years earlier, and the saxophone in the Fourth Violin Concerto is a continuation of the tango. There are many things that join Alfred's works together.

An inner change took place directly before or after his illness. Some people think that the Cello Concerto, written at that time, seems to provide evidence of this. But already in the String Trio, written before his illness, I find the quintessence of his suffering, or even the whole of his struggle to find some unearthly power that might enable him, if you like, to overcome the force of gravity. Written before the illness, the String Trio has a lucidity that anticipates the definite sense of luminescence of later works. Generally speaking, talking about his illness as a definite point of change, I would say that there he had a presentiment of the illness even before it came. The String Trio and even moments in the Second String Quartet are evidence of this. After the illness there was further development of this feeling. As he himself said, a new time began for him. Perhaps that is so. I hope he has enough time left for new changes of direction, but the essence has remained the same. To me Alfred is a special kind of seismograph. That is where his value lies. His music is not emasculated or calculated; it is full of his defeats, his diffidence, his doubts, his inhibitions, whatever you like, but there is in it a power that goes beyond the bounds of what is ordinary. Perhaps this power lies in the fact that ultimately in music he is not afraid of being himself, and perhaps after his illness he is less afraid than he was before it.

IVASHKIN: Many of my Russian friends living in the West believe that it is impossible for someone in the West who has never lived in Russia to understand Schnittke's music and all it stands for. What do you think, as someone who performs regularly in the West? I was surprised by the ecstatic reception his music had today.

KREMER: I don't find it surprising. I have played this work (the Fourth Violin Concerto) in various countries, and the music has a profound effect on many people, even the uninitiated. Certain things are more comprehensible and accessible to people living in the Soviet Union or under the Soviet system, but Alfred's language is universal. In the West a common reaction to modern music is to say, "Yes, very interesting." That happens in the Soviet Union, too. I find it extremely insulting when people come up to me after a concert and say, "Very interesting." It is such a commonplace remark.

It seems to me that "very interesting" is precisely what one must not call Alfred Schnittke's music. There is something spellbinding about it, but in it there is also what he refers to when speaking of his Concerto Grosso: a similarity or parallel with Thomas Mann in his story *Tonio Kröger*, where in one passage the main character talks about the power of vulgarity or ordinariness in human life, and about how vulgarity and banality are not in opposition to human beings but are part of them. And it is this that enables us to feel and understand the music, because through its imagery we can more easily identify ourselves with it. You see, if we are presented with something beyond our understanding, we say, "That's interesting," or "We don't understand that." But Alfred forces us to be alert to those inept emotions that we should like to hide and of which we are somehow ashamed. This is what he shows us, this is the language he uses, and this may be why he is closer to us on the level of imagery. And this is not confined only to people living in the Soviet Union. Human beings are weak not just where they are oppressed, but unfortunately also where they enjoy all kinds of opportunities and where everything is spread out in front of them.

From an interview conducted in 1989. Russian text published in *Besedy s Al'fredom Shnitke*, compiled and edited by A. V. Ivashkin (Moscow: Kul'tura, 1994), pp. 238–245.

35

GENNADI ROZHDESTVENSKY ON SCHNITTKE (1989)

ROZHDESTVENSKY: If I am not mistaken, the first time I came into contact with Alfred's music was many years ago, in the early 1960s, when we were trying to organize an audition in the Bolshoi Theater of his opera *The Eleventh Commandment*. But nothing came of it. Then I performed the First Violin Concerto with Mark Lubotsky and recorded it for radio broadcast.

IVASHKIN: Did you have any difficulties in performing his music?

ROZHDESTVENSKY: None at all. I recently went back to this work and performed it in Siena with my son, Sasha, as soloist.

I retain a clear impression of listening to a recording of Alfred's Piano Quintet at a meeting of the Melodiya Studio Artistic Council. The effect of the music was so powerful that I immediately phoned Alfred at home and told him that, in my opinion, the work required symphonic treatment. He told me that for the moment he couldn't conceive that, but that he would try to do so. And he did so quite quickly. I performed *In Memoriam* [the orchestral version of the Piano Quintet] and then recorded it.

I don't want to talk about the first performance of his First Symphony in Gorky—that is too well known. I remember the first rehearsal in the Great Hall of the Conservatory of Alfred's Third Violin Concerto—with Oleg Kagan and Yuri Nikolaevsky. On that occasion I had the distinct feeling of the healing of the wound created by the death of Shostakovich. It became clear that the bridge hanging over the precipice was now finished.

IVASHKIN: What common features do you see between Alfred and Shostakovich?

ROZHDESTVENSKY: I see them in the chronicle of time, in the chronicle of the intonations of time, and in the way they use their material, including everyday material. I think that Alfred, like Shostakovich, is a chronicler of his time, a composer who turned the next page of the history of the art of music in Russia.

IVASHKIN: It is remarkable that today at concerts of Alfred's music there is exactly the same atmosphere as there was for Shostakovich's music in the early 1960s.

ROZHDESTVENSKY: Yes, and that is easy to understand.

IVASHKIN: Do you often return to Alfred's early music—do you now see it differently?

ROZHDESTVENSKY: No, for me any music by Alfred is a breakthrough, an explosion. I've always had that impression. In that sense, too, one can draw a parallel with Shostakovich and his early works. Alfred's First Symphony is something quite amazing!

IVASHKIN: Did it strike you as something new?

ROZHDESTVENSKY: Yes, something supernatural. I found it a shocking experience, although I could sense the roots and threads linking its music with the past. The work played an enormous role in my life.

IVASHKIN: Was it your idea to perform Alfred's First Symphony with Haydn's *Farewell Symphony*?

ROZHDESTVENSKY: Yes, it was. I don't think his First Symphony can be performed with anything else.

IVASHKIN: What is your impression of the works Alfred wrote after his illness, after 1985? Can you see any new style in them?

ROZHDESTVENSKY: Yes. What is most moving is the wisdom, the clarity, the simplicity. One is constantly struck by the way he can keep reminding us what a triad is—quite remarkable! The appearance of a simple triad makes the most powerful impression.

IVASHKIN: Don't you find that in his later works there is a harshness of sound not there before?

ROZHDESTVENSKY: No, I don't think so.

IVASHKIN: Not even in the Fifth Symphony?

ROZHDESTVENSKY: In the Fifth Symphony I feel something else: that we cannot give outward form to his conception. In my opinion, the present-day technique of modern instrumentalists makes it impossible. That is why I had the idea of doubling the brass with voices. Alfred tells me that in the Concertgebouw the symphony was performed without this doubling. That is possible. But I think that this leads to excessive strain. So when I recorded the Fifth Symphony in Moscow the whole of the brass was doubled: a voice for each. Otherwise, in my view, it would be impossible at present. Just as, in its own time (in 1913), a performance of Stravinsky's *Rite of Spring* seemed physically impossible. There are similar difficulties in Alfred's Third Symphony. We are not yet prepared for them today. While the Fifth Symphony is extremely complicated to perform not only physically but also in respect to the need to make all its polyphony clearly audible, in a recording the sound engineer can help here.

In fact, in my opinion there are many works today that are not suitable for performance without technical means—modern technical equipment and a skillful sound engineer. For example, Alfred's First Cello Concerto. It is impossible to perform without sound enhancement. The way many composers, including Alfred, relate to their material, to the sound in their heads, is inseparable from modern recording techniques. Take any harpsichord or celesta part in a tutti passage that has an important function in the whole material—without increasing their volume, these instruments cannot be heard. And I believe that is not a miscalculation, but something quite deliberate.

IVASHKIN: I shall never forget your performance of Shostakovich's Fourth Symphony with the State Symphony Orchestra in Moscow when the spirit of Shostakovich seemed to be hovering in the Great Hall of the Conservatory. Can you sense any hidden symbolism, any subtext, in Alfred's works, like those that are so obvious in your performances of Shostakovich's music? And, in connection with this, do you think that Alfred's music is a Russian phenomenon?

ROZHDESTVENSKY: I think it is just as much a Russian phenomenon as is the music of Shostakovich, Prokofiev, and Stravinsky. And the reason it is Russian is precisely because it is international. The most vivid example is Scriabin, a very Russian composer who, under the closest examination, reveals no common roots with the Russian musical tradition. And something else is important: the scale of things. You could not compose the *Poem of Ecstasy* in Holland, no matter how clever you were. It simply would not work!

IVASHKIN: Many musicians in the West think that Alfred's music is for domestic consumption in Russia; much of it they do not understand. Can you explain that?

ROZHDESTVENSKY: By the fact that life is different. I played Shostakovich's Fourth Symphony with the Cleveland Orchestra—the players found the scherzo funny: "It sounds like the clatter of horses' hooves," they remarked. When you tell them about communicating by tapping on radiators, they are amazed. As far as they are concerned, radiators are for heating.

IVASHKIN: How many of Alfred's works have you performed? Alfred counted thirty-five... and in many of them you collaborated in the composition....

ROZHDESTVENSKY: What does "collaborate" mean? Any conductor with a brain is a "co-author." Only Stravinsky said that a conductor could not be a co-author, that he was merely someone who reproduced the composer's text. But that is unrealistic, even if the composer performs his own works. I devised a suite from *Revizskaya Skazka* [The Census List] with Alfred's approval and under his supervision. I arranged the second part of *Music for an Imaginary Play* for four flutes, but only after Alfred agreed to it. And of course I made refinements to the scores in the process of rehearsing for performance.

IVASHKIN: Alfred is known to make many changes to his scores during rehearsals. This irritates some conductors. How do you feel about it?

ROZHDESTVENSKY: I think this is like Mahler, because the revisions always depend on the acoustics of the hall where you are performing. When you get to another hall and start rehearsing, you have to change it again.... When Mahler arrived in Munich from Hamburg he found himself in a different concert hall and thought his instrumentation was wrong. And the more performances he gave, the more versions appeared. It seems to me that various editions of Mahler's symphonies are a kind of guide to the concert halls of Europe. They show you where one thing works and where it doesn't.

IVASHKIN: Don't you think that Alfred's orchestrations are too traditional? Apart from using guitars and keyboard instruments he always uses the traditional form of orchestra....

ROZHDESTVENSKY: No, I don't. And I have always been against guitars. You can't always get them, and when you do, it turns out that the guitarist cannot read music. If suddenly you find he can, you feel like going down on your knees. I remember that in one performance of *Faust* they had to tie strings to the guitarist's legs so that someone could give them a tug when it was his turn to play.... But Alfred's guitar is not just a guitar, it's a basso continuo, a large harpsichord for today.

From an interview conducted in Stockholm in 1989. Russian text published in *Besedy s Al'fredom Shnitke*, compiled and edited by A. V. Ivashkin (Moscow: Kul'tura, 1994), pp. 248–251.

CHAPTER 36

VLADIMIR YANKILEVSKY ON SCHNITTKE
(1989)

YANKILEVSKY: Alfred's and my relationship gradually grew more involved, but it started in a very simple way.

IVASHKIN: When was that?

YANKILEVSKY: I think it was about 1965, just at the time when Alfred had written the music for an animated film, *The Glass Harmonica*. Soon afterward Andrei Khrzhanovsky introduced us. For some reason it happened on the street. The first thing I heard of his compositions was the Violin Sonata [No. 2, *Quasi una Sonata*], performed by Luba Edlina and Mark Lubotsky in the concert hall of the Krupskaya House of National Arts and Crafts.

IVASHKIN: And were you introduced to him as someone involved in the artistic avant-garde?

YANKILEVSKY: No, for me the word "avant-garde" had no significance. The idea of the "avant-garde" is connected with so much speculation that few people understand what is really meant by it. Some people imagine that members of the avant-garde wear yellow trousers, others that they walk about on their hands, or write incomprehensible music. It always seems to mean something vague, all the more now, when the expression has been completely devalued and the avant-garde has become so "comfortable," has acquired a meaning so much the opposite of its true sense, that I now try to avoid it altogether. It is no longer a word with a definite dictionary meaning, but something quite indefinite. No, Alfred never seemed to me to represent any kind of avant-garde current in music. When I first met him, my initial impression was at a purely human level: I saw someone whose spiritual aura was close to my own. Even physiologically he seemed close to me, almost like a near relative. After a brief conversation with him I trusted him completely, and straightaway we began to talk to each other in a very honest way. There was none of what is called in battle "reconnaissance." And it was immediately clear that within him there was concealed a massive and complex layer of various impressions of the world, that he was a personality with a deep understanding of life. And later, when I came to know his music, every time I heard it opened up more of the reserves that I felt he had inside him. Everything I heard came as no surprise. All his works came from the same world I had recognized in him at our first meeting.

IVASHKIN: You both belong to the same generation and could even be said to be moving in the same direction. Alfred's music has changed over the years. Outwardly it has become simpler. What is your impression of this evolution? Do you feel that something similar has happened in your own work? What does this simplification mean? Does it have a kind of symbolic significance (that is, that the simple elements, which turn into symbols, have a very profound subtext, and it is only on the surface that they appear simple), or is it merely a kind of traditionalism, which appeared in the 1970s and 1980s, but which was absent in the 1960s? How would you define it?

YANKILEVSKY: Right away I object to the word "simplification." "Simplification" is one word, "simplicity" is another, and the two things are different in principle. I prefer to speak more precisely of music that is simple in a majestic sense. There is no more unnecessary fuss, everything has become more monumental, clear, and precise. And this is a very logical development for any great artist, because art, like any way of looking at the world, is a philosophy, a life experience. With this experience, one grows wiser, music becomes wiser, and wisdom is simplicity. But I should like to add something on the question of evolution. I think that all great artists have an idée fixe, a conception. In fact, they are born with it. As Einstein once said, he always had only a couple of good ideas, everything else was the interpretation of these two ideas. But they were so vast that they seemed to take in the whole universe. I think that Alfred too had a few good ideas and that they became the basic concept of all his creative work. These ideas, as they gradually penetrated all his work, enriched it, and at the same time simplified it. The enrichment developed paradoxically, looking from the outside like simplification. What had preceded each successive work became an integral part of it. And the image of the world that was created became vaster, but it was still a continuation of the same idea. At the very beginning the idea could be expressed in the two sounds that created the space, fixed the vision, fixed the world... but then to be able to perceive these two or three sounds is to define one's creative destiny. One person has these sounds, while someone else will never perceive or hear them. What is also important is the fact that art is multilayered, consisting of many levels. There is an outer surface layer—a kind of subjective and actual comprehension of the world. Many artists are fixed in this layer: children of their time, they live on the ideas of the time, adopt the texture of the time. But when this time has passed, when the people for whom it was actual are themselves no longer living, what they have done loses all its meaning. But if in a work of art there are other layers of eternal problems, cosmic layers, then everything fixed in these layers can no longer come to an end, but lives on in encoded form. Subconsciously it enters the human psyche, the spiritual world of human beings, and it then reveals itself gradually, influencing them and their lives. And perhaps the longer this process lasts, the greater its effect.

That was once the case with Bach, when his contemporaries could not understand his music. A hundred or more years had to pass for his full greatness to be appreciated. I think this has happened in every age. There are artists of their own time and there are artists whose orientation seems to be toward eternity, who have no concrete time. Of course they live at a particular time, but in actual fact they live in the past and the future, as though they were stretched out in time. Artists are extremely fortunate, and Alfred especially, if, having a profound understanding of human life, they also have the remarkable ability to give their understanding an actual texture. This provides a bridge, an emotional conduit, over and through which people with little understanding, and perhaps not altogether ready to perceive the depths of this "iceberg," come to an understanding—and many things become more accessible to them. Sometimes they are deceived, perceive the conduit only, and think they have understood everything. I am sure many people think like that. I know that it is the actual textural layer that makes the greatest impression, but Alfred has nothing to fear from that, inasmuch as beneath the surface layer there is another rich and deep layer of what is eternal. I think he is a lucky man because, while his works have a deep foundation, he can still have a conduit to link him with his audience, and this is very important.

IVASHKIN: So you don't think his art is elitist?

YANKILEVSKY: There is a sense in which I regard all art as elitist. It cannot help being elitist. But there are certain levels at which an audience is affected, as happens with a shaman. No one understands how this works, but it crosses some sort of emotional threshold, when people do not understand very well how they are being affected, but begin to be affected. But this is not important. This is the specific character of art. It acts like an injection: when someone gives you an injection, you don't necessarily know what they are injecting, but then certain processes begin in your body.

There is the art that is in code, an art that in fact contains a great deal, but what it contains is very remote. A long time has to elapse before it can begin to work. There are artists and composers in history whose work has been in code for their contemporaries and which has only later begun to operate.... I think that this encoding is sometimes seen as elitism, because it is not at once comprehensible. But this is a problem of the time.

IVASHKIN: Do you think that in time Alfred's code will be deciphered? Or is it the kind of code that gets more remote the more you listen to it, like an image in a series of mirrors? Or is it perhaps just a failure to understand his language at a particular stage, a difficulty that will later disappear?

YANKILEVSKY: Alfred's music can always be deciphered in an obvious way. For example, the paradoxical combinations that he used in his First Symphony: puzzling collages, combinations of musical trash, banality, and vulgarity, and at the same time music that is profoundly classical. For many people that is as far as an appreciation of his music went. But behind this, of course, there is something deeper. And when I speak of something encoded I have in mind precisely what at first sight is invisible. What is hidden in his mathematical calculations, what he did in his Fourth Symphony, when he made use of Catholic and Lutheran chants, and what he did in the Third Symphony. All of these are things that most people find difficult to understand at first hearing. And of course you could call it elitist. I am convinced that in many respects art operates through the subconscious. Apart from an outward and accessible level that seems to be clear, there is also a subconscious level (assuming of course that the work has one). Nowadays we have artists who make a profit by using social themes. It is a whole trend—"socioart"—they paint hammers and sickles, pictures of Lenin and Stalin, this and that. And as something actual and topical this affects people, it stirs them. But most of these artists have nothing deeper to offer. What will be left when people have forgotten who Stalin or Brezhnev were? There is none of this in Alfred; he has a deeper level, much more significant. I even think he could vary the surface level, change it about, have a game with people, tease them. It is like a mask you can change for another one, but behind the mask there is something even more important, and this is the tragic basis of his work.

IVASHKIN: How do you react to his music? Does it seem close to you, something related to your own artistic practice, or do you react to it through the musical traditions and styles you know? Do you think that there is something in common between his method and yours?

YANKILEVSKY: Alfred recently told me he was writing an opera. In it there is to be a scene, the action of which is broken in two by an entr'acte. And I immediately remembered my own broken pieces. Joining together different states in a paradoxical way—by breaking them apart—is the only way of uniting such opposites as life and death. That is what I do. The way I have found, using a black hole, for example, is a paradoxical joining together. And in this sense the forms and methods we use are very similar. So we may be searching in the same direction.

Shostakovich's music, which I love and worship, seems to be just that—music. By comparison with Alfred's music it looks like music, because in it everything is as if it were confined within a single musical form. In Alfred's case the music contains many paradoxical elements; that is it is not created according to classical laws. It seems to have been destroyed, and at first one cannot understand just what it is.

Sounds are often heard in Alfred's music that make you wonder whether he wrote them himself or whether he has introduced a quotation: Is it a collage? Some of the fragments he has written have a striking effect; they sound like genuine seventeenth- or eighteenth-century music. This has been his way of searching for the image of life he wanted to create in his music. In the Second Violin Concerto there are pauses. Then various insertions are used to fill the spaces left by the pauses. What in the early works had sounded *musical*—like elements of an actual sonata, like musical elements—in major works began to mix with insertions from others. It seems to me that from the dramatic point of view they had the same function—the further away, the greater the effect. It was in this force field that he was able to work and express his view of the world. This was a remarkable development. It became a new musical form.

IVASHKIN: Speaking of form, what is your impression of his small-scale works in comparison with the large-scale ones? He has after all written five symphonies and many concertos, and they are all different. He himself says (and I feel this myself) that he takes no account of traditional forms, or, to be more precise, only does so at the beginning. For example, the first part of a symphony starts like a sonata allegro, but then that collapses. And as a rule the form never continues to the end of the work. Any indications of circularity are merely external: something from the beginning makes an appearance at the end, but in fact this is not a question of form, it is purely symbolic.

YANKILEVSKY: You know, the expression "large scale" bothers me somewhat, because monumentality is more a concept on an existential plane, not a matter of size.... I have said that you can take two sounds and use them to define the extent of something. And in Alfred's case even certain small things look monumental and occupy considerable space. So in this case the term "large scale" is a mere convention. But I can say something about the way this is close to my own ideas. It seems to me that in almost all his major works there is a personal beginning that tries to define *its own* space, in conflict with what surrounds it. This is a perennial problem for the individual human personality and for music. In all the concertos and symphonies there is always a solo opening, a kind of theme, which defines its relationship to what surrounds it. Maybe I'm talking in a roundabout way. But it is something that runs painfully through Alfred's work.

I am not speaking as a musician. I am not a musician, and I don't want to pretend that I understand this as a professional musician would. I am speaking as a human being reacting purely intuitively and able to draw parallels with what I myself do. But not at the level of musical analysis, so I ask your forbearance. What I understand, and what I feel is close to me, is the problem of expanding or destroying my own box (I can show you my latest pictures, and that will make it clearer what I mean), because each individual human personality has its own social and existential box. All human beings have their own structures and live in them.[1] The human personality tries to break its social box or at least to keep struggling to escape it. And it seems to me that the most powerful part of Alfred's music (at any rate this is how it works on me) is when the personality, the personal principle, comes into violent opposition with the elements of mass culture, with what destroys freedom, with what always prevents a human being from living. So many of his works contain passages where a highly active and dramatic struggle is taking place. And there are passages when the human being achieves harmony with his surroundings and possibly attains some kind of goal. Some of his works end without a result; the human being cannot find harmony. But his perennial theme is the elucidation of the relationships between the human personality and the world, the attempt to define oneself in this world. And this is what all human beings are engaged in, and it is in this that the vast human significance of Alfred's work lies, its human significance. One reacts to this directly and emotionally. No decoding is needed.

IVASHKIN: But if one speaks of time in his compositions, is it circumscribed in each one of them *separately*? Or is every opus a new phase in a single large work? The way I see it, his musical forms are not closed. They form a kind of spiral, never a circle. A

---

1. There are sketches of this on Yankilevsky's walls. —ed.

spiral winding away into endless associations. They are not closed either in respect to meaning or in the purely formal sense. Do you think that in the temporal sense the quality of being closed is essential? I am returning to the idea of a so-called large-scale composition, meaning one that stretches over time. Do you think that this requires closure? Do you have a sense of this in his symphonies and concertos?

YANKILEVSKY: I want to be clear about this. By closure do you mean a certain uniformity of meaning, for instance?

IVASHKIN: To a certain extent, yes. That's why any kind of closure is a cliché difficult to avoid.

YANKILEVSKY: Now I understand what you are getting at, and I want to say something quite definite. Alfred's works have a multiplicity of meanings. In that sense they are not closed. It is more that they supplement each other in the way they depict the world. They form a kind of series of depictions from various angles and distances.

IVASHKIN: How would you define your own artistic language—as "symphonic"? What is the meaning of your language as a painter, its elements, and of what elements is it made up? I should like to know so as to compare it with what happens in Alfred's music.

YANKILEVSKY: When I began my career, you understand, I tried to create my own language. But perhaps first I ought to say this. In the broad sense there are two types of artists. There are artists who know what an artist is, what he should look like, what clothes he should wear, how he should work, and what an artistic masterpiece is. The work of that kind of artist is directed at creating a masterpiece. That kind of artist knows what a masterpiece is and what it should look like. The second type does not know what an artist is, how an artist should work, and what a masterpiece is. They try to depict the world, as it were, artistically. And for this purpose they create their own language, without knowing how to do this, and create it afresh every time. Incidentally, Leonardo da Vinci spoke of this. "Each time I start anything new," he said, "I feel like a dilettante." I believe this is the attitude of the genuine artist. The first type is the so-called gallery artist who paints pictures for galleries, gives exhibitions, sells his works, and spends his life doing so. Whereas the second type, as a rule, rarely has any social success. Rarely. Which sort of artist you are depends on your destiny, and I think Alfred is extremely lucky in this respect—he is definitely the second type. Perhaps the most vivid representative of this type of artist is Van Gogh... his destiny was, as it were, the classic destiny of an artist.

I am not talking about the quality of my own work (it is not for me to judge), but in principle I too am the second type. Because I don't know and have never known what an artist is. Furthermore, whenever anyone told me how I should paint a picture, I got very annoyed and tried to define for myself how to paint it. Even a rectangular form did not suit me, and I tried to find another one. I tried to find a relationship between the form and the inner content of a picture, between its *inner* configurations and its *outward* form. So I started, as it were, from absolute zero, at the very beginning. And as I made a picture I tried to make it like a picture of the world, for this purpose creating a depictive language. So I was concerned with the problem of order and chaos.

In this respect I cannot see any direct parallels between what I do and what Alfred does; but in the way we strain to depict the world as a whole, we do have a lot in common. To me, he too seems to be trying to embrace the whole of reality, in all its dimensions, and to create a musical system in which he can do so. The line along which both he and I are moving is the same. If we have anything in common, that is what it is.

IVASHKIN: Does this mean that each successive work contains what has preceded it as a component?

YANKILEVSKY: I have invented the word "existentium." By that I mean the space occupied by a human being's existence. And all artists describe the existentium as they understand it, on the scale and in the size they can conceive. Each one sets the parameters of this existentium. One artist depicts the hammer and sickle. And the whole of his existentium is enfeebled, because there is nothing else behind it. It would appear that what is most vivid and realistic in this system is in fact what is most dead. It seems to me that Alfred does the same in his monumental symphonies as I do in my major works, when he creates layers of spatial music extending into the past and into the future.

An artist simultaneously depicts, as it were, several states. To put it more precisely, there are several types of experience. Experiences of what happens outside the window or, if we are talking about painting, outside the frame—"there." Then the viewer becomes a kind of observer of what is happening outside the frame, and he or she experiences events taking place "somewhere," "at some time," and with "someone"; he or she is merely an observer. The second type of experience is when the events take place in front of the frame, with the viewer, and he or she takes part in this experience. And the third type is when the viewer does not really have an experience, but simply establishes something. For instance, the window itself, the frame itself, in which there is nothing but the fact that it exists. This is not a look into the past or the future, it is simply something that happens, but still....

A traditional picture always depicted what was happening outside the frame, and I think that in music too listeners have always been observers, not participants. A complete experience must encompass both what is happening in front of the frame and what the frame itself is. This is what I am trying to do, and I think Alfred is doing so, too: trying to encompass the entire experience. To force the listener or the viewer to be a participant, you have to include the kind of material, use the kind of texture, that ensures that something happens to the viewers, next to them, near them. They must experience this actively, not look at it from outside, as they do in the cinema.

From an interview conducted in Moscow in October 1989. Russian text published in *Besedy s Al'fredom Shnitke*, compiled and edited by A. V. Ivashkin (Moscow: Kul'tura, 1994), pp. 251–259.

MSTISLAV ROSTROPOVICH ON SCHNITTKE
(1990)

IVASHKIN: You worked with Prokofiev and Shostakovich. Now that you are playing Schnittke's new Cello Concerto, written especially for you, do you see him as continuing the same tradition?

ROSTROPOVICH: Absolutely! I have been very lucky in my life. God has granted me friendship with this composer of genius. Alfred is a continuation of those pages in my life that began with Miaskovsky. I was very fond of Miaskovsky, and he acted as my patron. Indeed it was he who brought me into close acquaintance with Prokofiev. Later my creative link with Shostakovich began. Our close friendship dates back to 1943, when I was in his instrumentation class at the Moscow Conservatory. It seemed to me that this line of innovation, as well as the line of human emotions and feelings, was really coming to an end. Then I met Schnittke and simply fell in love with his music. I delight in performing and conducting it, happy that I am alive at this time.

IVASHKIN: Do you see in his music the continuation of a certain Russian tradition, or do you think it is more universal?

ROSTROPOVICH: I think it is more universal. But many of my friends, who listen to his music, find deep Russian roots in it. I didn't find them straightaway. As far as I am concerned, the most remarkable thing about Schnittke is his all-embracing, all-encompassing genius. He encompasses everything he has to. They build bridges nowadays of metal and plastic—everything human beings have invented. Schnittke is like that—he uses everything invented before him. Uses it as his palette, his colors. And it is all so organic: for example, diatonic music goes side by side with complex atonal polyphony. I regard this as unbelievably individual.

IVASHKIN: What is your impression of his new Cello Concerto in comparison with the vast number of cello concertos you have performed?

ROSTROPOVICH: I am in love with it, in love with it.... It is incomparable! There has been more than one woman in my life, and I loved them all.

From an interview conducted in Berlin on 28 November 1990.

38

SCHNITTKE AS REMEMBERED BY
MARK LUBOTSKY (1998)

All this happened a long time ago, but even today I clearly recall that sunny afternoon in 1962, when spring in Moscow was in full bloom. At the entrance to the Small Hall of the Moscow Conservatory, I was approached by a polite young man. He was a composer, and, like me, had recently completed a postgraduate course at the Conservatory. Having introduced himself, he told me in a few words about his violin concerto and asked me if I could find time to have a look at it. I said I could, and he handed me the music. Then he introduced me to the shapely young lady standing beside him—his wife, Irina. We went down the Conservatory steps together. They both were young, handsome, and smart, and they seemed very happy. We walked along Herzen Street to the Manezh, where at the time there was an exhibition of work by young Moscow artists, soon to be labeled by Khrushchev as "pederasses"[1] and "avant-gardists."

As I went through Alfred Schnittke's Violin Concerto, I liked it more and more. The only problem with the violin part was that it was overloaded with three- and four-note chords following each other in rapid succession. Alfred agreed with my suggestions that this be changed. We met often and became friends.

I first played the revised version of the concerto with piano accompaniment for a committee of the Composers' Union. Then it was broadcast live twice from the Moscow Recording House with the Bolshoi Radio Orchestra under Gennadi Rozhdestvensky. Soon afterward our performance was recorded.

David Oistrakh heard it on radio and reacted favorably. The artistic director of the Moscow Philharmonic, Moisei Grinberg, had a high opinion of it and included it in a subscription concert given in the Great Hall of the Moscow Conservatory. There was just over a year between the first performance on 29 November 1963 and the first public performance in the Great Hall on 12 February 1965.

Even more often than we actually met, Alfred and I had long telephone conversations. We had a great deal in common. We often talked about literary subjects. One of them was Boris Pasternak. Pasternak was Alfred's favorite poet, and he saw him as a wonderful example of human and civic courage. Alfred was still considering whether to write a work based on the "Gospel Cycle" of poems from *Doctor Zhivago*.

On two wonderfully joyous occasions we saw in the New Year together. There were three couples: Alfred and Irina; me and my wife, Natasha, an orientalist;

---

1. This spelling shows how Khrushchev pronounced the word "pederasts." —ed.

Rostislav Dubinsky, the first violinist of the Borodin Quartet, and Luba Edlina, the pianist. Each couple prepared and recorded on tape a special humorous New Year program, and on New Year's Eve we all listened to the programs together. It was a kind of wit competition: each of us tried to be as witty as possible. But it was a waste of time to try to compete against Alfred. His humor was remarkable for its inexhaustible imagination and brilliance. And his laughter was so hearty and infectious!

I played the First Violin Concerto several times in succession, in Donetsk, Novosibirsk, and again in Moscow. The concerto was well received everywhere, and in Novosibirsk we repeated the last movement as an encore.

Meanwhile Alfred was finishing his violin sonata. I gave its first performance on 28 April 1964 in the concert hall of the Gnesin Institute. The program included both classical works and works performed with their composers: Nikolai Karetnikov's dodecaphonic sonata for violin and piano and Schnittke's First Violin Sonata.

In conversations with Alexander Ivashkin, and earlier with Dmitri Shul'gin, Schnittke has talked in some detail about each of his important works, including the First Violin Sonata. There is little to add, except to emphasize that the sound image and symbol B*A*C*H [B-flat*A*C*B-natural] in his works has its beginning in that sonata. First heard in the passacaglia and then in the climax of the last movement, this motto is opposed to the wild ugliness of what is commonplace and vulgar.

It was only a few years ago that Alfred told me he was beginning to move away from the BACH motto theme. It had been present in his music for decades.

On one occasion Alfred asked me if I was familiar with the name and works of Nikolai Roslavets. When I said no, he told me about him in a few words. Several days later he brought me a sheet of paper, both sides of which were covered with his handwriting. He had made a special trip to a reading room (possibly at the Lenin Library in Moscow) so that he could provide me with a written biography of Roslavets, various things he had said, and articles about him written by critics who had "torn him to pieces," as Alfred put it. Shortly afterward I acquired the music of the Fourth Violin Concerto by this highly original composer, and in later years learned and played all of Roslavets's violin sonatas and other works.

Alfred was not satisfied with his First Violin Concerto. We often argued about this. In the first place he was not happy with the second movement, the scherzo, and asked me to omit it in performance. I disagreed. Only once in Leningrad did I do what he asked, but regretted doing so. Comparatively recently he said to me, "What do you see in this concerto? There is only one reasonable main theme in it, on which, in fact, the whole work is based. But what else is there?"

In July 1965, when I played Schnittke's First Violin Sonata with the pianist Vsevolod Petrushansky at a musical festival in the Finnish city of Jyväskylä, the Finns were ecstatic. The festival organizer, the composer and music critic Seppo Nummi, suggested to Alfred that he write a concerto for violin and chamber orchestra for the next festival.

In the mid-1960s Alfred was working exceptionally hard. In particular, work for the cinema took up much of his time. He got very little sleep and suffered badly from headaches. When we met we exchanged news and discussed our plans. My wife, Natasha, loves the poetry of Marina Tsvetaeva. I told Alfred what we thought of it and presented him with a small volume of her verse. Shortly afterward he played for us on the piano a short vocal cycle he had just completed, based on three of her poems. He explained that, as he composed it, he had tried to keep himself free of any kind of definite technique of composition, relying exclusively on his direct reaction to the words, on his musical intuition, not on any particular method.

In 1965 the American harpsichordist and composer Joel Spiegelman visited Moscow. Even before that he had been in close contact by letter with Alfred and with Edison Denisov. During his visit, at Alfred's request, Spiegelman and I recorded several items in the baroque style with a small chamber orchestra for the musical accompaniment to Elem Klimov's film *Adventures of a Dentist.* In another of Klimov's films, *Sport, Sport, Sport,* there are several remarkable "baroque" miniatures by Alfred. I thought it unwarranted that this wonderful pure music—written by Alfred wearing an eighteenth-century costume, but without in the slightest degree compromising his good taste, imagination, and bold wit—should be used merely as film music. I tried to persuade Alfred to combine several pieces of "Schnittke baroque" into a suite "in the old style" for violin and piano, but at first he refused point blank. These charming compositions were later published and immediately became extremely popular. But Alfred often said that when he heard them he could not accept them as his own music, in short, he was embarrassed by them. I could not understand this and often included the suite in my programs.

In Moscow at that time there were many interesting artistic exhibitions, some officially organized and some officially prohibited. I recall that in the late 1960s or early 1970s Alfred invited us to go to an exhibition by the officially banned artist Pavel Filonov at the Nuclear Research Institute. We went to Falk's apartment, where some of the paintings of the disgraced dead artist were on display. Alfred also took me to the studio of his friend, the "avant-gardist" Vladimir Yankilevsky.

During summer vacation, when we were separated, we occasionally exchanged letters. I once received from the House of the Creative Arts at Kurpaty a thick postal package containing music manuscript paper. It turned out to be a miniature opera with parts for soloists, choir, extras, and so on. It was Alfred's way of telling me about his travels and holiday with Irina at the Kurpaty resort.

Alfred and I once arranged to attend a concert by a certain brilliant up-and-coming young musician. His playing was undoubtedly virtuosic, and his program—although calculated for success—was interesting and varied. We were somewhat put off by the fact that he was very skillful at creating an effect by his playing. It was as if he were toying with the audience, doing his best to keep them happy, sometimes making it obvious that he expected them to be impressed with him. As one piece was coming to an end, he increased a tempo that was already stunningly quick, and after an unexpected ritardando, took the last note as if he were flirting with it. He also exaggerated the accents and in the pianissimo passages played so softly that he was almost inaudible. On the whole everything was highly impressive, particularly the numerous encores. Alfred and I sincerely joined in the enthusiastic applause. The next morning Alfred called me. "About yesterday's concert," he said, "I enjoyed it. So did you. Then two or three hours later... nothing, there is nothing left. And you begin to realize how cleverly you have been cheated."

I remembered this incident when, in Alfred's article about Alexei Liubimov, I read, "The greatest virtue of a performer is indubitably to affirm the music he is playing, not to affirm himself."

Generally speaking, Alfred had a negative attitude toward encores, "concerts inside concerts," and such "confections." He disliked it when the success of a program was inflated into a giant soap bubble.

"Why did you do that?" he once asked me reproachfully. This was as recently as the 1990s, when our quintet, in which Irina Schnittke was playing the piano part, gave an encore of the last movement of his Piano Quintet—in response to numerous calls from the audience. I was surprised. "Why did you do that?" he repeated and added, "There's no need for any encores at all. And in this music least of all: people die only once, you know."[2]

Alfred's Second Violin Concerto, written in 1966, has only one movement. (When the concerto was still in its planning stage, Alfred asked me what I thought of the idea of a violin concerto with a choir. Later he abandoned this idea.) The composer himself defines it as "a serial work, with aleatoric elements, and G as the central note," and in many respects it has no parallels in the violin repertoire. Each of the twelve string parts in the orchestra is independent (individualized, as it were), while the double bass contraposes the solo violin, distorting and parodying the musical utterances of the soloist.... "What could it all mean?" I wondered. At first Alfred refused to comment, although he dropped a hint, relying on my acuity. Then I got the idea that the "Gospel subject" of the concerto was not so much Alfred's version of his reaction to one of the actual biblical gospels as the result of the influence on him of the "Gospel Cycle" of poems at the conclusion of Pasternak's *Doctor Zhivago*. The music of the concerto, as it were, "rhymes" with these poems. Alfred himself later gave a fully concrete description of everything that takes place in the Second Violin Concerto, analyzing it literally bar by bar. I can add only that the vividness of the musical scenes and images he presents to us is amazing and unique.

By the time he was working on the Second Violin Concerto Alfred already had a remarkable knowledge of the violin and had evolved his original violin style, which is inseparable from his ideas as a composer and which became one of the elements forming an organic part of his musical world. In the Concerto hardly anything had to be changed because of "un-violin-ness." Only two pages before the coda, where the fundamental G was on an open string and moving toward an irresistible ostinato in sixteenths, were changed in several places at my request to avoid complicated leaps that might make the ostinato passage drag. All the rest sounded so organic that it seemed unlikely that Alfred himself had not tried it out on the violin. Later the questions he put to me about the violin part in the works he composed were directed not at the problem of "un-violin-ness" but at the creation of some timbral effect (for example, a musical image identical to that found in the piano cadenza in *Quasi una sonata*) or concerning indications of tempo or details of dynamics (*Suite in the Old Style*, Third Violin Concerto). In general, as was made clear in one of our conversations about the problems of instrumental music, Alfred took

---

2. The Piano Quintet was written in memory of Schnittke's mother. —ed.

a negative view of a composer who is an outstanding instrumentalist concerning himself unduly about composing music to be "comfortable" on the instrument. Inasmuch as profound musical ideas are more important than what is "comfortable" for the performer, surmounting new technical demands actually increases the potential of the instrument. Hence music must not be too "comfortable"; by over-coming what is uncomfortable new types of virtuoso challenges arise, which are closely linked to innovations in the language of music.

My father's funeral took place on the morning of 26 June 1966. Alfred came with us in the rental bus. The weather was oppressive. No sooner had we arrived at the Vostriakovsky Cemetery than a violent thunderstorm broke, with a heavy down-pour. The coffin was lifted out of the hearse. And at that moment, first from one side of the cemetery and then from the other two sides, other funeral processions stretched out past us, headed by brass bands. Each band was playing an out-of-tune funeral march—and every march was different. As my father's coffin was being lowered into the grave, the rain stopped, and a single, final thunderclap pealed. The impressions of that day, as Alfred himself has written, especially the "pile-up" of funeral marches, is reflected in the score of the last movement of his First Symphony.

The story of the first performance of Schnittke's First Symphony in Gorky is widely known, as is Alfred's own account of it. It was a remarkable event in the musical life of our country... primarily connected with the ban on its performance in Moscow. Even before and after this, other bans on the performance of Schnittke's music were often enacted. I remember how Alfred and I traveled to Voronezh for a performance of his Second Violin Concerto. Alfred had decided to play the piano part himself (the piano has an important role in the orchestral score). The conductor was Yuri Nikolaevsky. We had several rehearsals. After the final rehearsal on the day of the concert Nikolaevsky phoned me at my hotel and told me in despair that the director of the Voronezh Philharmonic, following the orders of the regional Party secretary, had requested that Schnittke's concerto be replaced by another work that evening. Nikolaevsky had refused point blank. I managed to ring the Party secretary. He listened closely when I told him we were playing a work by the Soviet composer Schnittke, that we had permission from Moscow to perform it in Voronezh, and that we could not understand why he was banning it. He briefly replied, "You are mistaken. The regional committee and the Party are not banning anything. They simply do not think it necessary to recommend it." Nevertheless, wearing our concert clothes, we arrived at the Philharmonic Hall half an hour before the start of the concert. At the box office hung a notice announcing that it had been canceled.

Thus permission was never obtained to perform the Second Violin Concerto in the halls of the Moscow Philharmonic. It was heard there for the first time in the Hall of the Composers' Union only seven years after its first performance in Finland. And this was after I had played it in London, Berlin, Amsterdam, Copenhagen, Stockholm, and Madrid. When Rozhdestvensky and I played and recorded it in Leningrad, Melodiya decided not to release it. It was sold to Eurodisc, who first issued it.

When Alfred tried to publish his *Quasi una sonata,* he encountered a special problem. It was dedicated to Luba Edlina and myself. But after we had emigrated, there could be no question of mentioning our surnames. By Soviet logic the name of anyone leaving the country was permanently erased from Soviet history. Alfred refused to have the sonata printed without the dedication, and it was printed with a dedication to Luba and Mark. But apparently the publisher got into serious trouble about that.

One of my most powerful musical experiences was at an evening with the Schnittkes when, on his old Becker piano, Alfred played for me and my wife, Natasha, the *Requiem* he had just completed. The instrument was in a battered state, and while he played, Alfred sang softly, sometimes making comments. What an unforgettable experience. Incidentally that same Becker piano gave rise to a misunderstanding. In his First Violin Sonata Alfred uses the device of having the piano strings in the lower register pressed by one hand (creating a kind of muted pianoforte effect). He tried this out on his Becker, on which the position of the board between the strings does not correspond to its position on a modern Steinway or Yamaha. This creates extra problems for the pianist.

The *Requiem*, the Quintet, and the day of Alfred's mother's funeral in the German cemetery in Moscow are indissolubly bound together in my memory. They are part of a particular line in his works that continued in his string and piano trios and is heard in the Third Violin Concerto and on the tragic pages of many of his other works.

After the death of Shostakovich, when I asked Alfred if he intended to write a short work in his memory (maybe for violin, I added hesitantly), he said no. But less than a month later he showed me his *Prelude in Memory of D. Shostakovich* [*Prel'udiia pamiati D. D. Shostakovicha*] for two violins or for violin and tape. At my last concert in Moscow I played it in the same set as a violin sonata by Shostakovich. Later I often gave concert performances of it and recorded it twice, both times with myself playing the tape-recorded second violin part.

The account of how Alfred wrote a cadenza for Beethoven's Violin Concerto is connected with the piano arrangement of the violin concerto made by Beethoven himself. As is well known, for this version Beethoven wrote cadenzas for the piano accompanied by tympani. I once attempted (it turned out that I was not the only one—similar attempts had been made before) to transcribe these highly interesting cadenzas for violin. In 1972, performing a concert with orchestra in Prague, I played the Beethoven concerto with my own transcription of the cadenza for the first movement, with tympani accompaniment. To my surprise in a review of the concert that appeared the next day I was harshly criticized. The reviewer considered it inappropriate for a young musician, who had shown his understanding of Beethoven's style, to play a cadenza that was alien both to this style and to good taste. Of course the Prague critic was not obliged to know about the piano version of the concerto and, reflecting on the matter, I had to acknowledge that my version for violin and tympani had not worked. Several years after I met Alfred I told him about this incident and asked him if he could write a violin version of the Beethoven cadenza. He looked at the music and then gave it back to me, commenting that the very idea of a cadenza for violin and tympani was unacceptable. Tympani can combine with a piano (since the piano, he said with a laugh, is also partly a percussion instrument), but, as far as the violin is concerned, a large-scale cadenza entirely with tympani accompaniment is impossible. Several months later I was delighted to get a phone call from Alfred, telling me that he had something for me. "Don't be surprised," he added, "and don't be too hard on me. My apologies."

Talking with Dmitri Shul'gin, Alfred has given a precise account of the construction of this unique cadenza, the second half of which consists of a collage of themes arranged over several bars from concertos by Bartók, Shostakovich, and Alban Berg. I should add that I cannot listen calmly to, let alone play, the transition from the climactic catastrophe based on Berg's music to the celestial D major of the coda of Beethoven's concerto. It is like a promise of peace and light after the impenetrable darkness, suffering, and horror of our age.

The first time I played this cadenza was in Perm, with Lev Markiz conducting. When I played it in 1976 in Eugene Ormandy's Beethoven program, one critic wrote that while I was playing the cadenza he came to the conclusion that I had gone mad and was spontaneously improvising on themes from other violin concertos. When I told Alfred about this on the phone he merely said, "Well, my apologies."

In April 1976 my family and I left the USSR and settled in Holland. I kept up a correspondence with Alfred, albeit an irregular one, but his letters were unusually dry and restrained. Meeting him later, I was very embarrassed when he said to me reproachfully, "How can you have forgotten it all so quickly and write to me as if you were not aware that everything is read and censored?" I realized that I could have made life difficult for him and was horrified at my thoughtlessness.

In one of my first recordings for Philips, I included *Quasi una sonata* and *Prelude in Memory of D. Shostakovich*, along with the Shostakovich Violin Sonata. The director of the Dutch firm Philips, Rob Edwards, who was extremely well disposed toward me, nevertheless was reluctant to record music by a composer unknown to him. To my surprise he agreed to spend two days in Vienna with me, where at that time Alfred was giving lectures at the invitation of the Music Academy. After our trip to Vienna, all of Rob's doubts vanished.

In the 1980s I tried not to miss any chance of meeting Alfred in the West or of attending premières of his latest works. The *Faust Cantata* in Vienna; the ballets *Othello* and *A Streetcar Named Desire* [making use of Schnittke's music], and *Peer Gynt*; the Fifth Symphony; the operas *Life with an Idiot* and *Historia von D. Johann Fausten*; the Concerto for Viola and the two cello concertos—all of these and many others I heard at rehearsals and concerts given by the best performers.

In the winter of 1987 I was invited to a summer music festival in the English town of Darlington. I proposed to play several short concertos with a string orchestra, and also a short work especially written for first performance in Darlington.

I called Alfred in Moscow. He said at first that he could not write anything for violin and strings in the near future, but that he had a suggestion. He had recently transcribed for strings a canon by Alban Berg, adding several voices to it. "The theme," he said, "is unique. You could increase the number of voices almost to infinity. And it will have a wonderful sound. I'll add a solo violin part and send it to you." The next time I phoned Moscow, the solo part had already been sent off. But Alfred said he had been unable to write the last bar. I got a piece of paper, and he dictated it over the phone. Then he paused and said, "No, that's no good," and dictated another version. Then he had second thoughts, told me to cross out the first two versions and dictated the last one, this time the definitive one.

It is probably no exaggeration to say that the Second Violin Sonata or *Quasi una sonata*, which marks the beginning of a new period in Schnittke's work, was also a revolutionary breakthrough in the violin repertoire. Never in the violin or chamber repertoire had the performer been presented with such a task. First of all we may refer to the actual atmosphere of the music, permeated by a flow of high tension, in which the pauses ("freeze frames"), held to the absolute limit, raise the temperature of what is already white hot. Here the absolutely unique variations on the BACH theme are expressed through innumerable stylistic allusions to Beethoven, Brahms, Liszt, Franck, even as far as Stravinsky-like rhythmic structures. The piano and the violin individualized to the limit, the rampant G-minor triad, endlessly drumming in the coda, as if in the throes of hysterical protest—"So you want simple tonality? Here it is!" Before long the same chord turns up in Schnittke's *Faust Cantata* as the climactic center of devilry, in the terrifying tango danced by Mephistopheles disguised as a woman.

Oh, that demonic tango! It is one of Schnittke's numerous intuitive visions, like the pauses in *Quasi una sonata*, like the use of a microphone to increase the volume in the First Cello Concerto, like the terrible major chord in the quintet, as if the heavens are opening—the miraculous birth of a choral sound in the orchestra... and so much more!

Seven years ago the leading professorial position for composition at the Hamburg Hochschule für Musik became vacant. It had previously been occupied by the famous György Ligeti. The composer Rataard Flender and I went to Bad Kissingen, where Alfred was at that time, to invite him to take up the position and to give him the details. After discussions with the Hochschule and the Hamburg Senate, he decided to accept. Alfred moved to Hamburg, where Hans Sikorski had his music publishing house, which for many years had worked with leading Russian composers. The world-famous ballet dancer and choreographer John Neumeier worked there. He had already produced several ballets to Schnittke's music.

From 1986 I was teaching violin classes in the same Hamburg Hochschule, and after Alfred and his family moved there I was able to meet him regularly. With Alfred and Irina I went to music festivals in Evian (France). There Schnittke's Piano Trio (arrangement of the String Trio) had its première with Rostropovich, and other works of his were included in the program. He also received a special prize there. In London we recorded a CD, with Irina playing the Second Piano Sonata, the *Quasi una sonata* (transcribed for violin and orchestra, with the English Chamber Orchestra, conducted by Rostropovich), and the Piano Trio (with Irina, Rostropovich, and myself). Alfred was also in London, for the editing of our recording.

In 1992 we traveled together first to Moscow, where we gave several concerts of his music, and then to Tokyo, where Alfred was awarded the Praernium Imperiale, the equivalent of a Nobel Prize for people in the artistic world. In Tokyo we played his chamber works.

At the beginning of 1994 Alfred decided to fly to the United States for two important premières. His Sixth and Seventh symphonies were performed by Washington's National Orchestra under Mstislav Rostropovich and by the New York Philharmonic under Kurt Masur.

Soon after his return from New York, Alfred phoned me and invited me to visit him. Together we listened to the recordings he had brought back from America. Then he handed me several sheets of music manuscript paper. On them was written the third and last sonata for violin and piano. He let me look through the manuscript and asked what I thought about the possible tempi in the second and third movements.

Later in 1994, in connection with his sixtieth birthday, I took part in public festivals in Moscow and London. This time Alfred was not along: his serious illness made travel more and more difficult for him. However, he continued to work productively.

The effects of his penultimate stroke were particularly terrible and had grave consequences for Alfred's final years. When I visited him and Irina in their Hamburg apartment, I was amazed by the fact that—in spite of his affliction, which made it almost impossible for him to move his hands—he was still composing. Somehow he managed to overcome the reluctance of his hand to write down what he had finished composing in his head.

Sitting at his desk, he handed me twenty or more pages of the manuscript of a symphonic work. Within a short time there were more than a hundred pages. He gave me to understand that the Ninth Symphony was already finished in his head.

Naturally he could not attend the Ninth Symphony's première in Moscow on 19 June 1998. I was present at this performance and the presentation to Alfred of the "Gloria" prize (Irina accepted it on his behalf).

Returning to Hamburg from a concert tour in the latter half of July, I learned that Alfred had suffered another stroke. This time it was to prove fatal. I spent several days at his bedside with Irina before his death in the Hamburg Eppendorf Clinic. He was breathing with difficulty and gradually losing consciousness. He passed away on the morning of 3 August.

Written in 1998. This essay has not been previously published.

INDEX OF NAMES & TITLES

Page numbers in italic type refer to illustrations.

ALEXANDER IVASHKIN is Professor of Music at the University of London. He is also Director of the Centre for Russian Music at Goldsmiths College, University of London, and Artistic Director of the Adam International Cello Festival/Competition. He has published a biography of Alfred Schnittke. As a concert cellist, he is the dedicatee of a number of Schnittke's compositions.